SAMSON

SAMSON

A SAVIOR WILL RISE

DURING WORLD WAR II, JEWISH MEN WERE FORCED

TO BOX ON SATURDAY NIGHT FOR NAZI ENTERTAINMENT.

THE WINNER GOT EXTRA FOOD.

THE LOSER WENT TO THE GAS CHAMBERS.

SHAWN HOFFMAN

W Publishing Group

An Imprint of Thomas Nelson

Published in Nashville, Tennessee, by W Publishing Group. W Publishing is a registered trademark of Thomas Nelson.

The views or opinions expressed in this book, and the context in which the images are used, do not necessarily reflect the views or policy of, nor imply approval or endorsement by, the United States Holocaust Memorial Museum.

Thomas Nelson titles may be purchased in bulk for educational, business, fund-raising, or sales promotional use. For information, please e-mail SpecialMarkets@ThomasNelson.com.

Unless otherwise noted, Scripture quotations are taken from the King James Version. Scripture quotations marked NIV are taken from the Holy Bible, New International Version®, NIV®. Copyright © 1973, 1978, 1984, 2011 by Biblica, Inc.™ Used by permission of Zondervan. All rights reserved worldwide. www .zondervan.com. Scripture quotations marked NKJV are taken from the New King James Version®. © 1982 by Thomas Nelson, Inc. Used by permission. All rights reserved.

Library of Congress Cataloging-in-Publication Data

Hoffman, Shawn.
  Samson : a savior will rise / Shawn Hoffman.
    pages cm
  "During World War II, Jewish men were forced to box on Saturday night for Nazi entertainment. The winner got extra food. The loser went to the gas chambers."
  ISBN 978-0-8499-6468-8 (trade paper)
  1. Holocaust, Jewish (1939-1945) 2. Concentration camp inmates. 3. Boxers (Sports) I. Title.
  D804.3.H594 2013
  940.53'18--dc23

                          2013014111

Printed in the United States of America

13 14 15 16 17 RRD 6 5 4 3 2 1

Special thanks to Saul, the Auschwitz survivor I met who told me stories of his experiences, stories that inspired me, stories that haunted me, stories that needed to be told . . . His confirmations of my research were invaluable, and thus this book was written.

The following is inspired by true stories and based on real events. Some of the characters in this book are amalgamations of more than one person, and certain dates and sequences of events have been altered for the sake of the story.

CONTENTS

ONE	1	EIGHTEEN	195
TWO	5	NINETEEN	205
THREE	19	TWENTY	219
FOUR	31	TWENTY-ONE	229
FIVE	39	TWENTY-TWO	241
SIX	49	TWENTY-THREE	253
SEVEN	61	TWENTY-FOUR	265
EIGHT	73	TWENTY-FIVE	277
NINE	79	TWENTY-SIX	299
TEN	91	TWENTY-SEVEN	311
ELEVEN	107	TWENTY-EIGHT	321
TWELVE	115		
THIRTEEN	127	*POSTSCRIPT*	323
FOURTEEN	145		
FIFTEEN	155	*ACKNOWLEDGMENTS*	327
SIXTEEN	171		
SEVENTEEN	181	*ABOUT THE AUTHOR*	329

They have invented a myth that Jews were massacred and place this above God, religions and the prophets.

— Mahmoud Ahmadinejad, Iranian president, denying the Holocaust actually happened, as quoted on CNN.com, December 14, 2005

In any free society where terrible wrongs exist, some are guilty—all are responsible.

— Rabbi Abraham Joshua Heschel, *The Big Little Book of Jewish Wit & Wisdom*

He will swallow up death in victory; and the Lord GOD will wipe away tears from off all faces; and the rebuke of his people shall he take away from off all the earth: for the LORD hath spoken it.

— Isaiah 25:8

ONE

AT FIRST, ALL HE COULD HEAR WAS THE SLOW DRIP of blood into a metal bowl.

Samson Abrams's mind fought the darkness. His sense of smell came back to him next. The odor of formaldehyde. The dank dustiness of wet concrete walls. Samson inhaled deeper, struggling for recognition, his mind becoming clearer with each second of consciousness. The sour smell of an open wound. The bitter reek of decayed flesh. He wondered if a corpse was nearby.

Dried blood held Samson's eyelids closed. His hands couldn't move to scratch the blood away, but he could feel the same blood on his face and taste it in his mouth. He strained against the pressure on his eyes until the crusts on the lids gave way. His eyes fluttered open, and he glanced about the room.

It all came back. Block 10, Auschwitz. Experimentation ward. December . . . 1941.

A single lightbulb struggled against the dark far above Samson's head. He could just make out his surroundings. Nearby on a bench lay surgical tools and blood-soaked rags, scalpels, and broken needles, the equipment for a long, slow death. Specimen bottles lined a shelf far to one side. An IV fed something into his arm. Saline, Samson guessed, just enough to keep him alive. He caught a murky reflection of himself in a stainless-steel urn on the table. He swallowed, his throat painfully dry.

All he could see at first was the side of his jaw. Samson shuddered. That same jaw had once been sharp and keen, the jaw of a middleweight champion boxer. Samson could take a hit from any man, stay standing with a grin, and then pound back his revenge. His opponents said he hit with the force of a heavyweight, earning him the nicknames Heavy Hands, Sledgehammer, and The Lion of Zion. He'd dominated his opponent at the 1936 Olympics, but two judges and a referee disqualified Samson after he knocked his opponent unconscious. They handed the decision to the other man, but everyone in the arena knew Samson had been robbed. Samson had set his jaw in defiance and pride and walked out of the arena without a word.

That same jaw was now skinless.

The muscles in Samson's lower jaw were visible, like someone had begun shaving him with a straight edge but had cut too deep and kept going. Samson could see the backs of his hands looked the same. The tops of his feet. The fronts of his thighs. The surface of his stomach. He couldn't see his back, but by the mind-numbing agony he felt behind him, he didn't doubt his back had also been stripped of skin.

Pain shot across Samson's chest with each breath, and a dull ache throbbed in his shoulder joints. Both arms were held at the wrists, arms stretched wide. From the corners of his eyes, he could discern he'd been strapped to some sort of operating table that was propped upright. Metal surgical spikes pierced both of his hands and held him fast on a vertical medical gurney. Leather straps went around his wrists, taking the pressure off the spikes, prolonging the agony. He realized that he had been nailed to a cross.

Two thoughts rushed at Samson—how long would the torture go on? And where would he be today if he'd made a different choice that afternoon on the street in Kraków nearly a year ago? Was it worth everything just to do the right thing and show compassion to his fellow man? Had it been worth it to risk his life and the lives of all those he loved, just to help one less fortunate?

Samson let his mind wander. He could feel the hugs of his twin daughters again, tiny arms that once squeezed him in the afternoon sunlight. He could hear his young son's voice, strong and full of laughter. His brother, Zach, and Zach's fiancée, Esther—so much potential in that young couple. His aging parents, their presence as comforting as the smell of freshly baked bread. The shape of his wife's body, warm and curved under their bedroom blankets at home.

There was no sunlight anymore.

No voices.

No blankets.

No home.

Now, there was only one reality. Dr. Josef Mengele, the Angel of Death. He was the owner of the steel gurney Samson was strapped to. The operator of the bloody scalpel. A *Hauptsturmführer*, captain, in the Nazi army and a medical doctor by profession, Dr. Mengele had spearheaded the practice of human medical experimentation on prisoners at Auschwitz. He also selected many who would be gassed. The remembrance of his eerily calm Teutonic voice floated through Samson's mind.

"My promise to you," the doctor had told Samson before he passed out from the pain, "is that I will extract my revenge. It will come in the form of the slowest, most painful death that today's science can provide. On that, you have my most solemn word."

His mind now clear, Samson wanted to fight. He wanted to break free from the gurney. To smash the contents of the experimentation room and set it on fire. He wanted to tear down the walls of the concentration camp and destroy every tormentor who held free people in their clutches. But now Samson's strength was gone. It was a strain even to lift his head. Samson would never fight in a boxing ring again. Perhaps he'd never even heal enough to live life without a wheelchair.

Perhaps he would not live at all.

Samson held out one hope of rescue—Commandant Rudolf Höss. An unlikely savior, the commander was on the same side of the war as the Angel of Death. But as the senior SS officer in charge of Auschwitz, Commandant Höss had displayed an ironic penchant for keeping Samson safe within the confines of the camp. The commander's loyalty was strictly with the Third Reich; there was no doubt of that. But the commander had powerful reasons of his own for wanting Samson alive.

A choke caught in Samson's throat. The sound of one man's footsteps echoed down the corridor outside the walls of the experimentation ward. One man was coming, and only one man. In this isolated part of the camp, there were only two options.

Was it Dr. Mengele coming to continue his tortuous experiment in prolonged death?

Or was it Commandant Höss coming to intercede?

Samson braced himself as the door swung open.

TWO

KRAKÓW, POLAND

NINE MONTHS EARLIER, MARCH 1941

SAMSON ABRAMS HAD NEVER BEEN AFRAID OF anything. He was a muscular thirty-five-year-old, hands hardened and covered with scars as thick as sea barnacles. When it came to a fight—either in the ring or on the street—Samson was always the last man standing. Still, as his sharp, dark eyes stared out from around the corner of a building and peered across Kazimierz Street, Samson couldn't stop the shiver that ran down his spine.

A simple glance up and down the block reminded Samson that his native Poland was no longer herself. The *Oberkommando des Heeres*, OKH, was Nazi Germany's "Army High Command," and its presence could be felt everywhere these days. On one wall hung a poster that showed a virginal-looking Polish girl handing food to a hook-nosed Jew with a shadow like Satan's. Samson's nose had always been considered small by his Jewish relatives, almost Gentile-like, but he hated that poster propaganda as much as anyone.

Another poster next to the first screamed the slogan *Juden=Läuse=Flecktyphus*. Jews=Lice=Typhus. A shop window next door displayed a large picture of a Jewish skull with lines indicating a smaller circumference, and therefore lesser intelligence, of the Judaic brain. The collective implication was that Jews were all flea-infested, moronic seducers of the Gentiles.

A year and a half earlier, on September 1, 1939, Nazi Germany had flexed her muscles and pushed beyond her borders. Poland, though filled with brave fighters, was outmatched from the start. Germany was a munitions powerhouse. Day and night her factories churned out tanks, planes, and machine guns. The Polish army fought back with all it had, even managing to destroy a quarter of all German planes, but it was never a fair fight, particularly after the Soviet Union began fighting against Poland too. They called it the *Kampania wrześniowa*, the "September Campaign," and in just over a month, by October 6, 1939, it was all over. General Wilhelm von List's armored divisions drove steadily north from the Sudetenland, tanks rolling down the same boulevard where Samson now crouched behind the corner of a building, staring across the street.

At first, the occupied land was divvied up. The Soviet Union grabbed a portion; Germany took the rest. Polish cities under German control became military districts ruled by Nazi generals. Streets and cities were given new, Aryan-sounding names. Kraków became the new capital of Germany's central government. All Polish citizens were made to register with the new government and given identity cards. All Jews—men, women, and children—were forced to identify themselves by continually wearing a Star of David patch or armband.

Then food became short. One day you couldn't buy bread. Soon after you couldn't buy milk. Then you couldn't find enough fuel to heat your home. The December winds blew off the Vistula River, and people everywhcrc shivered as shops and restaurants were seized and shut down. Churches, museums, libraries, universities, and even high schools were soon shuttered—after all, Germany didn't want Polish people thinking *freely*.

Months went by. It became hard to find doctors. They, along with Polish teachers, priests, university professors, and other Polish leaders, were arrested and sent to prison. Other people simply vanished. One day you were talking to Sigismund, your next-door neighbor; the next day he couldn't be found. The lucky Polish children with blue eyes and blond hair were sent to Germany for "testing." If they passed, the youths were reeducated in German institutions. If they failed, even though they still had mothers and fathers back in Poland, they were shipped to orphanages—or worse.

Samson, along with all the adults in his extended family, had lost his job soon after Poland's fall. They were thrown out of their homes and forced to share a tiny four-hundred-square-foot apartment—all eleven of them—in a walled area of the city known as the Kraków Ghetto. The friends Samson had labored with as a journeyman steelworker disappeared, all the Jews were fired, and many of the Polish men were forced to work for the Germans making artillery and other weapons.

Some days, Samson was sent out on work detail. He picked up odd jobs here and there in an effort to try to make ends meet, but rations and compensation were always scant. He'd quickly learned to blend in on the street as a Pole, to stuff his Star of David armband deep in his pocket, and to speak Polish with a decent Polish accent. He thought it might be a good thing that his nose had that Gentile look his relatives teased him about.

This morning in March 1941, it had come to a point of desperation. Samson blew on his hands, trying to warm them up, and scrutinized the layout of the storefront across the street. Scratched-out words on a sign read *Jüdisches Geschäft*: Jewish Store. By the scent emitting from its walls, Samson knew the store was still in business, albeit under new ownership. German bread and pastry makers had moved into the formerly Jewish establishment. Samson knew exactly what he wanted and made a quick calculation of the risk. If he was caught outside the ghetto without being on a specific work detail, he would be beaten, shot, or immediately shipped to the camps.

He shook the thought from his mind when the front door opened, and a baker set out the first of the morning's wares on the shallow shelf—a large basket of fresh bread loaves covered with barbed wire. A padlock held the base and domed wire together, a precaution meant to stop hungry Poles from helping themselves to the goods. The bread could be smelled by passersby but purchased only if the vendor opened the padlock and separated the dome of barbed wire from the base. Samson's eyes locked on to the warm, steaming bread, the smell wafting into his nostrils from just yards away. The aroma brought thoughts of his own family to the forefront of his mind, the family he loved more than life itself.

They were the reason Samson got up in the morning, the reason behind what few smiles he had left. It had been weeks since any of them had eaten a good meal. Three days since any of them had eaten anything at all.

Within three months of meeting her, Samson had fallen in love with and married Rebecca, an ebony-haired young Jewish woman with a smile that made Samson glad to come home every night. Eleven years of married life later, Samson still adored her.

They had a son named Simon, now ten years old, a boy of strength and arts. He could play piano and violin with the skill of accomplished musicians ten years his senior.

Petite, seven-year-old, identical-twin daughters rounded out his immediate family: Rachel, a precocious math genius; and Leah, a little comedian, gifted in writing and languages. Twins on the outside, but completely different girls on the inside.

Samson's Orthodox Jewish father and mother, Abraham and Hannah, shared the apartment with them. Every day they grew frailer with age and hunger.

Samson's younger sister, Sarah, who also shared the tiny quarters, was showing signs of malnutrition, growing weaker and more exhausted every day. Sarah had a baby boy, Elijah, who often cried from not having enough to eat. Sarah's husband had been captured and sent to the trains after attempting to smuggle food to them.

A slender, young Jewish woman named Esther also lived in their apartment. She was without siblings, and her aging mother had passed away shortly after Poland's fall, leaving Esther without any family. She was engaged to Samson's younger brother, Zach, a bookish, slight-of-build intellectual, and they had pledged to maintain their chastity until their marriage date, even sharing the close quarters as they were. It was a strange mix of feelings they exhibited—excited that life was continuing forward for them, yet worried and haggard from the effects of the occupation.

Samson's mind snapped back to the task at hand. He was bound and determined to come home with food that day, one way or another. Samson stayed low and out of sight; he ducked behind a Nazi tank that lumbered along in front of him and crossed the street. After edging around a corner, he stopped, momentarily mesmerized by what he saw in the gutter near the corner.

One solitary flower stuck out of the cracked cobblestones, the earliest spring victor against winter's darkness. The tiny flower looked so out of place, such uncommon beauty in the midst of a city now cloaked in steel and death. He picked the flower, keeping the roots intact in the small clump of dirt, being careful not to crease its petals, and tucked it inside his jacket pocket. Along with the bread he'd vowed to bring home, the flower would bring a bit of joy to those he held closest.

Samson ducked back behind the building and turned his attention back to the vendor of the newly German bread shop. The baker was busy with a customer on the street. Samson stealthily moved ahead and slipped behind the German pastry sign, hiding just a few feet from his target. Now was his chance. Quickly, he slipped his hand inside the sharp metal wire, cutting himself on the iron as he pulled powerfully and forced the barbed wires apart. Within moments he was back in the shadows, down the back-alley steps, the bread safe in his jacket, one hand pressed against his bleeding forearm. Moving carefully behind the wall, Samson disappeared from the view of anyone on the main street.

A scream stopped him in his tracks.

Within seconds the scream came again. Samson turned, spotting an Orthodox Jewish boy, about thirteen years old, probably on his way toward the day's work detail. The boy was out on the street a few steps from the sidewalk; two SS officers ringed him on either side. The SS weren't any common German soldiers. They were a small, cruel, elite branch of the larger Nazi army—the lead branch tasked with purging "undesirables" from occupied countries. One officer held the boy's left *pais* in his hand. He'd just sliced off the long lock of hair on the side of the boy's temple with an infantry bayonet.

"Edict forty-four-ninety-one. You know better than to be out of Jew Town!" roared a big, square-shouldered officer. Samson felt his fists clench, but he stayed in the shadows of the alley, unmoving.

Laughing, a shorter, stocky soldier cut off the boy's other *pais*. This time, the bayonet sliced across the boy's ear and into his temple. A trickle of blood ran down the boy's cheek. He screamed again.

Samson checked himself. He knew better than to interfere, but a memory flashed in his mind, a memory he couldn't set aside. Years ago, when he was about the same age, he had been the only Jewish child on his block, a walking target for any neighborhood bully. One day an older boy spit on him when he walked to school. Another day, a gang of boys loaded shotguns with rock salt and blasted Samson's legs and back while he walked home. On yet another day, two boys started a distraction in front of Samson while two more snuck up behind him and hit him in the back with a three-foot-long pipe.

The bully work had proved an excellent training ground for a young fighter. He fought everyone. Boy after boy, bully after bully. Samson learned how to bob and weave, how to take a punch, and how to punch *through* his target. He'd lashed two full ten-gallon water buckets, about eighty-five pounds each, to a length of pipe and clamped the lids on. Every day before school he lifted the pipe over his head in repetitions of ten, military-press style. After school he lingered at the playground monkey bars, doing pull-ups from a dead hang. Twenty-five. Fifty. Seventy-five. One hundred. He'd taken boxing lessons at a nearby Boy's Club, all the while honing his strength and fighting skills. In time, the only boys who dared to tangle with him were older and bigger, the surly cowards who singled Samson out and came against him in groups of four and five at a time.

When Samson was fifteen, a bulky man had grabbed his mother's purse along with a bag of groceries she carried. Nearby, Samson heard his mother call for help. The man was much bigger and older than Samson, but by the time the police arrived, they needed to pull Samson off the purse snatcher. The man's face had been ground into the dirt, his nose broken, both eyes blackened. Samson's hands were clenched tight around the man's throat, poised for the kill.

The boy screamed again, breaking into Samson's thoughts. The taller officer laughed and swiped his bayonet at the boy's other cheek. Blood ran down the boy's face now. Fury rose in Samson's heart. He paused for a moment to kiss a tattoo of the Star of David on his wrist. He'd got it when he turned sixteen, much to his father's dismay. Tattoos were forbidden in Jewish culture, but Samson's rebelliousness had developed into an almost unbending condition. He was immediately labeled as stubborn and defiant in high school. The first time he was suspended, his father begged him to be quieter, more cooperative. The second time he was suspended, his father just shook his head. But defiance had proven helpful over the years; it had a way of working to Samson's advantage.

Fueled by the painful memories of bullies and anti-Semitic gangs, Samson ran to the opening of the alleyway and slanted sideways, disappearing into the rubble of a half-demolished post office. He moved quickly and quietly, mapping out his attack.

The shorter officer held the boy from behind, one of the officer's thick arms around the boy's windpipe, while the taller officer hit the boy's face.

"A perfect example of why all Jews should be taken care of like diseased rats!" The taller officer leaned into the boy's bleeding ear and whispered loudly, "You're about to take a nice little train ride, and on the other end there are lots of ovens for you to play in."

The boy pushed with everything he had. He managed to turn his throat enough to get some air into his lungs—just enough to cry out a single word: *"He-e-e-e-e-e-lp!"*

Crack!

The taller officer was knocked off his feet.

Samson lashed out again, fighting with the old, familiar rage. The shorter officer doubled over from a slug to the gut. The taller officer struggled to rise as he reached for his gun. *Snap!* A fist broke his nose, blood sprayed, and the big Aryan was knocked out cold. The shorter officer rose, unhooking his holster. Samson broke the officer's jaw with a devastating left hook.

The bleeding boy wiped the tears from his eyes and stared up at his savior.

"Move!" Samson yelled. "Run!"

But the boy stood, shaking, immobilized by fear.

"These two weren't alone," Samson hissed. "There is no God to save you. Run or die." A police whistle sounded down the street.

Samson grabbed the boy and tugged him backward. SS reinforcements were fast on their way. Distant rifle chambers opened, ammunition loaded, guns cocked. The shrill sound of weapon fire crackled overhead as Nazis blasted warning shots. Standard procedure with so many innocent bystanders.

Samson threw the boy over his shoulder and ran. The Nazis were less than fifty yards behind. He darted down an alley, hoisted the youth over a fence, and dropped him on the other side before jumping the fence himself. He picked up the boy again and lugged him over to Zablocie Street, a grim industrial district not far from the bank of the Vistula River.

The boy finally found his feet, and Samson wrapped one arm around the boy's shoulders, squeezing him tight, pretending to keep him warm to any onlookers while moving him quickly forward, half lifting him with each stride to increase their speed. Samson needed to keep his wits about him. It was going to be a chess game from here to home, and he knew it.

The Nazi guards on patrol stopped, eyeing the two Jews curiously—the only Jews on either side of the street. They had obviously been separated from their work detail, and the SS guards traded looks with each other, smirked, and pulled their clubs out. Their faces were easy to read: *This should be good for a bit of sport, something to pass the time on this dreary morning.*

Samson pulled the boy tighter and whispered, "Scratch your head and body." As he began to scratch his own head and body, still walking quickly, Samson explained, "The Germans think we all have lice. But if that doesn't work . . ." The SS guards eyed Samson's scratching. They slowed their approach but did not stop. The boy still had not begun to scratch, not understanding the ploy. Samson continued, ". . . then start coughing, a real fit, they'll think we've got typhoid."

Samson started coughing violently, nearly doubled over. The boy joined in, finally understanding the act, coughing loudly, following Samson's lead. The guards slowed more, reluctant to get too close. People on the street suddenly parted like the Red Sea for the two "sick" Jews. Samson spit phlegm, then, searching for the words in his mediocre German, he called out to the oncoming SS, *"Flecktyphus! Flecktyphus! Wir haben unsere Blauscheine!"*

The Nazi guards were now just a few feet away as Samson reached into his jacket pocket and whipped out his *Blauschein*—a blue card proving Nazi-legal work detail. The disease-fearful guards stopped in their tracks, not wanting to risk a closer inspection. Samson continued coughing violently, stuffing the *Blauschein* back in his jacket as the two pariahs continued their quick shuffle down the street. Samson and the boy crested Vistula Bridge to see the ghetto gate of "Jew Town."

Get home safely. The thought ran through Samson's mind over and over again. *See my wife and children again. Don't get shot.*

Jew Town was the ghetto where many of the displaced Jews had been forced to go when they were thrown out of their homes. The SS took great pride in forcing them to congregate like rats in a sewer. Samson had been born in Poland but raised in America from the time he was five years old. His parents had poured their sweat into building a new life in the land of opportunity, a better life than they'd known in Poland. But like many Jews they knew, the dust storms and droughts of the Great Depression forced them back to their homeland to start all over again, living with extended family. The Abrams household had returned to Poland more than ten years ago. For the past decade, the Abrams family had built back a life in Poland, not a rich life, but a decent life, only to have it ripped away again at the start of World War II.

Other families had already lost more. Some Polish families of Jewish origin had lived in their homes for decades—generations even. They built prosperous businesses in Poland and constructed beautiful properties. All that changed with the occupation. As the Jewish families were removed, they were often forced by the SS to stop and watch new residents move into their former homes. Those same Jewish families were marched into the ghetto and piled on top of one another. But as bad as it was, many soon came to realize it was far better than being forced onto the trains. No one was coming home from the trains. News of that infamous fact was spreading.

Still on the run, Samson eyed the front gate to Jew Town. The gate's scalloped ramparts suggested elegant gravestones. Broken glass cemented atop the nearly ten-foot wall dissuaded any thoughts of escape. Living behind a wall that looked like tombstones was part of the Nazis' deliberate psychological torment of the Jews. A sign in Yiddish above its arches read *Jüdischer Shtot*: Jewish Town. This was the Kraków Ghetto.

The barking of dogs pierced the air. Samson snapped back to attention and shot a glance behind him. In the near distance he could make out the two officers he'd bested. With them now were two Dobermans straining on their leashes. The officers had caught up with the disease-fearful guards, and an additional group of Nazis were with them, joining in the pursuit.

Several bands of tired, gaunt-looking, slave-labor Jews walked through the ghetto gate on their way to work. Others were heading home from the night shift. Samson pulled the boy quickly now, cutting in line toward the front of those waiting to get back into the ghetto. He stole another glance back at the oncoming Nazis, then stopped as they reached the checkpoint.

The ghetto gate guard took his time eyeing Samson. *"Blauschein?"* the guard finally asked.

Samson and the boy fumbled for their work cards, tearing through their pockets, nervous. *Slap!* The gate guard backhanded Samson across the face, then chuckled. *"Zu langsam, zu langsam,"*[1] the guard said.

Samson seethed, fists clenched. He was not one used to taking a shot to the face without returning fire, but he knew better than to lash out now. The SS were bearing down, less than half the length

---

1. "Too slow, too slow."

of a soccer field away, and Samson knew their only chance of surviving was for him to take that punch, swallow his pride, and get the boy and himself out of this predicament alive.

The boy showed his *Blauschein*. Red-faced, Samson yanked his card out. The ghetto guard took his time checking out the two cards. Samson stole a look out of the corner of his eye. The SS had reached the top of Vistula Bridge. In a few more seconds they would easily spot Samson and the boy.

The gate guard handed back their cards and waved them into Jew Town. Samson and the boy hustled through the gate. As soon as they were inside, Samson pulled the boy into an alley.

"Run as fast as you can. Talk to no one. If they catch you, you don't know me. You were not saved by me. Understand?"

The boy nodded. Stuttering badly, he spoke his first words to Samson. "You . . . your na . . . na . . . name is . . . ? So I ma . . . may tha . . . thank you . . ."

Samson smiled. He could not help himself. The boy looked so gentle, so sincere, and his halting stutter made Samson immediately empathetic. Samson wiped some blood from the boy's cheek. "No names," he said. "Just run home. Run as fast as you can."

The boy reached up, hugged Samson's shoulders, and nodded again. He sprinted down the street. Samson checked over his shoulder. The SS officers were conferring with the gate guard.

Samson took off sprinting, but not before the soldiers spotted him. The tall Aryan officer, the one with the newly broken nose, pointed at Samson and shrieked, "*Du! Stehen bleiben!* Stop, you! That's the one!" Whistles blew. Dobermans barked. Out of the corner of his eye, Samson saw a group of guards coming after him. He looked straight ahead and continued on at breakneck speed.

Samson cut in and out of various crowds of people, knocking

over carts, dodging through alleys. He had better knowledge of the ins and outs of the ghetto than his pursuers, and he used that edge to his advantage like an aggressive chess player. He leaped over a broken rubble pile like an Olympic hurdler, cut through a back alleyway, and ducked under a broken fence.

When he chanced to look behind him again, there was no one in sight.

The nose of the tall SS officer throbbed.

He stopped running and blew his whistle again, signaling the other guards in his group to gather around him. They wheezed up, wiping their brows. The Dobermans' tongues lolled out of their mouths, frothing.

"Let's be smarter about this," the taller officer said. He pointed to one of the junior officers. "You—go contact the *Sonderkommando*.[2] A Jew who fights like this must have a reputation. Find out who this rat is. And you—" He pointed to another guard. "Ask around. Someone will soon see a young orthodox Jew-boy without his *pais*. We'll locate these vermin if it takes all day."

The officers dispersed in groups of twos and threes to inquire with the ghetto police and shake down the locals. They knew their power. No one wanted to be on the bad side of the guards.

The taller SS officer stood unmoving on the street. He reached up and probed his broken nose with his fingers. It was swollen like a grapefruit. He kicked the dirt, swore in German, and smashed a nearby window with his fist.

---

2. Jewish ghetto police.

THREE

Samson smashed a side window. Breathing like a freight train, he crawled through the broken shards and into the ghetto apartment building. It wouldn't be smart for him to be seen going through the front door. The stark sunlight through the side window showed his surroundings in pale strength. Staying low to keep out of sight, Samson rolled into the hallway, panting and bruised but in one piece. Catching his breath, he quickly searched his jacket pockets. He smiled faintly and nodded. His presents were still there.

He pulled out his key as he bounded up the staircase, a smile creeping across his face. It wasn't the first time he'd outsmarted an enemy, but his triumph that day somehow tasted sweeter. It had been costlier, the stakes taken to a new level. Samson didn't second-guess his decision to help the boy. If he had not intervened, the boy would have been beaten, tortured, and sent to the trains. Samson would do it all again if handed the same set of circumstances.

He burst through the door into his family's little hovel and quickly closed and locked the door behind him. Bedsheets hung from lines stretched across the room. Sparse sticks of furniture dotted the

19

cramped apartment. Clothes boiled in pots on the stove, acting as a makeshift laundry for the whole household. His ten family members were busy setting up Shabbat dinner in the one-bedroom pen.

Ten-year-old Simon ran to him quickest and threw his arms around his father's waist. The boy was never able to contain his affection for his father. "Daddy," he yelled, "I'm so glad you're home."

"How is my little ghettomench?" Samson said with a grin. He scooped Simon off the ground with one arm and tousled his hair with his free hand.

The twins rushed to their father, barrelling into Samson with glee. Rachel and Leah, the seven-year-olds, threw their arms around him. Samson hugged his girls close. "My babies," he said lovingly.

"We're not babies anymore," Leah reminded him, smiling.

"Ah, that's true," Samson said. "You're both growing up so fast." He kissed his twins on their cheeks.

Samson's wife, Rebecca, smiled, then slipped behind Samson and gave him a gentle squeeze around his middle. "Successful day?" she whispered. The faintest curve formed in her lower abdomen. Rebecca was two months pregnant, just barely along, and as far as Samson was concerned, she glowed like the morning star.

He paused and turned. The whole family was looking at Samson now. His parents, Abraham and Hannah, sat huddled in shawls near the stove. His younger brother, Zach, and Zach's fiancée, Esther, sat by the window holding the books they'd been reading before Samson came in. They looked at him expectantly. Sarah played with her baby, Elijah, on the floor. Despite Samson's best efforts to shelter his family members from the difficulties he faced outside the apartment's walls, they always seemed to be aware of his dangerous forays for provision.

"Well, I couldn't get challah, but I think this will do." Samson pulled out the fresh German bread, kissed Rebecca's pregnant belly, then kissed Rebecca again—a long, lingering kiss, the kind that normally would be done in private, but these close quarters afforded no privacy. The family turned away, embarrassed . . . and Samson kept right on kissing the woman he loved, no end in sight.

Finally, Zach, clad in the clothes and prayer shawl of a Talmudic scholar, pushed up his bifocals and held out his hand to stop the public display of affection. "You know, big brother, you are not making my last week as a single man any easier."

Samson paused from his tight embrace with Rebecca and spoke to Zach, although he never stopped looking at Rebecca. "You will have to forgive me, little brother. I am addicted to my wife. She is like fresh spring water I must drink regularly."

Zach was the opposite of Samson. He was extremely academic, and even though Samson's school test scores had been consistently at the top of his class, he had always picked running around outside, playing in the streets, over sitting inside and reading like Zach.

Regardless of their personality differences, Samson had always been highly protective of Zach, who was over ten years younger. Samson had once caught wind that some older boys at Zach's school were pushing Zach around, bullying him, and humiliating him regularly. So Samson showed up at Zach's school, his hands wrapped tight with boxing tape and wrist wraps. He grabbed the two bullies by their shirt collars and shoved them up against the wall. Politely, he asked them which hospital they wanted to go to when he was done beating them. The bullies pled for their lives. Samson told them that if he ever heard they were picking on his little brother again, no one but God himself would be able to save them. From then on, no one had messed with Zach at school—the former bullies saw to that themselves.

Samson kissed Rebecca again, pulled out the flower he'd picked outside the bread shop, and handed it to his wife. She smiled and smoothed the petals back. Samson could tell she liked the thought behind the flower even more than the flower itself. "I saw something so beautiful in the midst of so much darkness . . . it made me think of you."

Sitting down, Samson motioned to his little girls. He grabbed them both up off the ground and plopped them down, one on each knee. "Who wants to play Ride-Over-the-Nazis?" he asked.

Rachel and Leah squealed with delight. They'd played it many times before, unaware of the deeper implications of the game. "Me! Me! I want to! Me! Me, Daddy!" they both said.

Samson bounced them up and down on each of his knees, playing his version of "horsey." He held each girl's shoulder so she wouldn't fall off the makeshift ride and cried, "Galloping over the Nazis, it's a hoof to the head! Another Nazi down! Hurray!"

But as they continued to play, death was hatching a game of its own. It was only a few blocks away, preparing, getting ready to move in for the kill.

On the south side of the Kraków Ghetto, the shorter, thicker SS officer was exacting his revenge on the stuttering Jewish boy Samson had saved, slamming the boy's face into the concrete again and again. The taller SS officer looked on, a bemused smirk on his swollen face, while two members of the ghetto police ringed the boy on either side in case he tried to bolt.

The shorter soldier poured out his anger on the child. He was furious and humiliated for the beating he and his fellow officer had taken at the lightning-fast Jew's hands. Catching his breath, almost winded from doling out the beating, the stocky Nazi grabbed the boy's hair and gave him his final warning. "His name! This is the last time I will ask kindly. If you refuse to cooperate, we will not kill just you. We will kill your mother, father, sisters, and brothers—all before the day is over. Understand, you Jew-dog piece of filth? Not one left. Not one!"

"I told you b-b-before," the boy stuttered as he spat blood. "He didn't give me his n-n-name."

The officer yanked the boy upright and pulled out a silver-handled cudgel with tiny swastikas on the grip. He whipped off the boy's coat and pulled the boy's shirt over his head. The officer paused, ornamented club in hand, and examined purplish splotches on the boy's back.

"You are no stranger to beatings, I see," the officer said. "Hitler Youth?"

The boy nodded.

"They have done their jobs well." The officer struck the boy near the spine with his club. The boy shrieked and collapsed on the sidewalk. The officer yanked him standing again and raised his club. It looked as if the boy was about to say something. He was reaching the breaking point. They all did eventually. But with so much blood in his mouth, all the boy could do, apparently, was sputter.

"You are remarkably stiff necked," the officer said. "All you Jew-rats are." He struck the boy again, harder this time.

The boy cried out and fell to the pavement again, writhing in pain.

"Think of your mother." The officer stood over the boy this time. "Your baby sister. How will they look to you with a knife to their throats? Do the responsible thing and tell us what you remember about this man. You *do* remember something, don't you? Tell us, and we'll let you go home. Your mother and baby sister will stay safe."

The boy hesitated, spat blood, then nodded.

The stout SS officer turned gentle, seemingly concerned, feigning care as well as any professional theater actor. He pulled the boy on his feet again, took out his handkerchief, and wiped the blood from the boy's mouth and face. He tucked the boy's shirt back in his trousers and handed him back his coat.

"My dear, sweet boy," the officer said. "What's that? I didn't quite hear what you said."

The battered boy stuttered for a moment, then, extreme pain written on his face, he gurgled a whisper. "H-h-he . . . he had a t-t-tattoo."

The officer shot a questioning look to the *Sonderkommando*. "Do you know this man?"

One of the ghetto police nodded. He looked down at the boy. "A Star of David? . . . On his wrist?"

The boy nodded again, then lowered his head.

"Abrams," the *Sonderkommando* said. "Samson Abrams. His family's apartment is not far from here."

The taller SS officer exhaled loudly. He would have his revenge on this Samson Abrams. This Jew of surprising strength and cunning would pay with his life for what he had done.

The Nazi smiled at the bloody, battered boy. "You're a good little Jew," he said, and he patted the boy's head as one would pat a dog.

———

Samson patted Simon on the head, tousling his hair. "You are a fine violin player, son. What was that song called? I don't think I've heard it before."

"*Zog nit keynmol az du geyst dem letstn veg,*"[1] Simon said. "A boy taught it to me on the street. The tune is spreading like wildfire all throughout the ghetto."

"Ah, hearing you play always brings me great joy and pride." Samson patted him on the back.

Samson's younger sister held her one-year-old baby on her hip. Sarah was known for her fiery personality, lithe figure, and curly ringlets of shoulder-length hair. As she helped her mother set the table, she eyed Samson all the while. Samson had been a teenager when Sarah was born, and he'd become much like a second father to her. People said they thought alike, talked alike, acted alike. Sarah was one of the few family members who could speak bluntly to him, and whenever she sensed Samson's dangerous antics, she offered him no slack.

She sidled up next to Samson and spoke pointedly. "I can see it in your face, Samson. You're never this happy unless you're causing trouble." His sister leaned in and spoke softly. "Don't lie . . . what have you done?"

Samson shrugged, trying to play it off. "Nothing any other man wouldn't have done if he were in my position."

Samson's father shook his head. He, too, knew his son and knew that his daughter's intuitions about Samson were often correct. The old man adjusted the ornate yarmulke on his head and shot a knowing look to his wife. Hannah looked away, fingering her mezuzah necklace idly, pretending she did not hear. But Abraham was not one to ignore an issue. "Your little sister is wise beyond her years," Abraham said. "Come, tell us, Samson, what sort of trouble are you in?"

---

1. "Never Say That You Have Reached the Final Road."

Samson rarely answered this type of questioning unless he absolutely had to. This was beginning to feel like one of those times. Simon placed his violin in its case, and Samson grabbed him heartily, fake wrestling, playing for time. The twins joined in, and all three children wrestled with their father on the floor. He squirmed out of Simon's headlock and added, "Can't a man just enjoy his family?"

Abraham looked to ponder Samson's question before answering. "No, son . . . not anymore. Not unless the Messiah comes and changes all this."

Samson's smile faded and he looked away from his father's gaze. Samson once had a strong faith; some would say an unshakeable faith. Like all Orthodox Jewish men, he'd learned lessons from the Torah and rabbinical traditions since he was a little boy. The pictures flooded his mind now—the nightly routine of his youth when his father would gather him under the lamplight, and they'd pore over the Scriptures together. But his faith had been chipped away, piece by piece. The hardships of the Great Depression that sent them back to Poland had started the cracks. The Nazi invasion had deepened the fissures. The occupation had crumbled his foundations, ruining his belief that things would ever get better.

The question that swirled in Samson's mind now on nights when sleep wouldn't come was this: How could a good God allow so much evil? How could a supposedly loving God, the God of the Israelites, the God of Moses, the God of King David, the God of Solomon, the Father of the chosen people, apparently abandon them? Samson couldn't escape the facts that his people were being harassed, robbed, thrown out of their homes, and shipped away on the trains. What kind of father would permit this to happen to his children without intervening?

Each new day reminded him of the direness of his family's predicament. The Nazis, the lack of food on his family's table, a tiny apartment filled with eleven hungry people—ten of whom looked to him for provision—these were Samson's realities. Samson's father had always taught him that hope was the blueprint of faith, and that faith itself was the building materials, the wood and cement. But Samson had lost hope and faith—he had no blueprint, no goal to move toward, and no materials left to build with. He remembered the rabbis saying to hope in the Messiah. But what kind of hope was that? To Samson, the idea of a Messiah was a vague hope at best. The Messiah was supposed to save them. But when? He hadn't shown up yet. And if the Messiah was still coming, he was sure taking his time. So, although Samson loved and respected Abraham and he would have killed to protect his aging father, the idea of a Messiah was a sore, painful topic to bring up.

Samson now turned and looked directly at Abraham, speaking slowly and deliberately. "There is no Messiah," Samson said. "So I will enjoy my family until I no longer can."

Out in the street, the ghetto police led the two SS officers toward Samson Abrams's apartment. Several other Nazi soldiers had joined in, along with a squad of *Einsatzgruppen*. Their full name—*Einsatzgruppen der Sicherheitspolizei und des SD*—was well known throughout Poland.

They were the most feared of all Nazis. Easily identified by their special lightning bolt SS armbands, the *Einsatzgruppen* wore long overcoats and carried machine guns over their shoulders. Each *Einsatzgruppe* division was specially trained as a lethal, legal, and official death squad. Mass killings were their specialty. Jews were their favorites. But they didn't discriminate. Intellectuals, political dissidents, doctors, handicapped people—the *Einsatzgruppen* killed them all.

At the corner of the street where Samson's apartment sat crumbling, two older Jewish men spotted the *Einsatzgruppen* walking down the cobblestones. The men hastened out of the way, flattening themselves against the brick wall of an adjacent building until the squad passed.

Up ahead near the entrance of Samson's building, three Jewish children danced in the alley. At the sight of the militia, the children stopped dancing and stared wide eyed. Even in their short lives, they had learned the sight of impending death.

Inside the apartment, Samson took Rebecca by the hand and led her out on the floor in the middle of the tiny living area. Simon also grasped Esther's hand, and she pulled Zach along with her, then Rachel and Leah grabbed hold of Zach too. *"Hava nagila, hava nagila, hava nagila ve-nismecha . . . ,"*[2] they sang, stepping left foot across to the right, left foot in back of right, dancing in a circle, slowly gaining speed.

The rest of the family looked on. Hannah and Sarah continued prepping for Shabbat dinner. Baby Elijah played on the floor, cooing and clapping his hands at the music. Abraham couldn't help tapping his foot.

The dance finished. Sarah smoothed the tablecloth. She wasn't

---

2. "Let us rejoice, let us rejoice, let us rejoice and be glad."

letting her previous question drop. "You are too happy, my brother," Sarah said. "You're never this happy unless you're causing trouble. Come on, Samson, let us in on your secret. What have you done?"

"Maybe he did nothing," Rebecca answered for her husband. She could feel her shoulders tense against the repeated question. "Maybe he has the rare gift of hopeless optimism"—Rebecca gave Samson a kiss on his lips—"which I find very attractive in a man."

Samson pulled his wife closer to him. He was not one to hide secrets from her for long. She gave him another kiss, and he bent over and whispered in her ear, "God's people struck a victory today."

Rebecca's smile faded. She clung to her husband even tighter as her brow furrowed. Rebecca had seen Samson push the confines of the new slave-labor laws before. But by the look on his face, she could see that this time something was different.

Oblivious to the conversation, Zach eyed Samson and Rebecca holding each other, then looked longingly at Esther, who smiled gently, blushing.

Esther whispered in his ear, "Just one more week, my love. Then we will be married."

Zach looked deeply into her eyes. "Yes, my love, and what a long week this will be."

At the same moment, the Nazis reached the base of Samson's apartment building. The tall SS officer, still wiping blood from his broken nose, barked orders. The SS fanned out, surrounding the base. He gave the sign. In unison they locked and loaded their rifles, storming into the building through all entrances.

FOUR

SAMSON COULDN'T HELP THINKING THAT THE SINGLE
loaf of stolen bread on the table made for a meager Shabbat meal.

He eyed his family members all sitting around the table.
Abraham said a short prayer before wrapping the tefillin. Also
called phylacteries, meaning "to guard or protect," the small set of
black leather boxes contained scrolls of parchment inscribed with
verses from the Torah, the first five books of the Hebrew Bible.

Abraham wrapped the tefillin's attached leather strap around his
upper arm, hand, and fingers. It was the same tefillin that had been
passed down for seven generations in the Abrams family. Abraham's
father, Zachariah Ben-Haim Israel Abrams, had passed it down to
him, and Samson expected it to be passed on to him as the eldest
son of Abraham at some point, although he felt that Zach's zeal for
Talmudic law would make him a better candidate to receive the honor.

Wearing tefillin on Shabbat was prohibited by the rabbis, and
Zach could not help noticing. "Father, why are you wrapping tefillin
on Shabbat? You've never done that before."

Abraham nodded. It was true. "The Torah, the Word of God,

states that tefillin serve as an *oth*, a reminder," responded Abraham. "It explains that one wears tefillin only on those days when one requires a reminder of God's blessings. One does not normally wear tefillin on Shabbat because Shabbat itself is a reminder of his blessings. But this night I need a special remembrance of God. So I am wrapping tefillin because your old father has reached a point where he does not want to go on living in this misery. I would rather join my forefathers than continue in this way."

Abraham finished wrapping the hand tefillin before reciting a second prayer that preceded the wrapping of the head tefillin. Once that prayer was finished, he took his time wrapping the head tefillin, or *shel rosh*, and set it above his forehead. The family's stomachs growled, but Abraham was determined not to be rushed.

Sundown was approaching fast. Hannah lit two small candles representing the dual commandments to remember, as well as keep, the Sabbath day of rest. After the lighting, she waved her hands ceremonially over the candles, welcoming in Shabbat. Then she covered her eyes so as not to see the candles before reciting the blessing, part of the tradition.

Abraham began the traditional Shabbat prayer in classic sing-song fashion. The whole family responded, praying in unison: *"Barukh atah Adonai, Elohaynu, Melekh ha-olam, asher kid'shanu b'mitzvotav v'tzivanu—"*[1]

A knock interrupted the prayer. The knocking was urgent, repeated, quiet—too quiet for soldiers. Samson moved quickly to the door and unlocked it, braced the door against his shoulder, and opened it a crack.

---

1. "Blessed are You, Lord, our God, King of the Universe, who sanctifies us with his commandments, and commands us—".

"Mr. Abrams!" came a familiar voice. It was the neighbor boy from two floors underneath them. "They're here, Mr. Abrams. Here—for you." The boy disappeared down the hallway. Samson closed and locked the door and turned to face his family.

Abraham found his voice first. "My son," he said, and glanced at the little children as an indication he was speaking in code. "Go take a bath—quickly."

Simon looked around the tiny apartment, the boy's eyes questioning his grandfather's words. "A bath? At this time of day? Why would Daddy do that? And where?"

Samson hung his head, knowing what his father meant. He nodded. "I'm so sorry," he whispered, and moved quickly as if to hug his wife.

"No time!" Abraham's voice was firm. "Go now! Promise me you will not come out, no matter what you hear."

Loud footsteps could be heard from the far end of the building. Wordlessly, Samson rushed to the hall closet, Zach close on his heels. The brothers pulled coats aside as Samson reached the back wall and yanked open a trapdoor set flush against the woodwork. Samson ducked low and climbed inside. Zach shut the trapdoor with a quiet click, then rearranged the coats in front and closed the closet door. From inside Samson could peer out through a narrow peephole.

At first, the knock thudded like a boot against the front door.

When it came again, the knock splintered the door above the lock. A hand reached through the ragged opening and forced open the lock. The door slowly creaked. An *Einsatzgruppe* captain entered the tiny room, his revolver drawn. Four others were with him. Samson could hear more soldiers outside in the hallway. The sight of the SS armbands raised within him a mix of rage and fear for his family.

The captain lifted his chin and smelled the air with disdain, the way one does when driving up to a pig farm. He was tall, with a sharp, crooked nose. Samson couldn't help thinking he looked like a shaved rat. The captain eyed the unarmed Jews in the room. His gaze lingered over Rebecca, then fixed on the young, lithe Sarah.

"Where is he?" the captain asked simply.

No one said a word.

The captain nodded.

Immediately, the soldiers kicked over chairs, overturned the table, and knocked over rows of pictures with their truncheons. A framed photo of the Abrams family smashed into pieces directly in front of Samson's view. Every member of the family, even the little children, pulled out their *Blauscheine*. Rebecca held Rachel and Leah close to her, both daughters trembling. Simon stood gripping his grandmother's hand. The soldiers stopped, as if awaiting another order from the captain.

Hannah spoke first, her voice loud and clear. "We are all legal workers for the Third Reich."

The captain chuckled. Slowly, he swung his gaze around at each member of the family, then stepped forward to Samson's mother and took the card she held in her outstretched hand. "This is your card, old woman?" He looked directly at her.

Hannah nodded quickly, then dropped her gaze to the floor.

The captain ripped her card in half. Didn't even glance at it. The two halves of the card fluttered to the floor at her feet.

Slowly, deliberately, the captain spoke again, enunciating each word as if talking to a young child. "You are not legal workers. Not unless I say you are. And the next time I need to repeat a question, one of your children will die. Now . . . where is he?"

"Whom do you seek?" Abraham asked. From inside the closet,

Samson winced at his father's deliberate ploy. He knew his father could play the fool. The elderly man was an exceptional actor in his own way, particularly when speaking to Nazi officials, and the tactic of playing dumb had worked before.

Slap.

The captain backhanded Abraham, knocking him to the floor, then yanked Simon away from where he stood next to Hannah. The officer aimed his revolver against the boy's temple. "I think I will start with this young one," he said.

Samson's body stiffened. He grabbed a small pickax set in the wall of the hiding cove, his fingers on the door latch, readying himself to spring.

Zach, smart and calm under pressure, interceded. "Forgive my father, sir. He is old and senile. Samson, the one you seek, does indeed live here as I'm sure you have been told."

Samson's jaw hit the floor, the shock of betrayal shooting through him like a punch to the gut. The family stared at Zach, but he went on as if there had been no reaction from his family at all. "But my brother has not come home yet, sir," Zach continued without so much as a twitch.

"Then . . . we will wait," replied the captain.

"Forgive me, sir. I don't want you to waste your time . . . My brother is too intelligent and cunning to return home if he has done anything risky or foolhardy."

The captain shifted his full attention onto Zach, then lifted his revolver and began tracing Simon's cheek with the gun barrel, expressionless. Quietly, Samson pulled the latch, ax in hand. Pin drop silence.

The bony Nazi stared at Simon as he spoke. "If he is so cunning . . . there is only one way to catch this criminal and make an example of him." The captain turned to his underlings and nonchalantly ordered, "Take them to the trains—now!"

Rebecca shot a glance toward the closet where Samson was hiding and shook her head. He could read her thoughts, *Do not come out.* He could see the horror so calmly announced as it sank rapidly into every adult member of the family. It was happening.

"But our things," Sarah said. "We need to pack our things." She was begging for more time, desperate to hatch a plan. Samson could see the look on his sister's face.

The captain walked slowly over to her. A lecherous stroll. He looked her up and down, then tapped her lower lip with his revolver as he emphasized each word. "What you are wearing will be just fine."

Guards grabbed each family member, including the children. Sarah carried Elijah in her arms. Rebecca shot one last look toward the peephole, locking gazes with Samson. The two sides of Samson's personality battled in that moment. The warrior in him wanted to burst out of the hiding place and ax every Nazi in the room. The other side of him, the chess player, knew it would be suicide to fight ten soldiers armed with machine guns. Not only would Samson be killed, but, having caught their prey, the *Einsatzgruppe* would murder his family, too, no longer needing them as bait to catch him.

Samson watched helplessly as his family was led out into the hallway. He could hear their footsteps walking farther away from him. The captain stayed standing in the middle of the room. Three soldiers came inside from the hallway and stood with the captain, their machine guns drawn. The captain took one long, last look around, then turned and headed for the door, issuing orders to his men as he strolled out. "Standard procedure. No stone unturned. Set to semiautomatic—it's quieter. If he is hiding, you will want to be able to hear his screams."

Samson crouched in the fetal position and braced himself.

Moments after the captain cleared out, the *Einsatzgruppe* unleashed their machine guns. A whirlwind of bullets blasted the room. Wood splintered. Chairs were reduced to kindling. Plates, pots, and pans shattered into a thousand pieces. A menorah exploded as bullets blasted through walls, floorboards, and the ceiling.

Bullets flew through the wall of Samson's tiny hiding place and whizzed over his head, missing him by a hairsbreadth. He could hear screams from upstairs as bullets riddled the rafters. A red stain formed on the ceiling, then it began to drip—the blood of some innocent victim above him. The *Einsatzgruppen* took no chances when it came to killing hidden Jews.

Finally, the gunfire died down.

One of the Nazis chuckled at the carnage. "If he was here, he's dead," he said.

The hiding place had been Abraham's plan. Nearly a year ago now.

It had seemed foolish to Samson at the time. The morning back then had been cold and rain soaked, and he and Zach labored for nearly an hour to lug the old cement bathtub up the four flights of stairs into their apartment. Abraham had found the shallow tub in a pawnshop and instructed Samson to purchase it with what meager rations they had. It had taken Zach and Samson another two hours to open up the framing surrounding the hall closet and set the tub inside, enclosing it afterward in wood panels, unseen and untouched. "Someday, my sons, this may come in handy," was all Abraham had said when he inspected their work.

Samson unlatched the trap door, stepped out of the concrete tub, and ran his hands over the bullets now embedded in the basin's side. He glanced around at the tiny apartment. At his feet lay the broken picture frame of the Abrams family. Samson stared hard at the family picture. A single tear ran down his face.

He brushed the tear aside, clenched his fists, and ran through the door of the apartment.

FIVE

THE NAZIS MARCHED SAMSON'S FAMILY THROUGH the center of *Plac Zgody*—Peace Square—past the gate, and out of the Kraków Ghetto. Rebecca grasped the twins' hands. Simon held on to his grandparents. Sarah clung to baby Elijah. Zach walked with his arm around Esther's shoulders as she leaned into him. The Nazis marched with their machine guns in the ready position—their necks craned up and down and swiveled side to side as their eyes searched, persistently looking for Samson.

Night had fallen, and when Rebecca glanced over her shoulder at the ghetto gate, she gave no indication she saw anything in the shadows. But Samson saw her. He lurked about forty yards behind, following his family through the streets, trailing them carefully. He longed to run to his wife, to call out her name, to promise that he would find a way to save their family. But he bit his tongue and remained invisible in the dark.

Samson moved low and quick. The gate leading out of the ghetto was heavily guarded. *That won't do*, he thought. He side-stepped the main entrance, spotted an unlit portion of the ghetto

39

wall, and found an old cart to use as a step-up. He paused before climbing and broke off a wooden slat from the cart's side, then scaled the wall to the top. He slammed the slat on top of the wall. Hundreds of tall, knifelike pieces of broken, cemented glass were embedded there. If he didn't make the leap, those jagged pieces of glass would inflict serious injury. The wooden slat was scant protection, but better than nothing. He backed up on the ledge and mustered the best broad jump he could, cleared the jagged edges, and landed safely.

Samson glanced to the right and left, then considered his options. He was outside Jew Town, and he had traveled this way many times before. But on other days he had walked these streets as a free man; later he walked them with Nazi permission as a slave of the occupation force. Now he was a wanted man. Very wanted. The *Einsatzgruppen* were famously consistent at catching their targets, one way or another, and even under cover of darkness, Samson knew every step forward he took was a life-and-death risk.

Samson clung to the shadows and sprinted down the street. He rounded a corner, froze, and ducked back into the darkness to avoid a group of soldiers heading his way. They were looking off into the distance, distracted, and Samson rounded the building from the opposite direction and dashed forward—all the time heading for the Prokocim train depot. To his left, he passed a restaurant sign: *No Jews or Dogs Allowed*. Samson slowed momentarily, ripped the sign down, then kept running.

The clatter from the rail yard was unmistakable, even from a distance. Train brakes whooshed. Guards shouted and barked orders. Samson slunk as close to the depot as he could, found a good position behind an unused ticket building, and surveyed the scene. Activity was intense on the train platform, and his family had disappeared into the crowd. Nazi guards roamed constantly, scanning all operations. Handcarts piled high with luggage lumbered by as Samson watched Jewish parents hoisting their children into the train cars before climbing aboard. Soldiers and clerks supervised this standard postmidnight shipment of "vermin cargo." Samson had no plan.

On the side of the train depot a sign read *Reichssicherheitshauptamt*. The Reich Security Main Office, or RSHA, oversaw the *Einsatzgruppen*, and Samson knew if he made any attempt to stop the RSHA from taking his family, the chances of any of them ever getting away alive were next to nil. All he could think to do was find his family. Make contact somehow. Let them know he was coming for them. His eyes strained through the lights, trying to spot his loved ones.

Samson spotted a huge cart loaded with luggage rolling past his hiding place. The cart looked to be headed for the caboose. But just when the cart rolled past the sight line of the hordes of people being jammed into the train cars, the soldiers pushing the cart turned sharply away from the caboose and pushed their load into another building. Samson followed, sticking to the shadows. He peered into a low window. His face fell.

There, in heaps upon heaps, lay clothes, toys, shoes, pictures— all the contents from inside the luggage in the carts. The truth brought a new wave of pain. If the luggage wouldn't be traveling along with the people on the train, then that meant two things— where they were going, there was no need for luggage . . . and nobody on this train was ever coming back.

Stunned, Samson turned from the wall, raced back to the unused ticket building, and resumed searching through the crowd. He froze. Less than ten yards away stood his family.

They were all being loaded. Samson stared at the horrific scene—the long line of slatted livestock carriages stretching into the darkness. Rebecca held their daughters tight. Rachel and Leah cried as they were forced into the cold, dark cattle car. Zach hoisted Simon up to Sarah who grabbed the boy with her right hand while keeping baby Elijah safely on her hip with her left. Abraham helped Hannah up, then his father adjusted his tie and climbed aboard himself.

The now-familiar officers—the broken-nosed SS and the shorter SS officer—stood just a few yards away, watching, inspecting every face. Both officers still wore the same clothes, bloodstained from Samson's beating. They held their rifles loosely at hip level, their eyes ever scanning the crowd.

As Samson studied the officers' visages, the truth rushed at him—there was no escaping the situation. He could see resentment set in the brow of the taller man, determination chiseled into the eyes of the thicker soldier. Even if Samson gave himself up, they would show no mercy. Not after the beating they had received. The officers would kill Samson's family just to send a message. Just to save face.

Samson studied the situation. He could viscerally feel the tug and countertug of each option he had in his mind. The trains were impenetrable. He could not rescue his family from the boxcars. He could not travel hundreds, perhaps thousands, of miles on foot through occupied territory, then break his entire family out of a heavily armed concentration camp. He was out of rational options. Yet the alternative was equally unthinkable. He could not simply stand by and watch his family be shipped to a place from which no one ever returned.

That left only one choice—and it was equally irrational.

The train whistle blared. Guards began to shut the doors of the train cars. Samson's gaze locked on Rebecca, standing near the front of the doorway. She was kneeling, clinging to their three children, fighting to hold back her tears. The guards made their final checks of the lists, then slammed and locked the train-car doors, one by one, as they walked down the track, but Rebecca's train-car door was still open.

The two SS officers made one final look around. The broken-nosed officer took out a pack of cigarettes, gingerly placed one in his mouth, and handed the open pack to the other officer. They lit the cigarettes, mumbled to each other, glared at the Abrams family in the train car, and exited the platform. Samson didn't trust the officers' moves. On one hand, their departure might have been a ruse. On the other, they might have figured there were enough other guards around that no one was getting out. The officers could go home at last and tend to their wounds.

Samson breathed sharply, his shoulders tense. He could see Rebecca hugging all three of their children, trying to calm them. A young guard reached their train car and began to slide the heavy door shut, darkness descending on the faces inside. The door scraped as it slid along the rusty rail. At the last possible second, a man burst from the shadows somewhere outside the train and thrust his hand through the opening. The door bumped and caught fast. The guard stared at the new sleeved arm in front of him, then at the strange man to whom it belonged.

"I need to be on this train," Samson said. The steel of the door pressed against the sinews of his wrist.

Rebecca's voice gave a little start, then called from inside the train. "No—this man should not be here. Don't let him inside. Don't do it, Samson!"

The young guard eyed the man's upper arms and saw no Star of David armband. He looked at his clipboard, shook his head, and smiled. He could not suppress a chuckle. "You are not on the list," he said. "Get away from here." The train inched forward.

Samson stared hard at the guard. "I'm a last-minute addition."

The guard eyed him warily. "It's your life," he said with a quick shrug. He opened the doorway just wide enough, and Samson jumped on the train.

The train whistle blew loud and long. The locomotive's wheels turned on the tracks. The guard slammed the heavy cattle door shut, locking everyone inside.

Samson stood in the dim light, staring at his entire family. All stared back at him. The train began to move, picking up speed.

Tears flooded Rebecca's eyes. She stepped close to her husband and hugged him tightly. Samson wrapped his arms around her and their children, each drawing strength from the other. The whole family embraced, all adults trying to make sense of the last hour of their lives that had transpired.

Rebecca was barely able to muster a whisper. "You had your freedom—and yet you came with us anyway? Why . . . ?" Rebecca's voice trailed off, unable to finish.

Samson wiped the tears from his wife's soft face. "Because . . . I can't lose you . . . any of you."

Sarah backed a step away from the group and shook her shoulders, pulling her baby closer to her chest. She pointed a finger at Samson and began to flare. "You did this! You're the one who put us here. Whatever you did to anger the Nazis, this is all your fault!"

Samson stayed silent. He knew his younger sister's default emotion was anger, just like his. He tried to put himself in her shoes.

"Leave him alone; this is not the time," Hannah interjected, trying to bring peace, but Sarah wasn't finished.

"First they took my husband. Now Samson's foolishness has sentenced our family to death. Have you not heard the rumors? These trains are death. No one returns . . . Where these trains go—everybody knows. These trains go to the death camps!"

"No, my sister, those are just deceitful rumors, preying on unfounded fears," Zach answered on his brother's behalf, the young man's tone reassuring. "Why would the Nazis kill us for no good reason when they can put us to work for free? We are a valuable commodity to them. No—they won't hurt us. In their minds, we will help them win the war."

Samson looked his brother in the eye. He looked at his sister, then around at his whole family, and took a deep breath. "The rumors are true. I saw them throw the luggage into heaps."

A new despair fell on the family. Momentarily, Samson second-guessed what he had just said. He saw the new hard truth play on their faces. He considered how it's one thing to hear a rumor, a whispering, a hunch of some kind of potential evil lurking on the horizon. It's another thing entirely to stare that evil in the face, or worse, to find that you have been marched into its clutches. But Samson didn't want his family to hold out false hope. He wanted them aware of their reality, able to make decisions based on fact. He took Rebecca's hand and then held her closely.

Abraham motioned the family together. Slowly, they pulled into a tight circle, closing out the other passengers in the cramped car. Samson's father pulled out a small sack, opening it steadily and carefully.

"No matter where we are going, money is still money," Abraham said. "Money screams; everything else whispers. And money can still buy freedom."

Inside the sack lay a roll of currency, Polish zlotys, and a cluster of small diamonds. Abraham smiled as he looked at the stack of money and jewels he had worked his whole life to save. It was not a treasure born of greed. He had been saving because he never wanted to be in the same position he had been in during the Great Depression. He wanted to make sure he had something to give to the ones he loved. He was saving for an emergency such as this.

"Stretch out your hands," Abraham said. One by one Abraham distributed the funds. "Everyone gets the same . . . three hundred zlotys each and one diamond. Two diamonds for each child. Put them in the best hiding place in your clothing you can."

Cash and diamonds dropped into every palm. Samson closed his hand on the money allotted him, but then he shook his head and handed his money and diamonds to Rebecca. "It may help you or the children," said Samson, hopeful that he was right.

Samson turned to the whole family and stood up straight, mustering courage derived partly from defiant anger. "I promise you," he said. "We will be free."

Time passed in the darkness. The family stayed close. After a while, Sarah stepped forward and put her hand on Samson's arm. He hugged her tightly. No words were needed between them. The train hummed steadily on the rails. Soon the twins, perched in Samson's arms, dozed on his shoulders. Simon stood upright, half-sleeping, propped against his mother. Abraham and Hannah stood against a wall, their eyes closed.

From out of the darkness, Samson felt the wedge of people in the boxcar part slightly. Someone was moving from the back of the boxcar to the front. A young hand tugged at Samson's shirttail. Samson looked down in the dim light.

The boy's face was battered, bloody, beaten horribly. It took a few moments for Samson to recognize that this was the same thirteen-year-old boy he had saved. The boy stared at Samson, the two holding a look of recognition. The boy's eyes said it all. They pled with Samson for forgiveness, then looked away, ashamed.

Samson put a hand on the boy's shoulder. "I never did tell you my name," Samson said quietly.

"You d-d-d-didn't n-n-need to," the boy stuttered.

"It's not your fault. You know that, don't you?"

The boy gulped. "It's n-n-not yours either."

"My name is Samson. Samson Abrams. What's yours?"

"Ye . . . *Yeshua*. Joshua."

"Hmm," Samson said. "A fine Hebrew name. A shortened form of *Yehoshua*, meaning 'the Lord is salvation.' *Yeshua* means 'savior,' doesn't it?"

"Y-y-yes."

"Are you on the train alone, Yeshua?"

The boy nodded, then began to cry.

"Many believe that God will save us, Yeshua," Samson said. "Is that what you believe, too, my friend?"

Yeshua sniffled, trying to dry his tears. "I-I . . . I hope so."

Samson smiled faintly in the dark. He pulled the boy closer to him, pulling him next to his own children, hugging the boy tightly.

SIX

THE AIR WAS BITTERLY COLD WHEN THE TRAIN stopped dead in its tracks. Outside, the night was pitch black, and Samson couldn't see anything through the cattle-door slats. They'd only traveled a short while from Kraków, but dawn seemed far off. Samson braced himself, expecting at any moment the train to start up again or the doors to open, but minutes ticked by and neither happened. Little activity could be heard outside the train.

"What's happening? Why are we stopped?" Sarah hissed in the dark.

Other people in the car began to wonder the same thing. Far away they could hear the sound of banging on a door in a different section of the train. People in other cars joined in, yelling, "Help us! We need water!" Shots rang out from a machine gun—*rat-a-tat-tat*. The noise from the prisoners quickly subsided.

An hour passed. Another. The children slept. Samson maintained watch through the slats. When a pink band of light began to show far in the eastern sky, Samson first glimpsed Auschwitz-Birkenau through the cattle-door slats.

Dawn continued to brighten, and Samson stared at the massive camp—it was bigger than many cities he'd seen as a boy in America. From his limited vantage point, he figured it to be about fifteen square miles, and it looked like it could easily hold tens of thousands of people. Electrified fences surrounded the compound. Two sets of train tracks ran the length of the camp. Row after row of barracks stretched into the distance as far as he could see. Leafless birch trees stood tall on the far flank of the camp. Samson eyed ominous shafts of charcoal-colored smoke rising into the sky from smokestacks.

"It's okay," he said to the others. "Everything will be all right."

The train's engines came to life again, and the train inched through the main gate. A broad sign hung over the wrought-iron gates. Zach read the sign aloud. *"ARBEIT MACHT FREI."*[1] The train halted inside the gates. Guards slid open the cattle-car doors one by one, prodding people out.

Samson stepped off the train first, helping others down. He clutched his family close. A row of truncheon-toting guards stood nearby. The guards stood silently for a few moments, letting the crowd mill about. A man called out. A woman screamed. A child began to cry. Chaos soon erupted. People pushed and jostled. Children searched for parents. Only then did the guards go to work, shoving, swinging, pushing people into lines. In the midst of the melee, Samson could not help staring up at the constant smoke rising beyond the birch trees on the camp's western end.

"Form three lines: men, women, children," barked a guard. "Empty all your valuables or you will be shot! You can have them back tomorrow morning!"

After several prompts and a few warning shots fired overhead,

---

1. "Work brings freedom," or literally, "Work makes you free."

all the captives around him started emptying their pockets as they formed the three lines. Samson's family held on to their diamonds and zlotys, dumping everything else. Samson wanted to stay with his family until the last possible second. He lingered near Rebecca and the children, keeping a close watch. Rebecca hugged Samson tightly. He gave her one long, last kiss.

Thud! A club slammed into Samson's back, square in the kidneys. He crumpled to the ground and writhed in pain. Rebecca screamed and knelt near her husband. A guard grabbed her from behind and shoved her toward the women's line. Samson struggled to his feet, his fists clenched.

"Was it worth that last kiss?" said a voice from behind.

A thin, impeccably dressed man stood before Samson, a club in his hand. Samson sized up the man who had just hit him. He was an SS officer, but much more relaxed than the typical guard, and about the same age as Samson. The officer looked educated, bookish yet athletic, like a man trained in medicine who lifted weights on weekends. His dark green tunic was neatly pressed. His face well scrubbed. His thumb rested on his pistol belt, and he smiled ambiguously at Samson before beginning to whistle a happy tune to himself as prisoners were forced into lines.

"Over there." The man pointed with his club. "Three lines. Find the men's." Samson stared hard at this oddly relaxed man, then headed toward his line. With all the pain and tears surrounding him, the man seemed utterly unaffected, like a child watching ants scramble under a magnifying glass on a sunny afternoon.

A scream pierced the morning air. Samson saw who it came from and rushed forward but stopped in his tracks when a guard leveled his machine gun at Samson's head, ordering him not to move. About thirty feet away, near the end of the women's line, a guard was wrestling baby Elijah away from Sarah. Another mother with a baby stood nearby, screaming just as loudly while another guard was trying to take her baby as well.

The impeccably dressed SS officer strolled over to the second mother, seemingly unfazed by all the screaming. He unholstered his revolver. Samson expected the man to point it at the woman, but instead he pointed it at the guard's head, the one trying to take the baby away. The guard flinched and stopped his attempts. Although he was standing less than three feet away from the guard, the officer called out to the petrified guard in a clear voice, loud enough so everyone within fifty yards could hear. "Tell me, were you trained for war or for courtesy?"

The guard's eyes fell. He said nothing. The officer kept his revolver pointed at the guard's head. He stepped calmly in front of the young mother and spoke to her soothingly, as a doctor would do when delivering bad news to a patient. "Such vitality in a child," said the officer with a polite nod. "Such red cheeks. Would you please hold your child up in front of your face?"

The mother hesitated.

"You and your child will be fine." The man's voice was silky. His revolver was still pointed at the guard. "Lift up your offspring."

The mother held her baby up, face-to-face with her. She nuzzled the infant, quieting her, gently kissing the girl's nose. With the mother's eyes transfixed on her baby, she had taken her eyes off the officer. Quickly, he swung his revolver away from the guard and aimed it at the back of the child's head. He pulled the trigger. The mother and her baby were dead before they hit the ground.

Samson's jaw dropped, stunned. People screamed. Mothers tried to jump back but were held in place by guards. With nonchalance, the officer wiped the blood spatter from his face and revolver. He turned his attention back to the guard and spoke clearly and loudly, his voice still soothing. "You see—if at all possible, kill both together. It saves bullets."

The officer stepped closer to the next mother in line—Sarah with baby Elijah. Samson fumed but held his place, the machine gun still pointed at his head. The silky-voiced man looked closely at Sarah and her baby. The officer's head tilted to the side slightly, like a malicious, inquisitive boy about to take a stick to a stray kitten. "What will it be?" the officer asked simply. He seemed genuinely curious as to what Sarah would do.

"Please, don't . . . ," Sarah said. "Please, he's just a baby."

"It's an uncomplicated exchange," the man said. "Hand the child to the guard, and you and your baby will both live. Keep the child, and you will both die." The man pointed his revolver at the back of Elijah's head.

Sarah trembled, her mind unable to cope. The man stepped closer to Elijah, then lowered his revolver and laid his free hand on the baby's back.

"Such vitality in a child," he said. "Such red cheeks in this one as well. Do the right thing, Mother. Here—hand the baby to the guard. All will be well."

Sarah nodded slightly. Her eyes flooded with tears. She kissed Elijah lightly and tenderly on the cheek, then handed him to the guard. Sarah fell to her knees and sobbed.

"You chose correctly." The man's eyes were colder now, his voice firmer. "Now get in line."

One by one, other mothers gave up their babies. The officer motioned to a guard with a flick of his wrist. All the babies were taken to the left. The mothers were forced into the women's line on the right.

With the three lines in place, each line was paraded in front of the strange man. The morning still cold, the man donned gloves and took out a short riding crop. Person by person, young, old, male, female, for each one he flicked the crop one way or another. Genders and ages alternated as they passed by him. The strong and young, he motioned to the right. The very young, the old, the sick, and the weak, he motioned the other direction—left, toward the gray smoke rising in the distance. Nearly every decision was made in a split second. *Right, left, left, right, left.*

The pointed machine gun was taken away from Samson's head, and he shuffled forward with the rest of his line. His eyes drifted to a side ramp. Bundles of supplies were dumped like trash—everything that the prisoners had carried in—blankets, coats, handbags, piles of bread, jars of marmalade, sausages, sacks of sugar spilling onto the gravel. He realized his family's money and diamonds were probably worthless here.

Samson's eyes shot to the front. Sarah, still fighting tears, was being pushed along to face the man with the riding crop. The line stopped momentarily as the officer stared at Sarah's youthful beauty, apparently having forgotten he'd just taken her child a few minutes earlier. The man laid his riding crop across Sarah's chest, tracing her outline, as casual as always, more like an owner inspecting his livestock than a man leering at a woman. *Snap!* He struck her chest with the crop—a vicious, bitter strike. Sarah's knees buckled and she fell to the dirt. The man chuckled, a deeply happy giggle. Striking a woman seemed genuinely humorous to him.

Samson's body lurched instinctually, charging forward. This was his sister. But a hand reached out and stopped him. Furious, Samson twisted and knocked the hand away.

"Think, my friend. There is a time and a place to be a martyr. Do you think now is that time?"

Samson looked at the man who had stopped him—not a soldier, not a guard, but a monk wearing the full garb of a Polish priest. The monk laid his hand on Samson's shoulder, patting him like a father would do. "Think . . . think logically, not with your anger. The only way to help those you love is to stay alive long enough to help them."

Samson swallowed, then slackened his fury.

"Walk with me a ways," the priest said. "A man of your build will undoubtedly go to the right. But who knows what they will do with a man such as me. If this is my last conversation, I had better make it a good one." He paused, chortled in a rueful tone, and offered his name quickly—"Kolbe. Father Maximilian Kolbe."

"Franciscan?" Samson asked in a whisper, shaking the friar's hand as he checked over his shoulder, seeing that Sarah was slowly standing back up. The priest wore thick, round, black-framed glasses. His hair was gray and smoothed back, but he did not appear much older than fifty.

"Yes. I had a friary in Niepokalanów where I hid Jews.[2] The last few months, the Gestapo had me over in Pawiak prison. I was transferred here today. Your name?"

"Samson Abrams. I'm a steelworker with a large family. All here. Tell me, the SS officer with the riding crop . . . what do you know about this monster? Is he the camp commander?"

"No—that *Hauptsturmführer* is the physician at Auschwitz," the priest said.

Samson shook his head as he watched the *Haupsturmführer* circle Sarah. *How could a man who was merely a captain have so much influence? And how could this vicious individual possibly be a doctor?*

"Dr. Josef Mengele is his name, but he is rumored to go by another—*the Angel of Death*. Hush now. We are approaching the

---

2. Maximilian Kolbe hid and saved some two thousand Jewish men, women, and children from Nazi persecution (Caroline Cox, *Cox's Book of Modern Saints and Martyrs* [New York: Continuum, 2006], 177).

front. Perhaps we may talk again in this lifetime." The priest stared into Samson's eyes.

Samson studied the man's placid face in return. For a man about to be sent to his death, the priest's peace was beyond understanding. Kolbe seemed to look at people deeply, like a man who could see into people's souls.

Samson turned away, catching sight of Mengele as he motioned Sarah to his right. Shaken, Sarah stepped in line with the healthier-looking group, still trembling, still in shock, still overwhelmed with pain.

Zach stepped up next, glancing back at his fiancée. Samson could see Esther holding her breath in anticipation. Mengele looked over the short, thin, young Jew, noticing in a moment his sparse beard, short hair, *pais* growing in six-inch curls below his ears. Mengele shook his head and chuckled. "It will be interesting to see how long you last," he said to Zach and motioned him toward the right. Esther breathed a sigh of relief.

Esther did not garner even a second look from Mengele. He waved her to the right quickly, mostly due to his looking beyond Esther at Samson's twins, Rachel and Leah, coming next from the children's line. There was a curious excitement in the doctor's eyes. "Step forward, little girls," he called, and placed reassuring hands on their shoulders. He circled the twins, inspecting them closely. "Identical in every way!" The doctor smiled triumphantly, like he had found a rare treasure.

Samson could feel his heart beating like a drum. His fists were clenched, ready to attack. He eyed the guard nearest him, about three feet away. The guard was not a huge man, and Samson knew he could quickly subdue the guard, grab the rifle, and perhaps even kill Mengele before he would be brought down in a hail of bullets.

But Mengele showed no sign of cruelty toward the twins. To the contrary, he continued smiling at the girls, scrutinizing every feature. He leaned closer to them and smiled broadly. "Tell me, sisters, do you like chocolate?"

Rachel and Leah looked too scared to respond, terrified by all the eyes staring at them. The doctor rustled in his pockets and pulled out two small bars of chocolate, offering one each to the girls.[3] The twins stood dumbfounded.

He motioned to the candy again, looked them in the eye, and nodded. "Go ahead, girls. You will be two of my special children. Yes. All my special children call me Uncle Josef. Yes . . . you little Jewesses will be very special indeed." The girls took the chocolate cautiously. Rachel put hers in her pocket, but Leah broke off a small piece and put it in her mouth. Mengele motioned, neither left nor right, but behind him where two other sets of twins and several exceptionally comely, healthy-looking children stood.

Samson stood confused, waiting. Why were his daughters sent neither left nor right?

Simon stepped up next. Before Mengele even had time to wave his hand, Simon began pitching every reason he could think of to validate his worth. Even at the tender age of ten, he was well aware that a selection process had begun. Samson could see it on his face. His boy had learned in school that it was bad to be picked last for team sports, so Simon knew to say everything possible that could give him a chance to stay on the "good" team.

---

3. Mengele was known to give out chocolate to ease children's fears so he could have their cooperation as he took advantage of them during his experiments (Jonathan Broder, "Mengele Twins to Tell of Horrors at 1st Tribunal," *Chicago Tribune*, February 4, 1985, http://articles.sun-sentinel.com/1985-02-04 /news/8501040524_1_auschwitz-nazi-death-camp-war-crimes).

"I can play the violin! I'm good. Very good! You have no one here who can play for you like me." Simon's voice carried a dose of desperation.

The doctor's eyes widened, almost as if he were caught off guard. The Nazi camp soldiers looked to Mengele as if to say, *Should we shoot him now?* Mengele stared at the audacious Jewish boy, then recovered his equilibrium. "I don't remember asking about your musical abilities, young man. Why would you speak to me about this?"

"Everyone needs music, sir," Simon said. "Music is the joy of life." They were words Samson had told him more than once, but the boy began to sweat as Mengele stared at him.

Mengele leaned back, considering, still unreadable. It proved a palpable pause, the horrible, uncomfortable kind that causes the hearts of even the most stalwart to miss a beat.

Simon looked up at Mengele, knowing he was in trouble. "Please give me a chance, sir. I'm a good violin player, sir. Very good. You won't be disappointed."

"Ah, you are precocious, but then again the good musicians usually are. Tell me, young man—can you play Mozart?"

Simon nodded vigorously.

"Alright then," Mengele said. "You will join our special group. And we will all soon hear you play the violin . . . *excellently*." His last words sounded sarcastic, but he motioned Simon to head neither left nor right, but dead center, right next to the twins—Mengele's "special" group. Rachel and Leah immediately hugged Simon, clinging to their big brother for strength and support.

A man leaning on a cane stepped up next. He was handsome and young, broad shouldered and strong. He looked to have been injured in an accident from which he would soon heal. Mengele drew his revolver and shot the man in the head.

The line of people jumped collectively, on reflex. Several people screamed. Guards dragged away the man's body and threw it in the back of a nearby truck . . . far off to the left.

Rebecca stepped forward next and stood before Dr. Mengele. She kept her face down and her arms to her sides. Mengele began circling Rebecca. The doctor eyed her like a cow, pondering whether to milk it or slaughter it. Deep inside Samson, rage rose at Mengele's blatant actions. He started to shake with anger, a bull seeing red, his body instinctively getting ready to jump into attack mode.

"You are with child?" the doctor asked. "We provide a special place here to care for expectant mothers."

"No sir." Rebecca wasn't in the habit of lying, Samson knew, but although his wife didn't know all the rules of the camp yet, her gut instinct must have been telling her to keep quiet about any news of pregnancy.

"Your cheeks, your arms . . . they look a bit rounder than usual—am I mistaken?"

"Water retention, sir. My cycle."

"Ah," the doctor said. "I might have sworn you were with child. That is indeed a shame." He flicked his crop to the right. "Next."

Samson stepped up. He liked the idea of being close enough to Mengele to kill him, but his face revealed nothing.

Mengele paused to consider Samson too. The doctor studied Samson's face, then walked around him carefully. Something sparked in Mengele's memory. He'd hit Samson before with his club, but that did not seem to register now—Mengele had hit a lot of men that day. His face showed a distant flicker of a long-lost hatred, some annoying memory of this man that Mengele could not grasp at the moment. "You look familiar," the doctor said. "I've seen your face long before this day. How do I know you? From where? Come, tell me. I would rather shoot your face than be frustrated by it."

Samson took his time answering. He considered the doctor's question as one might consider a chess move. He knew the answer—guessed it anyway. But after a few pensive moments, he looked back at the doctor and answered with the same matter-of-fact tone that Mengele had addressed him. "Don't we Jews all look alike?"

Mengele smiled, stepped away from Samson, and nodded. "True. But I never forget a face. And yours does not look that much like a Jew." Mengele tapped his own nose. "Your olfactory bulb is too small." The doctor shrugged and waved his hand to the right.

Samson exhaled as he joined a line next to Rebecca's. In the distance he glimpsed Yeshua. The boy had made it through the selection process somehow, despite his bruised face.

Samson caught Rebecca's eye and saw a new, strange look of pain. He studied his wife closely, furrowing his brow in question. She pointed quickly to the left, to another selection pool. Samson's eyes followed hers toward the other side. Abraham and Hannah stood there looking frail and afraid. Samson stared at his parents across the dirt field. They stared back at him. Everything within Samson wanted to protect them, to run to them and get them back on the right side. But he knew that was not possible . . . not yet.

A guard stood near Samson. He was younger, Nordic looking. Samson pointed to his parents. "When will I see them again?" Samson asked the guard.

The guard paused, considering perhaps whether or not to even bother answering this Jew. Aloof and indifferent, he looked at Samson and said the two words that Samson would come to know all too well . . .

"Tomorrow morning."

SEVEN

THE SUN SLOWLY CLIMBED IN THE GRAY EASTERN sky as the nightmarish day continued. The lines of people not sent to the left were prodded into a large cement-block room. It didn't take Samson long to figure out why. As his line inched toward the far end of the area, he spotted branding needles.[1] There was no cleansing alcohol to prevent infection. The guard getting ready

---

1. Auschwitz was the only Nazi concentration camp that branded its prisoners. The serial numbering schematic included *regular*, *AU*, *Z*, *EH*, *A*, and *B* series. The *regular* series was used to identify male prisoners, including Poles and Jews. (Female prisoners received numbers in their own *regular* series.) Identifying letters in the other series were usually burned into prisoners' skin preceding the serial numbers. Soviet prisoners of war received numbers in the *AU* series, while the *Z* series stood for *Zigeuner*, the German word for those of Romany descent. The *A* and *B* series, first issued in 1944, were originally meant to be numbered up to twenty thousand and were reserved for Jewish prisoners. The *EH* was for prisoners who needed "reeducation" due to poor quality work or a flat refusal to participate in forced labor, resulting in a stint at a concentration camp or a special labor education camp for a maximum of fifty-six days. The ones with *EH* were, by design, the only ones expected to survive the journey into hell (George Rosenthal, "The Evolution of Tatooing in the Auschwitz Concentration Camp Complex," The Jewish Virtual Library, http://www.jewishvirtuallibrary.org/jsource/Holocaust/tattoos1.html). Maximilian Kolbe's serial number was 16670 (Elaine Murray Stone, *Maximilian Kolbe: Saint of Auschwitz* [Mahwah, NJ: Paulist Press, 1997], 75).

to brand Samson noticed the Star of David tattooed on his wrist. He eyed Samson for a moment, smirked, then stuck the needle into Samson's skin, searing the serial number right over the Star of David, deliberately marring it.

Samson bit down. He would not cry out from the fiery heat on his wrist—he'd made a choice long ago not to let any enemy see his pain. But hearing a quiet wail from the woman he loved across the room struck Samson to the core. Rebecca was being branded. She looked up, her eyes huge and watery, and saw Samson staring at her. Simon, Rachel, and Leah were wailing, all being branded a few feet away from their mother. Samson started forward, instinctively moving to protect his children, but Rebecca cried out, "Samson! Don't!" He halted. She was right; he knew it. He would wait and find another way of saving their children.

After the serial numbers were branded into their skin, Zach edged up to Samson and whispered, "It's a good sign. The tattooed numbers mean we are worth keeping track of. Why mark us if they're just going to kill us? Right? Why bother?"

"I hope you're right, little brother." Samson's face was grim. He was still watching his family. "But ranchers brand cattle, and still the beasts are slaughtered. Something tells me our new numbers have more to do with record keeping than anything else."

Branding finished, the guards shoved the prisoners into a small courtyard area and began to push them into their lines again, but when Samson saw what lay ahead of him, he froze. Three figures swung from the ends of ropes in a public gallows—a man, a woman, and a child—the family all hung by their necks. This impromptu gallows at Auschwitz seemed an everyday occurence.

The ropes had already choked the lives out of the two adults. Their faces were tinged blue, their tongues lolled out, swollen. But the little boy still struggled, his body too light to break his neck when the chair was pushed out from under him. Seconds seemed like hours as Samson and Zach stared at this boy. The slow agony. The fight for air. There was nothing anyone could do. The feeling of helplessness was maddening to Samson.

"Where, Zach . . . where is God?" Samson said, almost to himself. Zach shook his head and turned his eyes away.

A flat voice from behind Samson answered his question. "He's right there . . . dying . . . hanging there on the end of that rope."

Samson turned to look at who had spoken. It was just another despairing prisoner. Nobody he knew. The line moved forward again. Samson stiffened himself, then walked forward into another cement room.

Rebecca was near the front of the line. Samson could see her long, beautiful hair fall to the ground in strips, a pile of her raven locks growing quickly on the ground. Sarah sat on the stool next. Her hair fell away quickly, as did Esther's. Samson felt pride rise in his chest as all three women stood defiantly when their turns came. He felt the blow to their Hebrew culture—a woman's long hair was her "covering," a sign of reverence toward God, so shearing a Jewish woman was a deliberate affront.

Samson's twin daughters cried deeply when their hair was shorn. The girls' faces could not help but register shock and confusion. There were no mirrors to look in afterward, but the girls could see each other—that was mirror enough.

Simon closed his eyes as the shaver ran over his scalp. Samson wondered if his son was pretending he was back in his

old neighborhood playing Kick the Can. Simon had learned how
to do this mental trick whenever something bad happened. He
and Samson had practiced it more than once. The boy would shut
his eyes and try to remember good things from better times that
seemed so long ago—playing the violin at his school recital, eating
a delicious cut of roast lamb with his family, getting a hug from his
mother, wrestling with his dad.

Samson and Zach stood stoically as their hair was shorn close.

Kolbe stepped up after the brothers were finished. The guard
with the razor glanced at the little monk's hair for only a moment,
then shook his head. Too short to bother.

In the next room they were stripped naked.

Men, women, children. All together.

They stood shivering as their clothes were thrown into an ever-
growing pile. Guards searched the pile for any goods or valuables.
When one of the guards came to Rebecca's dress, he thrust his
hand deep into an inside pocket, pulled his hand out, and gave a
little start. The guard hollered to the others, and they descended on
the spot. One by one, all the Abrams family's treasures were found.
All the cash. All the diamonds. Their financial savior was no more.

Still naked, the prisoners were marched into another cement
room and systematically inspected for lice and scabies. Acidic white
powder was tossed on each person—delousing powder. Sharp
brushes were used to scrub prisoners' bodies. Skin turned a painful, bright red, so raw in areas that it bled.

Where is God? Samson wondered again. He lined up with the
rest of his family and prepared to go into the next cement room.

In his office, near the head of Auschwitz, camp commandant Rudolf Höss looked in the mirror. The commander's cheeks were rosy and cognac tainted, and he smiled faintly as he gazed at his own reflection. He'd been in charge of Auschwitz for almost a year now.

Near his desk hung a picture of Heinrich Himmler, head of the SS.[2] Adolf Hitler's picture should have hung in Höss's office, but Höss liked Himmler better. Hitler was too emotional, someone better at swaying crowds. But Himmler was a wolf. Höss could identify with the unflinching military demeanor of the man.

Höss strode to the cabinet next to his desk, unlocked it, and pulled out a humidor of cigars. He removed a cigar, inhaled deeply as he ran his nose along the edge, then clipped the end, lit it, and puffed away happily. *Precisely what's needed on a cold morning*, he thought as he glanced out the window. The commander checked his watch, frowned, and got his overcoat from a rack near the door. Two guards flanked him as he walked down the steps of his office and began his inspection of the camp.

The commander strode over to the largest of the clothing piles, surveyed the area, asked for a quick report of valuables, and nodded in approval. "Burn that." He pointed to a priest's robe thrown on top of the pile.

The sight of the robe triggered discomforting thoughts in Höss's mind. Some forty years earlier he'd been born into a strict Catholic family. His father, a one-time army officer, had raised Höss with military discipline and strict religious principles. Höss had no

---

2. Heinrich Himmler was director of security for the party, later the commander of the Home Army, and one of the most powerful men in Nazi Germany. His direct actions and orders resulted in much of the Holocaust.

friends his own age as a child, and his father decided Höss would do best entering the priesthood. Constantly, his father instilled in him the role of "duty" in a moral life. Faith was only about sin, guilt, and the need to do penance, never about forgiveness, love, or mercy. Once, the boy had confessed to a priest about an incident of indiscretion at school. The priest broke the vows of the confessional and told Höss's father. Höss shuddered as he remembered the beating his father gave him. He wasn't sad when his father died a few years later. Soon after, all religion died for the boy too.

As a college-aged man, Höss had formally renounced his membership in the Catholic Church. He heard Hitler speak in Munich and soon joined the Nazi Party. In his early twenties, Höss and members of the *Freikorps*, German volunteer military units, beat up a man so badly that he died. The man, Walther Kadow, was a schoolteacher suspected of communism, and the local farm supervisor, Martin Bormann, oversaw the beating. Bormann, a former student of Kadow's, received a year in prison for his part in the murder and later became Adolf Hitler's private secretary. The murder proved a pivotal event in Höss's life. Höss smiled, remembering—after a man had committed murder the first time, it got easier and easier to do.

Commandant Höss continued his inspection. He came near Block 10, where row after row of new prisoners stood, awaiting their next order. The prisoners were clothed now in vertically striped work clothes with smocks buttoned to the neck. The commander scanned his prisoners, a habit he'd developed each time a fresh batch was brought in. The camp doctor, Dr. Mengele, stood nearby examining a group of children.

Abruptly Höss stopped his scanning. His gaze rested on Samson's face. There was something so very familiar about this prisoner. Höss looked closer, then made a beeline for Samson. The commander's personal guards kept careful watch, rifles in hand.

"You there . . . step forward," Höss ordered as he approached.

Samson saw Höss pointing directly at him. Chin down, Samson stepped forward. Höss moved close, the same look of recognition on his face as Mengele had worn hours earlier.

"Pole or Jew?" Höss asked.

"*Jude,*" Samson answered.

Höss shook his head, frustrated. He inspected Samson's eyes, nose, mouth, and jaw. He stepped back and looked Samson over from forehead to feet. Again, he shook his head, peering at Samson. "You look more like a Pole than a Jew. Have you seen my face before?"

Samson shook his head.

"Why do I know you then? Tell me, before I order you beaten."

Samson shook his head and uttered his familiar line. "All Jews look alike, sir."

The commander barked in German to a guard, then pointed at Samson, Kolbe, and Zach. Guards quickly grabbed them, roughly pulling them away.

Samson looked down and saw that his feet were trudging through half an inch of ashy dirt. The ash was falling, almost unnoticed, from the sky. Samson, Kolbe, and Zach marched together with a dozen other men.

"Something doesn't seem right about the ground of this camp," Zach said in a hush. "This ash-like dust settles around here like a constant rain."

"I know something of this place . . . something horrible," Kolbe said.

"Are you trying to scare us?" Samson asked.

"You wouldn't believe me if I told you the truth. But it will be clear to you soon enough," Kolbe replied.

Samson stayed silent. He was eyeing the guards. Each wore a skull-and-crossbones emblem on the upper right collar of his uniform. Samson recognized them as members of the SS-*Totenkopfverbände*, the Death's Head Units, a special subgroup of the SS responsible for instilling order in the camps. The SS-TV stopped the prisoners near a huge pile of clothes. Samson exhaled in relief. It was only their work detail, nothing more.

"Move the clothes inside!" shouted the leader. "You have one hour!" He motioned to a *Vorarbeiter* to keep watch, then marched off. The foreman was a thick man with a face like a bulldog. He stood in place and clicked his heels. Oddly, he clicked them again, then smiled at the prisoners. "Anyone moving slowly, I will report," he said. The smile fell from his face.

Each prisoner grabbed an armful of clothing and carried the bundle toward a nearby barrack. Samson carried a pile into the barrack, came back, and carried another. The work was not hard. He stooped down, gathered another bundle into his arms, but then froze. Beneath him lay an ornate yarmulke. Samson would have recognized it anywhere. Abraham wore it every day. Lying next to it was his mother's mezuzah necklace. She had owned a gold one once but sold it during the Depression. This one was made of a cheap metal, probably lead—the Nazis knew that, otherwise the jewelry would have been long gone. But the necklace was precious to Hannah. She, too, wore it every day.

For a moment, Samson could not move. A flood of memories

flew through his mind—his father playing with him as a boy, teaching him how to hit a baseball when they still lived in America, singing with him on Friday night Shabbat dinners, coming to Samson's boxing matches. His mother hugging him, kissing his cheek when he came home from school, making matzo-ball soup for Samson when he had a cold, sewing two pairs of his socks together for double thickness in winter, and telling him she loved him at least twice a day—first thing in the morning and last thing at night.

Kolbe crouched next to Samson, glanced over his shoulder, and began to gather a bundle of clothing. "The Lord God will wipe away every tear," the priest whispered. "You must get up, my friend. If the *Vorarbeiter* reports you, you will suffer."

Samson fought to control his emotions; there was still a chance his parents were alive. He gathered his parents' belongings, added other clothes to it, and straightened up. There was nothing else to do but keep working or face the business end of a rifle. Carefully, Samson carried the bundle into the barrack. Inside, he glanced left and right, then quickly palmed the yarmulke and mezuzah.

On his way back to the clothing pile, Samson spotted another work unit of prisoners in the distance. They were lugging some sort of carcasses toward the ledge of a ravine. Samson couldn't discern at first what sort of animals had been butchered.

Kolbe quickly moved up next to him again and laid a hand on his shoulder. "Do not stop," he said in a whisper. "Turn away from this sight and keep working."

But Samson continued watching. He grabbed another pile

of clothing and returned to the barrack again. On his return trip, Samson eyed the other work unit again, this time more closely. At once, he realized what it was that the other prisoners were dragging—bodies . . . human bodies. The elderly, the infirm, the frail, and the starved were being dragged naked through the dirt toward a pit. For a moment, Samson was unable to move. Another thought flashed through his mind. He had his suspicions of who might be among the dead, but he needed to confirm his thought with his own eyes.

Again, Kolbe was by his side, as if reading his mind. "No, you must let this go, Samson," Kolbe said. "Stay strong for your wife and children. You cannot afford a moment of weakness, not in this place."

The priest's words sunk in. Samson knew it was wisdom, but he could not get one thought out of his mind. He tore his gaze away, continued to the barrack, dumped his load of clothing, returned to the pile, and grabbed another load. Mechanically, still stunned silent, Samson followed Kolbe with his armful of clothes. Samson set down the bundle inside the barrack, then his mind snapped back in place. He eyed the *Vorarbeiter*. The guard's gaze was elsewhere. Samson followed Kolbe and the other prisoners a few steps outside, then ducked behind a girder. He shot a glance at the guard again, then sprinted alongside the building, running toward the ravine.

Forty yards from the pit lay another barrack. Samson slid behind the corner of the building, panting, watching other prisoners throw bodies in.

The moment of opportunity arrived. The prisoners left the site with the guards following. Samson snuck toward the edge of the ravine, looked over, and froze. Directly in front of him, twenty feet down in a pit, lay a mass grave. Mounds of corpses intertwined with one another, their lifeless eyes staring, their mouths agape. Samson faltered, stumbling backward.

Near the edge of the pile lay the bodies of his parents.

Samson fought to hold back his tears. His suspicions were right. His fists clenched so hard that blood stopped flowing to his fingertips.

The prisoners and guards were returning to the pit. Samson fell backward, then stumbled up and staggered back to the edge of the building and looked on, still in shock. *Sonderkommando* on four sides of the ravine poured gasoline on the mounds of dead.

A guard pointed a rifle at three Jewish musicians. Nervous and pained, they rosined the bows of their violins, poised, waiting. Six female Jewish inmates—all crying—held torches. A heavily uniformed guard held up his hand, then signaled to the women. At his command, they threw their torches into the pit. The flames roared instantly and spread wildly. The head guard gave a second signal. The musicians began to play Tchaikovsky's Violin Concerto in D Major—plaintive, soulful music. Simultaneously, the female inmates began to dance, the guards' guns pointed at their heads for "inspiration"—it was a forced dance as the fire incinerated the dead of their people.

A rage burned hotter in Samson than the flames he witnessed. He imagined how he'd kill the first guard—a quick blow to the windpipe. With a Nazi rifle in his hands, he'd kill the rest of the guards. Samson lurched forward, moving on pure fury—but before he got two steps, a hand grabbed his arm. Samson turned, struggling. The hand grasped him firmly. It was Kolbe, again attempting to hold him back from doing something horribly foolish. "Suicide will not help your family stay alive," said the priest. "Now, come quickly, or they will spot you."

A scream broke the air. Kolbe yanked Samson back behind the barrack. Another scream. Another. They looked toward the sound of the screaming. Guards patrolled the perimeter of the pit. A group of SS-TV walked toward them carrying five or six small, struggling children under their arms. The children were very much alive.

One of the female dancers broke free from the group and ran toward the SS-TV. "My baby!" the woman cried. "That's my little boy!" A guard promptly shot the mother, then kicked her body into the flames. One by one, the children were tossed alive into the fire.

Kolbe was straining now, struggling with all his might to keep Samson back. "You cannot save them, Samson. But your wife and children—they still have a chance!"

"Let me go." Samson was not fighting the priest. He was fighting his own instinct. Fighting the agonizing wisdom of staying in the shadows, unmoving. Samson could glimpse the far side of the pit, down to where the bodies were burning.

He stared, horrified, as corpses sat up. Limbs reaching, mouths open as if screaming. The corpses twisted and writhed. The crackling fire burned so hotly it animated the lifeless bodies, causing them to contort and spasm, temporarily coming to "life." The SS didn't even look fazed—they must have seen this phenomenon too many times already.

The priest laid a hand on Samson's shoulder, hushing the stronger man while firmly pulling him back toward the work detail. Samson could not help looking back, helpless and horrified.

"Where, Kolbe . . . where is God in all this?" Samson asked in a whisper. He pulled out his father's yarmulke and his mother's mezuzah from inside his shirt, trying to hold back tears he could no longer fight.

EIGHT

THE REST OF THE AFTERNOON WAS SIMPLE compared with the horror earlier in the day. More work detail. A supper of thin soup. Assignment into barracks. Evening roll call. Dismissal.

Samson slid the yarmulke and mezuzah into his shirt long before stepping inside Hut 57, hiding the tangible memories of his family from the guards. Kolbe and Zach followed him inside the same assigned barrack. The women and children were assigned different quarters in the camp. Samson didn't know where.

The events of the day stupefied Samson's mind and heart. He ached for his parents. He was enraged at the manner in which they died. Normally at the end of a day, he would relax with his family—even in their apartment in the ghetto. They'd all listen to Simon play the violin, or they would tell stories and jokes and do their best to entertain one another—anything to brighten each other's lives. But there was no humor anymore, no optimism left in Samson's personality. Any remnants of good cheer had been incinerated along with his parents.

Tired and sore, the men crawled into their bunks. Samson and

Zach hadn't slept at all during the previous night on the train, and now they found themselves in a particularly cramped bunkhouse. Samson and Zach shared one bunk while Kolbe lay on the floor next to them. The *Kapo*,[1] a prison orderly, had a face like weathered leather. He seemed to take an odd pride in doing his nightly duties. With a sneer, he counted the men again, then shut off the dim lights. Blackness blanketed the barrack, save for a sliver of light from the thin crescent moon outside.

Despite Samson's deep exhaustion, sleep would not come. He stared, eyes wide open, at the bunk above him, thinking, trying to make sense of the images in his mind. On one hand, he longed to gain a greater sense of all that was happening around him. He wanted to find God in the midst of this horror, to figure out how he could call upon the Almighty—if he did indeed exist—to help his family survive. On the other hand, Samson simply wanted revenge. He wanted to lash out with pure, unbridled fury and kill every Nazi

---

1. While the Germans commonly called them *Kapos*, the official government term for prisoner functionaries was *Funktionshäftling*. These were prisoners in a Nazi concentration camp assigned by the SS guards to supervise forced labor or carry out administrative tasks in the camp. The system was also called "prisoner self-administration," and it minimized costs for the Nazis by allowing camps to function with fewer SS personnel. *Kapos* were known for their brutality toward other prisoners. Many were recruited from the ranks of violent criminal gangs rather than racial or political prisoners. The brutality was tolerated by the SS and was an integral part of the camp system. Overall, the system was also designed to turn victim against victim, as prisoners were pitted against fellow prisoners in order to maintain the favor of their SS guards. If *Kapos* were derelict in their duties, they would be returned to the status of ordinary prisoners and be subject to other *Kapos*. Prisoner functionaries were spared physical abuse and hard labor, provided they performed their duties to the satisfaction of the SS guards. They also had access to certain privileges such as civilian clothes and a private room, even (many being convicts) the possibility of reduced sentence or parole ("The prisoner functionaries system," Mauthausen Memorial, http://en.gusen-memorial.at/db/admin/de/index_main.php?cbereich =1&cthema=10&carticle=85&fromlist=1; "Prisoner Administration," Wollheim Memorial, http://www.wollheim-memorial.de/en/haeftlingsverwaltung_en).

he saw. He could imagine beating his enemies, one by one, breaking their ribs first, then breaking their necks, slowly throttling them into an unconsciousness from which they'd never return.

"Samson . . . you awake?" It was Zach.

"Yeah."

"That soup we ate tonight tasted like rotten dishwater. I saw one small carrot in the bottom of my bowl—and it had mold on it."

Samson exhaled. "It's been a day of firsts for all of us."

Zach swallowed quietly in the dark. "Samson . . . tell me more of what you saw. Did you . . . did it look like our parents had been killed quickly? Please . . . I need to know."

"I don't know what else to tell you, little brother. All I can say is I'm not going to die like that. And neither will anyone else in our family. We will be free, one way or the other."

Zach sighed. "From what I have seen today, only the Messiah can save us." Zach had always loved his mother and father deeply. The news of their deaths had driven him to tears and despair.

"You can wait for the Messiah if you want to," Samson said, "like a fool who waits for a bird to pluck him out of the middle of a storm. But I'd rather fight with these." Samson held up his hands and remembered the many brawls he'd won.

"The Messiah has already come," said a voice from the floor. "Now it is up to us to fight with our spiritual weapons, not our physical ones." The voice spoke softly, but with conviction.

"Kolbe—that you? You still awake?" Samson peered over the edge of the bunk and looked at the priest on the floor. The light of the moon shone on the man's face. The priest looked somehow thinner on the floor, even smaller than he'd seemed outside during daylight. "Take my bunk. I can sleep where you're sleeping. I told you that already," Samson added.

"No, my son. Keep the bunk. It is you who needs your sleep. Not me," Kolbe said. His tone was the sincere tone of a father who wanted to make sure his son got the rest he needed.

Samson shook his head in the dark. "You're as thickheaded as my brother."

Zach rose up on one elbow. "Kolbe, answer me this. You're not a Jew, and the Nazis rarely take monks . . . why are you here?"

Samson peered over the side of the bunk again and looked at the man. The monk had hinted at the answer earlier, but Samson wanted to hear more of the story too.

At first, Kolbe didn't respond. He had found two small sticks from the birch trees, and he was staring intently at them in the moonlight. He tore a small ribbon of cloth off the hem of his prison garb and began tying the two sticks together in the shape of a cross. Finally, he answered. "I'm here because I was at my Father's work."

"Your father's work?" Zach said. "Is he here too?"

"My Father is always at his work to this very day, and I, too, am working. At my friary I hid Jews who were trying to escape the Nazis. When the Germans caught me, they would have killed me on the spot, but the officer who led the group was a parishioner of my church until recently."

"You knew of this place, yet you still risked being sentenced to Auschwitz?" Zach asked. "It's one thing to be Jewish and therefore a target. It's another to deliberately throw your life away. You're a fool!"

Kolbe smiled and chuckled lightly. "Well, my friend, the Scriptures say that the wisdom of God is foolishness in man's eyes. And the wisdom of man is foolishness in God's eyes."[2]

---

2.   1 Corinthians 3:19, paraphrase, and 1 Corinthians 2:14, paraphrase.

"Forgive my little brother," Samson said in the darkness. "His fiancée is in the camp, and they never consummated their love. A man such as he is so close to heaven—yet so far away—and he cannot understand how another man could voluntarily turn away from the pleasures of this life if given the choice."

Kolbe nodded. "Well, I've been called a fool before—both for taking the vow of celibacy as well as offering cups of cold water to the so-called 'least' of my brethren. But I tell you, my friends—when people are motivated by faith, especially strong faith, they can move mountains."

"Faith?" Samson's words bore a firmer tone. "No, my little brother has plenty of that. Same as you. But you and he are here in the camps, same as me—a man who has no faith at all anymore. If there is a God—or a Messiah—then how could he let this happen? Where is a good God in the midst of the horror of this very day?"

Kolbe continued working on his makeshift cross. For a while he said nothing, apparently weighing the gravity of Samson's question. His silence contained the air of a man who knew this was a sensitive question, a question that required time to mull before charging into an answer.

"I have asked God that," Kolbe said at last, "and the answer given me is simple and yet complicated. The same answer is available to you, as it is to everyone. Yet many who claim to be open to the truth, whatever the truth may be, are not truly open. Not as open as they think they are. I have a feeling, my friend, you are not ready to dig for the truth, even if I gave you a shovel."

"What kind of answer is that?" Samson looked at the priest again, studying the man's face intently. There was no hint of malicious intent in the priest's eyes. No ill will or sarcasm or the kind of puffed-up pride that could spring from either ego or having more knowledge or experience than someone else. Just a sincere look of compassion. It was clear to Samson that Maximilian Kolbe honestly felt that this was not the time to answer the question.

Perhaps, Samson wondered in the dark, the priest was right—a man who loved to fight as much as Samson did wasn't ready yet to listen with an open heart.

NINE

Samson's shovel dug deep into the ditch alongside Kolbe and the other prisoners. The rains fell almost daily, the air frosty in the mornings and evenings.

Samson ran a hand across the stubble of his chin. His face itched. He shivered, shaking the rain off his back, trying to stay warm. His arms felt heavy, his legs dull. Day after day, the only food provided was thin, wispy soup. Prisoners constantly complained to each other about hunger pangs. Each day they were forced to dig, and dig heartily. If a man didn't, he was pulled off work detail and never heard from again. The prisoners' growling stomachs kept them awake at night, and the days of hard labor combined with not enough food and sleep were taking their toll.

Even so, Samson made the most of his time outside. As he worked, Samson surveyed the layout of the camp. He took note of each fence and the rotation of guards, always measuring in his mind, always calculating how many steps to a destination, always mentally filing away all the outcroppings that could be used as hiding places on moonlit nights. This daily analysis of Auschwitz had become a regular pastime for Samson. He knew he would get only one chance for escape, and he was constantly searching for any weaknesses in the camp. Little by little, he found them.

Samson closely watched Kolbe as well. Something intrigued him about the little priest. Kolbe seemed to be constantly taking in his surroundings—but he wasn't looking for a way to escape. Kolbe was always noting the small nuances and gestures of others, always watching their eyes, always noting where those eyes were looking. He peered into people's thoughts and feelings deeper than most, constantly striving to find out what motivated people to do what they did. Through whispered conversations in the barrack at night, Samson discovered that Kolbe had read every biblical psalm and proverb more than five hundred times. The priest seemed to have gained quite a bit of wisdom and insight from them. Kolbe had also read Jesus' teachings repeatedly, and he always spoke and acted as if he desired to know people deeply rather than to judge them harshly. Kolbe explained to Samson his reasoning. The priest felt that if he could observe and understand people better, then somehow he would be better able to share the love of Jesus that so burned in his heart.

"Has anyone ever escaped this camp?" Samson whispered to Kolbe one afternoon as they dug side by side near an outside wall of Auschwitz.

Kolbe checked over his shoulder, then dug for several minutes before responding. "It is no surprise to me you're asking this question."

"What makes you say that?"

"Because you will never give up fighting—neither for yourself nor for your family. I have come to see that about you."

"You think it's wrong for a man to fight?"

"Not necessarily, although I choose peace whenever possible. A man should protect those in his charge who cannot protect themselves. I am curious, though, if you have truly calculated the cost. You are only one man, and there are a thousand guards with guns in this camp. For many other prisoners, even the thought of escape would seem futile."

"Is that what you think escape from this place is—futile?" Samson dug closer to Kolbe and gave him a long, sideways glance.

"No, not for you it isn't," Kolbe said. "You are a man who must try to escape. And I believe you will do it too."

"Okay, so answer the question then—has anyone ever escaped from here?"

"Many have tried." Kolbe looked far away. "Only one I know of actually reached his goal. He got outside the camp, the other prisoners tell, and for a while, he was a very free man."

"What became of him?"

Kolbe sighed. "Oh, they caught him eventually, poor soul. Rumor was that when they found him, they crucified him upside down."

Samson nodded, grim resolve still stoking his spirit. He dug another row, shoveling dirt on a board to drag over to a larger pile. "Well, at least the man tried to escape. Better to die on your own terms than theirs."

"Perhaps, Samson . . . ," Kolbe said slowly. "I'm curious, have you ever considered not trying to escape? On the day you attempt to scale walls and dodge bullets, you will not be able to take your family with you. They need you alive here with them, trying to protect them from inside the walls."

"Stay inside these walls?" Samson dug harder, venting his frustration. "No. I will come back for my family. All of them. These fences are not so impenetrable. With the right strategy, a successful escape will be ours."

Kolbe glanced over his shoulder again, then stopped digging a moment. He looked Samson in the eye. "May I ask you a final question?"

Samson nodded.

"A man who desires a great reward is often required to sacrifice much. Are you willing to pay a great price for your family's freedom?"

"I have no money here," Samson said bitterly. "It was all taken, same as everyone else's."

"That's not the price I'm talking about."

"What, then?"

"I'm asking if you're willing to lay down your life for your family. I'm talking about the cost of your life."

Samson didn't respond at first. He continued to dig, shoveling each load with determination. Then came his reply, slow and measured yet irrefutable. "I'm no martyr. I want to live . . . but I will tell you this." Samson stopped digging and looked Kolbe in the eye. "There is nothing I would not give for my family . . . nothing. Including my life."

"You answer well, my friend." Kolbe eyed him back with the same iron determination. "Whoever gives his life out of love is a man after God's own heart. Jesus said no man has greater love than to lay down his life for a friend."[1]

Samson thrust his shovel into the dirt. "No wonder he died."

***

Some forty yards away from Samson and Kolbe, another conversation was taking place.

---

1. John 15:13, paraphrase.

Commander Höss and his wife, Hedwig, a quiet and compassionate woman still holding the flower of beauty well in her thirties, and Dr. Josef Mengele walked with two immaculately dressed Nazi officers. The conversation party was surrounded by *Schutzstaffel*, the most elite German protection squad. As Samson recognized the two men who walked with them, his jaw dropped. The men were Heinrich Himmler and Adolf Hitler.

A small camera crew followed the group. The crew looked to be shooting footage for a movie.[2] Samson nudged Kolbe, who looked over and spotted the crew. Fake prisoners dressed in clean, new prison garb posed before the camera in a "work scene." The prisoners in front of the camera were smiling, healthy, well fed, and obviously working hard to present a false picture of the prisoners' camp life. Knee-deep in a ditch, Samson and Kolbe watched, astounded. Their shoes stuck in the muck, their hands blistered, their stomachs growling.

Hitler and Himmler broke off from the group and went to talk with a man who looked to be the director. From far away, Dr. Mengele spotted Samson and whispered something to Commander Höss. Samson ducked his head down and dug faster. He turned his

---

2. SS Commander Hans Günther forced Kurt Gerron, a Jewish actor/director, to make a twenty-three-minute film called *Der Führer schenkt den Juden eine Stadt*, "The Führer Gives a City to the Jews." The film was designed to assure international audiences that the inmates were not being abused. It was a massive, well-drawn hoax. The film was part of the well-oiled Nazi propaganda machine, and it was intended to be shown in neutral countries to counter anti-Nazi propaganda coming from the Allies about the persecution of Jews. Influential organizations such as the International Red Cross and the Vatican would be given screenings to appease their concerns. In return for making the film, Günther promised Gerron that he would live. Immediately after Gerron finished shooting the film, both he and the other cast members were sent to their deaths ("The Führer Gives a City to the Jews," National Center for Jewish Film, http://www.jewishfilm.org/Catalogue/films/city_to_the_jews.htm).

back to the officers and hissed at Kolbe. "Keep facing toward them. Tell me what they're doing."

"Their eyes are glued our direction," the priest said. "They're still whispering and nodding. Look sharp—they're heading our way." The priest continued to shovel.

Mengele and Höss walked directly toward Samson and Kolbe and stopped at the ditch's edge. Two armed guards stood nearby, weapons drawn. Mengele smiled broadly at Samson. It was a wry smile, the kind of smile received when someone knows a secret about you.

"Samson Abrams—come here," Höss ordered. His tone was polite. It sounded more like a request than a summons.

Samson didn't trust them. He felt a gnawing in the pit of his stomach. He glanced at Kolbe, kept his shovel in his hand in case he needed to use it as a weapon, and climbed out of the ditch. For a moment, the officers stood without speaking, looking at the prisoner. They eyed Samson up and down. It was more of an inspection than a glance. Then Mengele walked slowly around him. Höss did the same. Samson stood unmoving. He looked forward, his stare unyielding. He gripped the shovel tighter in his hands.

"I knew that I had seen you before," Höss said, grinning. His tone was almost joyful, a singsong fashion, like a boy at Christmas talking about his favorite new toy. "Samson Abrams—Jewish boxing star of the '36 Olympics. The fiercest middleweight ever seen. Born in Poland but raised in America since he was just a small child. Came back to Poland with his family when the Great Depression struck the United States."

Samson said nothing. He had not wanted to reveal his identity to anybody. Too much attention was only a hindrance to escape. Kolbe's eyebrows shot up. Samson quickly looked the priest's way, then focused ahead again. By the look on Kolbe's face, Samson could tell the man had no idea he had been befriending a champion boxer. Mengele unholstered his revolver, and Samson saw Kolbe jump. Samson began to raise his shovel but quickly halted as Mengele calmly proceeded to clean the weapon, apparently enjoying the power that came with being the "big" man holding the gun. Hedwig approached, eyeing Samson. He glanced at her, then averted his eyes. She was smiling at Samson, a careful, bemused smile.

Dr. Mengele took over the conversation where Höss had left off, but his tone was not nearly as joyous as the commander's. He spoke with a cold edge. "Yes. Samson Abrams. The same boxer who nearly killed two armed guards in Kraków on a routine arrest. A crime punishable by death." He continued to clean his revolver.

Höss waved Mengele off. "What a shame it was to disqualify a man from his chance at an Olympic gold medal after he knocked his opponent unconscious. Even if he is a Jew . . . and even if it was a low blow."

"I hit him above the belt," Samson said.

Höss chuckled long and heartily. "Oh, so I hit a nerve with you, did I? A nerve that unleashes a beast. Ah, it's the truth, of course. I know you hit him above the belt. Straight in the solar plexus. I was there myself, directly in the front row. Saw it with my own eyes. It was the only time I've ever seen a man knocked unconscious by a blow to the body. The man couldn't breathe, passed out right in front of me."

Hedwig had remained standing next to her husband, but now she took a step closer. Samson shot her another glance. She had not stopped staring at Samson this whole time. It was beginning to agitate his nerves. He couldn't quite tell if hers was a salacious gaze, or if she looked at him like she might look at an animal at the zoo.

"You saw the fight. You know who I am. What now?" Samson asked.

Höss nodded. "Ah, a bit of bullheadedness in you too. Good to see. Now we're getting somewhere. What we want from you, Mr. Samson Abrams, is entertainment."

"Entertainment?"

"You see, this place is not much fun for me, Samson. I'm a camp commander. That is my lot in life. Not much glory for an officer unless you're on the front lines. Not much money unless you're a general. But there is always the possibility of entertainment. That's what we've come to"—the commander paused to cough—"discuss with you."

"Go on," Samson said.

"Every Saturday night here in the camp, the officers and guards have entertainment. Oh, it's nothing really, some boxing, some singing, some harmless wagering—simple amusements to brighten our time. We have held boxing matches before, but a Jewish Olympian . . . well, that will be good for morale among the troops"—the commander coughed again—"very good *indeed*."

"Not interested. My fighting days are through." Samson's tone was polite, yet firm. His experience from boyhood had taught him that when you stand up to a bully, the bully will fold.

Höss chuckled again, long and loudly, while Mengele continued to load bullets, one by one, slowly. He finished loading his revolver, snapped the parts in place, and took the safety off. He never once took his eyes off Samson. Hedwig noticed Mengele's actions and took a step back. The look on her face told Samson that she did not trust the doctor, even though her husband was higher in rank and had overriding authority in Auschwitz.

Höss smiled again and motioned for Mengele to put away his

revolver. "It's true, Samson, you have not fought for a while. I can see how a professional such as yourself would consider his boxing days over. But we have not explained our terms. You see, we enjoy our entertainment very much around here." The commander's voice grew firmer at the end, like a man who'd grown completely accustomed to any and all prisoners immediately saying yes to whatever was ordered of them. "So it will be a good idea if you . . . come out of retirement."

Samson looked at the commander's face. Neither man said anything for a moment, a testing ground of adamant wills. A dare to yield first.

Hedwig made the first move. She shook her head briefly. "You boys and your tactics," she said, then turned to walk away. But her husband grabbed her arm, stopping her. The commander looked at Samson while holding his wife's arm tightly.

"Our terms are that the winner gets extra food . . ."

"I'm listening," Samson said.

" . . . and the loser goes to the gas chambers," Mengele said. His tone indicated he'd had enough.

Hedwig's nostrils flared. "I hate it when you talk this way," she said. The woman broke free from her husband's grasp and strode away. This time, the commander made no attempt to stop her.

Dr. Mengele unsnapped his holster, stepped toward Samson, and lifted the gun to Samson's face. "Look, we've had enough of your insolence, you filthy Jewish pig. If it was up to me, your throat would already be slit. But out of respect for my colleague," he pointed to Höss, "let me make this perfectly clear. You will box for us, and it will be on our terms. Our terms are the only terms—and our terms are ordered, not offered." He stepped closer to Samson. "Do you know why you will box, swine? It's because your children—twin daughters and a son, I believe—are so very sweet. Since coming to the camp, they have had only harmless experiments performed on them . . . but I have been known to change my mind."

"What do you mean, *experiments*?" Samson's voice was set like flint.

"The doctor doesn't need to answer questions from prisoners," Höss said, motioning again for Mengele to reholster his revolver. "You will box for us, Samson Abrams. That is all you need to know. This weekend will be your first match. I suggest you prepare yourself. Now, if you'll excuse me," he turned toward Dr. Mengele with a sigh, "I must go find my wife."

Höss walked in the direction of the film crew, the same direction Hedwig had gone, but Mengele remained in front of Samson. The doctor's expression had returned to serene, but there was a tinge of color in his neck, red from fury. He spoke carefully and coldly, exacting his words as if slicing meat with a butcher's wheel.

"It has often been argued," Mengele said, "that one can prolong the torture of a human for as long as twenty-one days before he dies. Do you believe that, Mr. Samson Abrams?"

Samson said nothing.

The doctor eyed him up and down. "Yet I believe science will show that with a strong enough human specimen—a man such as yourself, for instance—I can prove a man is able to withstand torture far longer than twenty-one days . . . thirty days. Perhaps forty. Can you imagine being tortured for forty days, Mr. Samson Abrams?" The doctor eyed the prisoner, then smiled broadly, his mind apparently carefree again.

Mengele turned his back on Samson and began whistling a happy tune. "I look forward to seeing your skills in the ring this weekend," he called over his shoulder. The guards followed, walking back to the film crew.

Samson never took his eyes off Mengele's back. He trembled slightly, not from fear but from rage, and he felt he could easily ram his fist through a brick wall—or the doctor's skull. With Mengele far away, Samson climbed back into the ditch beside Kolbe. He speared his shovel's blade deep into the dirt and turned over a huge clod of ground. He lifted the dirt high and flung it hard against the carrying board. Samson shoveled and threw with all his might. Again and again, he shoveled and threw. Half an hour went by, then an hour, and Samson never slacked. The other prisoners looked on, startled by such an outburst of vigor. Despite his lack of food, Samson's anger fueled his strength.

Finally the little priest edged closer to Samson, motioning him to slow down. "Careful," Kolbe said. "If you work like this, you'll bring trouble to the other prisoners. No man can sustain this pace for long."

Samson breathed heavily, but he wasn't spent yet. "What do you know about this doctor's experiments? What will he do to my children?"

Kolbe laid a hand on Samson's shoulder. "Shovel softly. We can whisper then."

Samson nodded.

"I do not know yet all the horrors of this place," Kolbe said. "I ask a lot of questions and talk to as many prisoners as are willing to speak. Many prisoners talk to me about their fears, and without confirmation, who knows if their fears are merely suspicions or the things they have actually witnessed. But I do know this—the doctor is routinely interested in children, identical twins, and pregnant women. That is verified. I have heard others describe in detail the experiments he performs on them. Terrible, unspeakable things.

If the doctor is threatening your children's safety, then you must know his threats are not idle."

The hair on the back of Samson's neck stood up. "I want to know everything, Kolbe. What does he do? Tell me—now."

Kolbe's face dropped. "When I uttered my vows to become a priest, I never dreamed of a day when I would need to offer such counsel. You are a man who has vowed to protect his family, even at the cost of your own life. So you have no other choice. If you refuse to box, the doctor will show your family no mercy. He will torture and kill each one, slowly and cruelly. That is fact. You must fight, Samson. You must."

TEN

THE PLACE WAS CALLED SOLAHÜTTE.[1]

Samson rattled along in the back of a truck. It was nearly nightfall, but he could still see a sliver of the Sola River as he rode to their destination. He was handcuffed to a rail of the truck's bed, and four guards rode with him, all puffing on cigarettes, their weapons resting loosely on their knees. Samson's grasp of German was rudimentary at best, but he could discern from the guards' talk that Solahütte was the name given to a little-known resort for Nazi guards, administrators, and auxiliary personnel of the Auschwitz-Birkenau Concentration Camp. It was part of a tiny subcamp of Auschwitz, located about eighteen miles south of the main camp. Samson glimpsed the outside of the main building at Solahütte as

---

1. Facts about Solahütte remained largely unknown until after 2007, when the Höcker Album of vintage Auschwitz photographs surfaced and was donated to the United States Holocaust Memorial Museum (United States Holocaust Memorial Museum, "Auschwitz Through the Lens of the SS: Photos of Nazi Leadership at the Camp," *Online Exhibitions*, http://www.ushmm.org/museum /exhibit/online/ssalbum/?content=1).

they drove up. It was long and rectangular, and it stood high on a treed mountaintop—a rustic getaway facility. A resort just outside of hell.

The guards uncuffed Samson and ushered him down off the truck's bed. Dr. Mengele met them in the parking area. Two guards flanked him. "This way," Mengele said with a bemused smile, and the doctor led Samson and the guards inside, through the officers' parlor, which was already full of drunken Nazis.

SS-*Totenkopfverbände*, top SS-*Sonderkommando*, leaders of the Gestapo (the secret state police), and high-ranking guards mingled with female auxiliaries. People ate and drank, laughed loudly, spilled beer, and told raucous jokes, a stark contrast from the image of self-disciplined perfection put forth in Nazi propaganda. Samson spotted some Schutzstaffel, who never moved more than an arm's length away from Himmler.

In the middle of the parlor, the show had already started. Samson wafted away dense cigarette smoke from his face, his eyes drawn to a makeshift boxing ring in the center of the room. Small circus dogs jumped through hoops in the middle of the ring. They balanced on their hind legs, performing tricks. Samson got the picture. He was, almost literally, part of a dog and pony show. A man among trained animals. The dogs left the stage with their trainers to a modest round of applause.

A drag queen took the ring next, microphone in hand.[2] An accordion struck up a song, and the painted man shook his fake bosoms and began belting out an upbeat German tune, sliding

---

2. Drag queen cabaret was quite popular at the time, seen as both hedonistic and humorous, a "fun" diversion from the horrors of war, according to some (Vern L. Bullough and Bonnie Bullough, *Cross Dressing, Sex, and Gender* [Philadelphia: University of Pennsylvania Press, 1993], 237).

femininely between the boxing ring ropes and gliding toward the bar. The crowd whistled and hollered, cheering for more.

Mengele led them through the crowd into a bathroom near the end of the building. It was a stark contrast to the parlor—a cement floor with a wooden bench. On a chair were boxing shorts, some old German fighting boots, and a pair of boxing gloves hung by their strings. Oddly, a single, yellow, potted flower sat perched on the ledge above the sink. The flower reminded Samson of the flower he had given Rebecca immediately before being brought to Auschwitz. It seemed years ago, though it had only been a few weeks.

"Undress. Lace up. A guard will tape your hands," Mengele ordered.

The door to the bathroom still stood wide open. Samson eyed the guards, their weapons still drawn, then removed his prison garb. Samson was a very muscular middleweight, lean and chiseled from decades of boxing and hard physical labor. He sensed Mengele's eyes on his unclothed body.

"It becomes a matter of ethnic study," Mengele said. "You're fighting a large Polack tonight. You may well fight a bobcat next week. Or an alligator, if I could get one." The doctor chuckled. "The question in my mind, always, is which one of the animal species is superior."

Samson pulled on his shorts and laced up the boots. He held a hand forward. A guard began to wrap his hand in boxing tape.

"Oh, and see that you put on a good show," Mengele said with a yawn. "Commander Höss has got a lot of money riding on tonight's fight. He's bet on you, you know—the Jew. Everyone else took the Pole."

"Who did you bet on?" Samson asked, his teeth gritted.

Mengele laughed. "I haven't made my wager yet. Undoubtedly the Pole, but I wanted to see both men's muscularity up close first."

A commotion sounded at the doorway to the bathroom—

scuffling, shoving, loud footsteps, German curse words bandied about. Guards came in first, followed by a tall, shirtless beast of a man. More guards came in after him as the lead guards led the fighter to the other end of the bathroom where he finished undressing, suited up, and got his hands taped.

Samson eyed his opponent. The man stood well over six feet tall, and Samson estimated he weighed about two hundred and twenty pounds. He was big boned and thick skinned, with a healthy amount of body fat still covering his large frame. He was built more like a wrestler than a boxer, but his height and weight advantage were immediately obvious to Samson.

The Polish fighter nodded. Samson nodded back. It was an emotionless exchange. They were both businessmen ready to do a job. One man would die. The other man would eat extra rations and get another night of restless sleep, but he would not get to go home like a normal boxer would. There was no home to go to. There was only Auschwitz, the barracks, and attempting to stay alive to fight another day.

Samson wondered if this man had a family like his. He wondered what had been threatened against the Pole to bring him into the boxing ring. He was probably a farmer, a big man who had once wrestled or boxed in school, and now he found himself a slave to the Nazis like all the others in occupied Poland, objects of tortuous play for the Auschwitz officials.

Another commotion at the door. Commandant Höss walked into the bathroom, along with a group of guards. The bathroom was packed.

"A hundred reichsmarks[3] on my Jew!" Höss called out with a broad smile. "Come now, men—who'll take my bet?"

---

3.   During World War II, one reichsmark equaled roughly forty cents in American currency.

The guards shouted in approval. A few who were lounging by the edge of the sink jumped to their feet. Mengele waved them away. "No, no," he said, his voice still calm. "Not yet." The doctor walked around Samson, eyeing his physique, running the statistics of a large heavyweight against a smaller but potentially quicker middleweight.

"Commandant, you have yourself a bet," Mengele finally said. "I consider it a scientific wager, research if you will . . . It only makes sense for me to take the larger, genetically superior, Aryan-looking Pole over the smaller, inferior Jew. I will take the bet against you, if only to prove my studies accurate."

Höss dropped two fifty-reichsmark notes onto the counter beside the sink. Mengele nodded, eyeing the cash. Slowly, studiously, Mengele laid down the matching currency. Samson studied the men's faces. He doubted the two men liked each other, much less trusted each other. They were both too ambitious and competitive. They respected each other, perhaps. After all, they were both in the same line of work—killing. They had clearly both learned to deaden the senses, crucifying their sensibilities in order to carry out their brand of heinous, depraved genocide. Samson guessed they recognized in each other the same murderous instinct.

Both fighters' gloves were laced tight. Mengele and Höss left the bathroom to head for the front of the parlor, near the ring. Armed guards began to escort Samson and the Pole through the crowd toward the boxing ring. The room was packed. Samson couldn't see the ring yet from his path along the floor as he inched through the crowd. He noticed the drag queen was gone. Instead of the accordion, the strident rise and fall of violin music now filled the room. The violin player was skillful, classically trained, Samson could tell—undoubtedly more used to playing Mozart than the German folk tune now pealing from his instrument with an underlying shrillness. The crowd clapped along in unison, cheering on the musician for more.

Nazi soldiers argued and strutted all around Samson and the Pole. They laid down bets as the two fighters continued to push toward the ring. Samson could make out some of their jeers. Some guards pointed at Samson and laughed. The Pole had him in height by at least five inches, in weight by at least fifty pounds. But other guards nodded toward Samson, noticing that Samson's physique was hardened, lean, sinewy. He wasn't a big man, but his muscularity made it evident to the soldiers that he was used to training and hard labor. Several large scars showed on his back. Clubbings from school days. The guards could see he was no stranger to pain. Reichsmarks hit the tables. Bets quickly piled high in outstretched palms. The live violin music rose and fell in the background.

The crowd parted slightly as the fighters neared the stage. The Pole walked ahead, blocking Samson's view of the ring. With twenty feet to go, Samson slowed his gait. The Pole was already at ring's edge, and Samson was never one to crowd another fighter's entrance. The bigger man jumped up, pushed through the ropes, and went to his corner. It was at that moment Samson got his first clear view of the violin player.

"Simon—!" Samson gasped and jerked forward.

In the center of the ring sat his son on a stool. The boy's eyes were closed, his face drawn. He played the violin with a deep intensity, like he was the only one in the room.

"Simon!" Samson shouted. "Simon!" The yelling of the crowd was too loud for the boy to hear his father's call.

Guards grabbed Samson by the shoulders, holding him back. A choke rose in Samson's throat. The sight of his son sitting alone in the middle of the boxing ring playing for the amusement of a crowd of drunken, gun-toting murderers nearly sent Samson into a blind fury. He raged against the guards, shoving against the hands that gripped his shoulders. He was a protective parent, a bear robbed of cubs. Samson pushed to the ring's edge, dragging the Nazi guards with him.

"Simon!" Samson shouted again. He leaped up onto the ring's sides and hurdled the ropes.

Simon's eyes popped open. His music faltered. "Daddy!" Simon yelled. The boy jumped up and ran to his father.

Rough hands held them apart. Three guards dragged Samson back to his corner. The ring guard hit Simon on the side of the face. "We didn't say to stop playing, little Jew," the ring guard yelled. A red welt rose on Simon's cheek.

Samson strained against the guards. Two others joined in and held him fast. The crowd roared. Samson locked gazes with his boy across the ring from him—rage, shock, and love swirled within him like lava nearing a volcano's surface. Besides the welt, his son also had the remnants of a black eye. The corner of his lip looked puffy and swollen. This wasn't the first time the boy had been struck since arriving at Auschwitz.

"Who did that to you?" Samson yelled. "Who!" The guards gripped Samson tighter. A ring guard picked up Simon and threw the boy over his shoulder.

"Daddy—help me!" Simon wailed.

The ref-guard held Simon roughly as the boy struggled in his grasp before breaking free and falling to the floor. The ref-guard cursed and caught the back of Simon's shirt, yanking him up and backward. Simon stumbled. The angry referee grabbed him by the collar and righted him, throwing him into a headlock with one arm. With his other arm, the ref picked up the boy's violin. He dragged Simon to the corner of the ring and hoisted him over the ropes to another guard.

"Simon—*lehisha'er khazak! Ani ohev otcha!*"[4] Samson cried out as he exploded. He threw the guards backward and began to run for Simon, calling after his son.

Click. A gun cocked behind Samson's ear. Even in the throes of rage, the sound was unmistakable. It stopped him cold. Samson knew the sound well. He'd heard the click of a gun so many times since the occupation that he had trained himself to heed the sound, if for no other reason than to protect his family. Samson slowly turned. Pointed in his face was Mengele's gun.

The room quickly quieted. Samson looked around. Dozens of rifles were trained on him now.

"We take our entertainment very seriously here, Samson." Mengele's voice was calm. "Sometimes the wisest thing a father can do is let his child go."

Samson looked to the side. A guard was carrying Simon out an exit door. The boy looked over the guard's shoulder, back at his father. Samson's and Simon's eyes locked across the distance, Samson desperately wishing he could protect his son.

"Is that what you want to do, Samson?" Mengele motioned with his head. "Run after your boy? You know that will bring about only one conclusion." The doctor waved his hand, palm up, around at the crowd. "These people are here to see you box, Samson. You wouldn't want to disappoint them, would you?" The pistol was still inches from Samson's face.

---

4. "Stay strong! I love you!"

It seemed a straightforward decision, but Samson held his ground, unmoving. He glared at the doctor, silently challenging him to pull the trigger. A question rolled through Samson's mind—which was worse? Punch Mengele in the face once and be brought down in a hail of gunfire? Or box in a life-or-death match against a man five weight classes above him with a huge reach advantage, a man as desperate to win as any man can be?

Then he remembered—the winner got extra food. If he won, Samson could share the extra food with his family. As much as he longed to break Mengele's jaw, the wiser choice was to take his chances in the ring. He knew the correct pathway to take, but still his stubbornness persisted. His fists were clenched tight. He couldn't turn his stare away from Mengele.

"Enough nonsense!" Höss called forth. "Samson—go to your corner."

Slowly Samson's fists relaxed. He turned and walked to his corner.

Höss turned his head and called out to the crowd. "What say you? I've got big money riding on this fight. Let's get on with the main event!"

The crowd roared their approval. An accordion started up again. More beer was poured. More money exchanged hands.

The Polish fighter paced around the ring, a crazed look in his eye. Repeatedly, he hit himself in the face with his gloved fists to psyche himself up for battle.

From his corner, Samson turned to the ref-guard, who had dragged Simon away from him. "How many rounds?" Samson asked.

"Rounds? There are no rounds. The fight ends when one of you can no longer fight."

Samson shook his head in disbelief. No rounds? What other rules had been changed?

The mob roared. The noise drowned out the accordion player who had begun playing when Simon was removed. Nazis clapped in unison; the din grew in a swelling howl. Those farthest from the ring pounded the walls in anticipation. Stacks of money shook from outstretched fists.

Out of the corner of his eye, Samson noticed Hedwig coming into the parlor through a side door. She saw Samson, looked him in the eye, and held his glance.

Ding! Ding! Ding! The boxing ring bell chimed. Samson quickly kissed the marred tattoo of the Star of David on his wrist. The fight was on.

Immediately, the Polish fighter charged at Samson. The Pole launched a haymaker, then another—powerful but lumbering, sloppy punches that Samson easily ducked with lightning-fast reflexes. Samson was fast—very fast—and the Pole noted this, changing his tactics. He began to circle Samson in an effort to better use his substantial reach advantage.

Samson sized up his opponent. The Pole held his gloved hands reasonably high; his elbows were kept fairly tight. That meant he had some boxing experience. But his moves told Samson that the Pole was not a professional boxer. He moved more like a heavyweight wrestler, his back and knees bent more than necessary. All in all, the Pole was desperate and strong, and although not a pro, he was seemingly trained just enough to be dangerous.

The Pole thrust a jab at Samson's head. Samson ducked. Seeing Samson was going to be a hard target to hit, the Pole tried to clinch with him, attempting to get one hand around the back of Samson's neck, probably an attempt to wrestle Samson down. But he could not do it. Samson was too quick, backpedaling, fighting in a constantly shifting, cagey style with swift footwork, invariably shifting positions, bobbing and weaving. The man was impossible to get a bead on.

The crowd began to boo and hiss at Samson for not charging his opponent. It was becoming obvious to them that he was fighting defensively. The Nazis hated this, which brought Samson a moment of unexpected elation. For the first time in a very long while, he held the power. He could either make the Nazis' night entertaining or frustrating. If they demanded entertainment—then he'd go the other direction. He'd make their show as boring as a technically gifted boxer could make it. Maybe, just maybe, if the fight proved boring enough, the Nazis would stop the fight in disgust and send both fighters back to camp.

Unfortunately, this momentary elation caused Samson to be unfocused, distracted for just one split second and . . . *thud!* Samson was caught with a vicious hook to the chin. He staggered back, shaken. His huge opponent went to work on him, taking advantage of a temporarily stunned Samson. The heavyweight landed punches to the front and back of Samson's head as Samson tried to duck and weave his way out of a corner. *Thud.* Samson was again pummeled with a hard uppercut to his face. *Thud.* Another shot to his ribs.

Samson quickly tied his opponent up in a clinch. He put his arms over the other boxer's upper arms, pulling his opponent's arms forward to temporarily prevent further punches. Samson breathed hard, catching his wind.

The ring guard separated them, pushing them apart to stop the clinch, forcing the fight's pace to increase. The Pole charged back at him, but Samson's head was now clear, fully recovered . . . ready. The Pole came at him with a series of wild, erratic blows. Samson responded with slippery speed. Faster than fast, he head-faked and stutter-stepped, bobbing right, then left. The Pole kept swinging. Samson moved like a snake, slipping in and out of punches, never allowing his opponent time to locate his attack, forcing the Pole to repeatedly miss.

The evasive work began to tire not only the Pole, but Samson as well. The difficult and tricky work of getting his opponent to commit to a certain angle to throw a punch and then miss was exhausting. Both men had been on Auschwitz's starvation diet for weeks now, and Samson had not been in a boxing ring for some time. As masterful as he was with the evasive maneuvers, he was finding it difficult to maintain his usual pace.

The booing of the Nazis increased. They were used to amateurs standing in the middle of the ring and slugging it out, not this professional backpedaling, ducking, and head faking around the ring. Samson had yet to throw a single punch. The soldiers' wrath rose. Höss hung his head. Mengele walked out. Himmler shook his head, bewildered.

Thud! Thud! The Pole landed two hard shots right on Samson's jaw. With a chin of iron, Samson shook off the punches and tied up the Pole in a clinch again. More booing ensued. In the clinch, Samson's gaze landed on the door. What he saw stunned him.

There, on the other side of the room, stood Mengele. The doctor gripped Simon's neck from behind. With his other hand, the doctor held his revolver to Simon's head. Mengele smiled calmly in Samson's direction. The implication was blatant—*Give us the fight we demand, or your boy dies.*

The dam broke in Samson's heart. Floodwaters of fury spilled forth. There would be no more toying with his opponent. No more deliberately slowing the fight in an endeavor to save them both. He had no choice. Samson unleashed his true strength. He shoved the huge Pole back, way back—ten feet back, half flying into the ropes.

The Polish fighter stared at Samson, getting his first taste of Samson's raw strength. Some Nazis looked stunned. They traded looks—*Where did that come from?* Samson flew at his opponent and landed a hail of blows to his face and body. The crowd cheered. The fight had just become interesting. *Slam!* Samson's left uppercut connected with the Pole's ribs.

The man buckled, wheezing, and dropped his arms to protect his midsection. That left his head wide open—a big mistake. *Crack.* In a flash, Samson landed a crushing right hook, breaking the big Polish boxer's jaw. The big man toppled to the mat. He was out cold.

All cheering subsided. Stunned silence fell across the parlor. Nazi faces showed confusion, slack jaws, and staring eyes. Samson's last punch had been so fast that some did not even see it. But Commandant Höss did. He stood, clapping loud and clear, and then pulled in a sizeable pile of reichsmarks from the numerous bets he had made. Samson looked around, spotting Simon as Mengele dragged the boy out of the room.

Without success, the ring guard tried to wake the Pole. The big fighter did not respond and showed no signs of getting up. The ref-guard shrugged and climbed out of the ring, leaving Samson alone with his unconscious opponent. Samson stared down at the Pole, saddened. He knew he had not only won a boxing match—he had sentenced a man to death. Deep remorse set in. Samson knelt next to the Pole and wiped blood away from the man's nose and mouth so the Pole could breathe with less effort. Slowly the Pole woke up. He was groggy. Dazed. Samson looked him in the eye.

"I am so sorry, my friend," Samson said. "I truly am. I know you were being forced to fight, as was I . . . please forgive me."

The big man slowly looked around, realizing what had happened. Still badly shaken, the fighter managed a nod in response. He was still getting over the surprise of awakening on his back. Still stunned to see his smaller foe kneeling over him, offering his condolences.

Abruptly, several guards pushed Samson aside, grabbed the Pole, and dragged the still-weak-kneed, half-unconscious fighter out.

Other guards grabbed Samson and shoved him between the ropes, escorting him from the ring.

Heinrich Himmler leaned over and whispered loudly into Höss's ear, "Which one was the Jew?"

"The loser, of course, *Reichsführer* Himmler," said Höss without missing a beat.

Himmler smiled broadly. Höss shot a look to all the surrounding officers that clearly meant *Shut your mouths.*

Dr. Mengele had taken Simon to a truck, then returned ringside. He leaned over and whispered to Höss, "A specimen like this Samson Abrams is rare indeed. One so muscular and handsome for a Jew is beyond atypical. I would love to run some experiments on him—for the sake of scientific research, of course."

"Don't even think about it." Höss held up his stack of money. "That Jew is too valuable to send to Block 10. You can't have him."

Mengele smiled. "Later then . . . later."

Höss tamped his stack of money into one solid wad of bills, nodded to Mengele, and made a beeline for the changing room. Guards had already dragged Samson into it, and Höss wanted a word with the night's victor. Already, the commander saw money dancing before his eyes. His head reeled at the thought of how much profit he could make off his new Jewish champion.

Samson wished he could hold a bag of ice over the bruise on his cheekbone, but the guards offered him none. One motioned to him with the end of a rifle. Another was busy at the far end of the room, gathering up the losing fighter's clothes.

"Get changed, pig," the first guard said. "Someone will bring you your winnings soon."

Höss burst into the bathroom, a large grin on his face.

Samson wheeled around and squared off on reflex, expecting a fight.

Höss took one look at Samson in his fighting stance and started chuckling. "If I wanted to fight you, I'd just shoot you . . . silly little Jew."

The commander tossed Samson a large, fresh loaf of bread, then fished deep in his trouser pocket, searching for something. He pulled out a thick length of salami, only the end was cut off, and laughed at his own foolish joke. He handed the meat over.

"I'm not a monster, Samson. I believe in honor. I keep my word and reward those who deserve their recompense. Besides, benevolence makes me look good to my wife." The commander laughed again and slapped Samson on the back. "Next time we'll need to be more inventive, eh? Find someone who provides more of a challenge for you. Maybe a fighter who comes with a reputation, hmm? Some brute of a man who keeps the wagering stacked against you."

"Next time?" Samson asked, his voice like gravel.

Höss smiled at Samson as he headed for the door, but then

he stopped and turned back, eyeing Samson for a moment. "Of course," the commander said flatly. "Did you think you would fight only once?"

The commander gave Samson no time to respond. He bustled out of the room. One of the guards followed, leaving only the guard at the far end of the bathroom with Samson. For a moment Samson considered running at the guard, overpowering him, and taking his weapon. But he shook the thought from his mind. There were far too many guards in a place like this.

Instead, Samson stuffed the bread and meat into his shirt. He glanced at the guard, saw he wasn't looking, and plucked the yellow flower from the pot on the ledge above the sink, roots intact. The flower brought back good memories for him, and his mind was hatching a different plan.

ELEVEN

I T W A S   A   C L O U D L E S S ,   C O L D   N I G H T   I N   A U S C H W I T Z , the kind of cold that reached all the way down to a man's bones. Adrenaline from the fight still coursed through Samson's body as he climbed out of the truck back at camp. His joints stiffened, involuntary shudders came over him, and he fought to steel himself against the chill. The moon shone brightly as guards transferred Samson to the watch of the *Kapo* from Hut 57, whose job it was to lead Samson back to the barracks.

Samson chewed the heel of the bread as the *Kapo* led him through the camp. Despite the cold, a new, curious spring showed in Samson's step. He was feeling a twinge of hopefulness, something he hadn't felt for a long while. He thought of the little yellow flower under his prison shirt, remembering the beautiful flowers in America. He thought of New York in the spring and remembered playing with his children, dancing with his wife.

The little man with the leathery face ogled his food hungrily. Although the *Kapos* had privileges, they were still prisoners themselves and not afforded the quality of bread that Samson was eating.

"We heard you fought well tonight." The *Kapo* licked his lips.

"Word travels fast," Samson said.

"What will you do with all that bread?"

"Oh . . . I don't know. I thought I might give some to my *Kapo* . . ."
The *Kapo* clasped his hands in glee.

Samson slowed his walk. His last line had been uttered to gauge the man's reaction, and the *Kapo* had taken the bait. The man was hooked at the mere possibility of extra food. Samson spoke again, this time quickly and under his breath, so the *Kapo* listened carefully.

"Let's make this simple and honest. I have something you want. You have something I want. Let's make a deal. You know which barrack my wife is in, and I want to see her." Samson tore off a sizeable chunk of the loaf of bread and then broke off a piece of salami. He held the food out in front of him. The *Kapo* stared wide eyed at the offer.

"If they found out, we would both be sent to the chambers." The *Kapo* couldn't take his eyes off the food.

"Then we both better not get caught." Samson's hand held steady.

The *Kapo* nodded. He grabbed the food from Samson's hand, quickly nibbled some meat, and stuffed the rest in his shirt. He motioned with one hand in the direction of the shadows. Without making a sound, the *Kapo* led Samson toward a wire fence around the Hut 17 barrack.

Samson and Rebecca stood on opposite sides of the wire fence. Both fought back tears. The *Kapo* stood guard nearby, warily watching for any signs of guards or SS.

Samson slipped his fingers through the fence and touched Rebecca's belly. Only once, about a week after their day of arrival, had they been able to catch a glimpse of each other. That had been a lucky occurrence when their two labor groups passed en route to a work detail.

"I've been praying every day that I would see you again," Rebecca murmured. She stroked the back of Samson's hand over the top of her belly. "I feel so lost without you."

Samson leaned his body weight against the chain-link fence and pressed his face close. Rebecca leaned in at the same time and kissed him through a square in the fence, seconds ticking by like hours.

"You are my entire life," Samson whispered.

Rebecca fought tears. "And you are forever my champion." She touched his lip, wiping away some blood. "Thank God you won."

Samson kissed her finger. He wanted to tell her everything, but he knew it would only cause her more pain.

"We don't have much time," he whispered. "Does anyone know you're pregnant?"

She shook her head.

"Good. Keep it that way—"

"One minute," hissed the *Kapo*, tapping his foot.

Samson shot him a look—*back off*—although he, too, understood the wisdom of hurrying.

The flood of emotions bore down on Rebecca, and she struggled to choke off tears. "Can you get to the children? Can you save our babies?"

Samson touched her cheek gently. He pulled out the yellow flower he had picked and handed it to her. She took the flower, crying deeply. "I will save you and our children," Samson said. "No matter what . . . I promise you. But the only way to free you all is to get out and come back with help. If I can find an Allied soldier and get word to his commander, then the outside world will hear of this place. That's what we need now for victory—a strong army on our side."

Rebecca caught her breath, then stared at him, realizing the implications of what he was saying. "Samson—you . . . you can't leave us here alone."

He gently hushed her with a finger to her lips. "No, it won't be like that. Yes, I will escape. But you will always be with me, and I will come back for you and our children." He looked like he was about to say more but abruptly switched gears. "Our children . . . I have seen Simon, and he's okay. Quickly, tell me—are our daughters all right?"

"I have seen Rachel and Leah twice now . . . from a distance. Just yesterday was the last time. But . . . oh Samson, it is so difficult. Everyone says such terrible things about Block 10 . . ." Rebecca's voice trailed off. She swallowed, her throat sticky, then continued. "Sarah and Esther are as well as can be expected, although we have not heard anything about baby Elijah. What do you know of Zach and your parents?"

"Zach is doing his best." The greater question made a lump run down Samson's throat. He did not want his wife to see any weakness in him. "But Elijah . . . I have heard none of the babies are spared once they arrive here . . . and my mother and father . . ." Samson could not finish his sentence.

Rebecca covered her face. She knew her husband well and could sense the bad news even without words.

Samson shivered the tension out of his shoulders, ripped the remaining loaf of bread in half, and pushed it through the fence to Rebecca, along with half the salami.

She eyed the food hungrily, then shook her head. "No. You need to keep your strength if you're going to save us."

"I will be fine. Quickly, my love. I insist. I would give it all to you, but I think I can get to our children with the rest."

Rebecca relented and took the food, hiding it in her shirt. "I will pray for you, Samson, that you would be successful . . . and that you would have all the power that comes from faith. Remember, my father used to say, 'A man with no faith has no real power at all.'"

The *Kapo* took a step closer. "Samson—long enough. We need to go . . . *now!*"

Samson glanced around him. "The *Kapo* is right. Quickly— kiss me again."

They kissed through the fence, but Rebecca held on to Samson's hand. She wiped the tears from her eyes and smiled. "I desperately needed a waistband to hold up my pants," she said. "So at the garbage dump, I found three fragments of twine. I felt like the richest woman in the camp." She showed him her new "belt" and grinned. Rebecca was always trying to lift his spirits. "Do not worry, my love. Everything will be alright."

Samson grinned back at her makeshift belt. He reached out and touched her face. Her skin had always been so soft, and even now, gradually starving more each day, the touch of her skin still felt like a warm fire on a cold night.

"I . . . I still blame myself," he said.

"No. I know what was said on the train. But promise me you won't blame yourself anymore. They would have gotten us sooner or later."

Samson nodded, struggling to hold back his tears. "I love you, Rebecca. I will return for you. No matter what—this family will be free."

"Don't even think about it," the *Kapo* said.

Samson eyed him coldly.

The *Kapo* led him past the "Black Wall"—a removable wall constructed out of logs and covered with cork that had been painted black. The Black Wall was to protect the beautiful brick wall behind it from bullet holes. The wall spanned the cement courtyard and connected the front of Block 10 with the front of Block 11. It was against this Black Wall that prisoners were regularly lined up and executed.

"What is it you think I'm going to do?" Samson asked.

"Look, I'm not a bad man. Just a pragmatist. You'll never be able to get inside. I can see the look in your eyes."

"You're going to stop me with your truncheon?"

"I won't need to. Look through the windows. Guards. Lots of guards. They wouldn't trust a *Kapo* to walk you back to the barracks if they thought you had a chance of doing anything dangerous."

Samson studied the building more closely. Just as the *Kapo* had said, armed sentries paced the hallways inside the windows. Samson leaned close to the *Kapo* as they continued walking, his eyes never leaving Block 10. "You said I'd never be able to get inside. But—here's the better question . . . can *you* get inside?"

The *Kapo* paused before answering, a thin, slow smile stretching across his lips. "Well, I've done it before, so I'm certain I could do it again. But I need to know, why would a prisoner such as you want so desperately to get inside Block 10? If I was a wagering man, I'd bet there's someone you want to see. It can't be your wife, because you just saw her. So I'm going to say children. A man who wants to see his children will do just about anything. Am I right?"

Samson stopped walking. The two men halted next to a ditch. They'd both seen ditches like it dug at various places around the camp. The ditches weren't for storm water collection. They were for graves, and it was there that Samson made his proposition.

"Half the food I have left. I'll give it to you right here, right now." Samson reached inside his shirt and held out the entirety of his remaining bread and meat.

"Go on," the *Kapo* said.

"Find my children—a ten-year-old boy named Simon. And two seven-year-old girls, Leah and Rachel. Last name Abrams. The boy plays the violin—he won't be hard to find. The girls are identical twins—there can't be that many in Block 10. Half the food goes to you for making the delivery. The other half to them. Understood?"

The *Kapo* stayed silent a moment, possibly pondering if he could negotiate, then nodded quickly. "Deal," he said, and took Samson's food. "You have my word."

"I don't need your word. I'm confident you'll keep your end of the bargain."

"Why are you so sure?"

"Two reasons—as long as I'm alive and fighting in the ring, there'll be potential for more profits from my victories. Do this now, and do it well, and there will be more food to come."

"The second reason?"

"Less than an hour ago, I beat a man unconscious with my fists and sentenced him to death." Samson eyed the *Kapo* coldly. "If I find out that this food does not reach my children—and I will find out—I'll put you at the bottom of this ditch myself."

TWELVE

The next morning dawned clear and frigid.

After roll call and a breakfast of watery soup, the prisoners headed out on work detail, same as always. Samson shoveled in the very ditch where he had threatened to bury the *Kapo*. All around the prisoners, ash drifted to the ground.

For once, Samson's face didn't itch from stubble. He'd shaved that morning for a very specific purpose. The *Kapo* procured a razor, and he'd agreed to loan it to Samson on the promise of a future food payment. The bruise over Samson's eye wasn't too noticeable either—he had endured many brutal battles before and was a quick healer. Samson had borrowed a bar of soap from the *Kapo* and had tried to scrub the grime and stench away from his body. Where he was going, he didn't want to run the risk of being smelled too closely.

Some twenty-five yards away, guards loaded two army trucks. Kolbe and Zach shoveled alongside Samson, following his eye line. Samson's stare was unyielding. He was careful to do his work, but even he, ever mindful of the guards' perceptive gaze, held his attention on the trucks too long.

Zach knew his brother as well as anyone. "Something unusual interest you in the trucks this morning?" Zach sneezed, wiped ash away from his nose, and continued to shovel.

Samson gave a start and snapped his attention back on the ditch, shrugging off the question. He continued to dig, and for some time, the prisoners shoveled in silence. In the distance, the guards continued loading. For a while, they rested, smoked cigarettes, then continued loading again. Samson's eyes stayed glued to the scene.

A small bird flew overhead and landed atop one of the army trucks. It opened its beak and began to sing a song of springtime, its voice sweet, clear, and free. Samson stared at the bird long enough to burn an image of it into his mind, a picture of freedom that he would hold on to. One of the guards picked up a rock and tossed it at the bird, shooing it away. The bird lifted, flying over the high fence and into a birch tree as Samson's gaze followed it. The bird continued to sing outside the camp's walls.

"Hard to imagine a bird could ever sing in a place like this," Samson said under his breath. "For one to fly so effortlessly out of Auschwitz is inspiring." He addressed his comment to Zach and Kolbe, but he was not talking to them. Not really. He was talking to himself, solidifying his inner image of freedom.

"They will catch you, brother," Zach said, guessing at Samson's plan. "You know that, don't you? They will catch you and kill you."

"No," Samson said. "I'll be just like that bird. I'll fly high over the wall and sing when I get to the other side. And when I fly back, I'll be leading an army of eagles."

Kolbe glanced over and noticed Samson's hands were shaking. An uncommon amount of sweat lined Samson's brow—not the sweat of exertion, but the sweat of nerves.

"I will pray for you, my friend," Kolbe said. "I believe you will have your freedom, one way or the other."

Samson turned away from the bird and offered Kolbe a slight nod. "If there is a God in heaven, Kolbe, then now would certainly be the right time to pray. *Right now*, in fact."

"*Right now?*" Zach whispered, one eyebrow raised. "You're going in broad daylight?"

Samson stopped shoveling. "The trucks never leave at convenient times, do they, little brother?" He took a deep breath, readying himself. The soldiers had finished loading the truck.

"Samson, wait—do you remember the first time you ever boxed, back when you were about thirteen years old?" Zach asked. The odd, ill-placed question caught Samson off guard.

"This is not the time for memories," Samson said.

"The fellow you fought—he was a big schlemiel. A real putz. You two hit each other at the same time, right on the kisser. Both of you went down hard. But you looked at the guy on the mat and said, 'Last one up is a fat schmuck.' You got up and he didn't. They had to cart him out in a stretcher, remember?"

Samson grinned and looked at Zach. He knew his brother was attempting to get his mind off the horrible challenge at hand. It was Zach's way of trying to ease the painful pressure. Samson loved his brother; he always had.

Zach stepped close, his own grin fading. "Samson, promise me this. If I don't get up—if I don't make it back up off the mat . . . when you come back, take care of Esther for me. I can handle the thought of me not making it out alive. But please don't let Esther die here. The thought of her dying makes me feel my life has been for nothing." His brother's plea was clear.

"You won't die here—and neither will she," said Samson.

"None of us will, if I have my way. And if the day ever dawns when you are no longer able to care for her, know that Esther will be well looked after." Samson squeezed Zach's shoulder, gave a quick nod to Kolbe, and turned away, checking to make sure no one was watching him. He kept his shovel with him, holding it tight to his body, then stayed low and sprinted to the side. As Samson disappeared behind the barracks, ash continued to gently fall around him.

Behind Hut 14, ash fell on the cigarette of a lone soldier who was sneaking a few drags before the military trucks departed.

Silently, Samson watched the other soldiers slowly climbing on the back of the truck with the supplies. He slid up behind the lone cigarette-smoking soldier and tapped him on the shoulder. *Crack!* Samson punched the Nazi so hard that a tooth flew out of the man's mouth. It was a two-hit fight—Samson hit the soldier, the soldier hit the ground.

Samson dragged the man to the shadows, threw down his shovel, and rolled the body into an alley between buildings to hide it. He took a deep breath and removed the man's helmet.

The Nazi's uniform fit tight across Samson's chest, but it was just about the right length at the wrists and ankles. Samson kept the Nazi's helmet pulled low, tossed the soldier's pack into the back of the army truck, and hopped aboard.

Some twenty-five other soldiers crowded into the truck. A glance told Samson their units were mixed—none of the men knew each other very well. They smoked and laughed. It was nothing more than a routine transport. Two large German shepherd guard dogs sat just a few feet away. Samson kept his eyes on the floor as the supply truck's engine came to life, rumbling. The truck slowly began to roll forward. Furtively, Samson folded his arms and sunk his chin beneath the high jacket collar to hide his face. His shave that morning had been no coincidence.

The two trucks rumbled past the main gate. He looked back at the gate, again reading the sign that Zach had read aloud when they had first arrived. *ARBEIT MACHT FREI. What a horrible lie*, Samson thought. It provided the prisoners with false hope that they'd see freedom again, if only they towed the line and worked unceasingly. But work would never make them free—not the Nazi definition of work. *A man makes himself free*, Samson thought.

A man who escapes.

Samson tipped his helmet down farther, pretending to nap. He buried his chin in his chest as he tried to feign sleep, but a young soldier sitting across from him leaned forward and nudged Samson's knee.

"Hast du 'ne Zigarette?" the soldier said.

For a moment Samson did not move. Then, slowly, hoping he had understood correctly with his rudimentary German language skills, he pulled a pack of cigarettes from his uniform pocket and held it out. Samson kept his chin low and didn't make eye contact.

The young Nazi took the cigarette and nodded thanks.

Samson's heart raced in his shirt, adrenaline pumping through his system. He wanted to pull out his newly acquired pistol, leap out of his seat, and shoot every enemy soldier in the back of that truck. But he knew better. He'd get a couple, but another truck full of soldiers was just ahead. They'd put him in the grave for sure.

No . . . he had to keep his head, fight his urge to fight, and quietly escape this hell.

The two trucks plodded through the countryside. Samson maintained his fake sleep, catching snippets of conversation from the Nazis surrounding him. About two hours from camp, the trucks pulled to the side of the dirt road. From what Samson could understand, it was time for a bathroom break. The soldiers filed out of the backs of the two trucks, yawned, and stretched. Some lit up cigarettes. Some ambled into the woods. Most just relieved themselves by the side of the road.

Samson kept his head down as he made his way out of the truck. On the edge of the woods he paused, reached into his uniform's pocket for the German's cigarettes, and lit one to blend in, glancing around him. He took a puff. For a moment he had an odd feeling of being one of a group. Just a regular guy again, a man among men, not prisoners. All around him men talked, laughed, shivered, and urinated—just like any other group of soldiers would do on a trip. These Nazis seemed so very human, yet it dawned on Samson how thoroughly brainwashed they'd become to believe he was their enemy.

Samson had never harbored any ill will toward any German until the war began. Now he hated these same men with every inch and fiber of his being. They had stolen his freedom and were systematically waging a war against his entire people. They'd taken everything from him—his family, friends, house, job, city, and country. Yet, for this one moment, Samson had a strange feeling they were just like him.

How did it ever come to this? Samson wondered. *How could a nation ever sink to the level that Germany has now?*[1] *It is a modern, refined, well-educated country, as a whole. But the Führer believes that his is a "Master Race" that deserves to rule the world, and his propaganda machine has done a masterful job of convincing an entire country he is right. Still, how can so many people follow this madman and succumb to this depth of evil?*

Samson let his cigarette fall to the ground. He stepped on it to snuff out the spark, relieved himself on a bush, then walked a few steps into the woods.

He checked over his shoulder. No one was looking.

In a flash, he was gone.

⸻

One by one the soldiers climbed back aboard their trucks. It wasn't an urgent mission, so they were taking their time, still enjoying a stretch.

In the back of the truck Samson had ridden in, all the soldiers

---

1. When World War I ended in 1918, the victorious countries demanded at the Treaty of Versailles that the defeated countries accept responsibility for starting the war, as well as disarm, pay reparations, and make substantial territorial concessions. Germany, one of the losing countries and largely bankrupt by then, bitterly resented the treaty and struggled to meet its terms. This resentment and economic struggle, in part, fueled the rise of a totalitarian state and Hitler's regime.

   Hitler's motivations for hating the Jews are more complex to discern. In some ways, he simply needed a scapegoat for his country's difficulties. The Jews, largely pacifists, proved an easy target. In other ways, his hatred was deeply rooted in a carefully crafted ideology of evil. Historian Yehuda Bauer summarized it as follows: "The basic motivation [of the Holocaust] was . . . ideological, rooted in an illusionary world of Nazi imagination, where an international Jewish conspiracy to control the world was opposed to a parallel Aryan quest. No genocide to date had been based so completely on myths, on hallucinations, on abstract, nonpragmatic ideology—which was then executed by very rational, pragmatic means" (Yehuda Bauer, *Rethinking the Holocaust* [New Haven, CT: Yale University Press, 2002], 48).

gathered except one. The trucks started their engines and began to move. Samson's former seat was still empty.

"Where is that man?" a soldier asked, confused. "Out in the woods still?"

All the soldiers sat for a moment, looking at the one empty seat. Their truck was rolling down the road.

As if a lightbulb was suddenly turned on, the soldier Samson had given the cigarette to shot to his feet, stiff as a board, and yelled, "*Anhatten! Halt den Laster an!*"

The truck screeched to a halt.

Samson ran through the countryside, the soldier's pistol in his hand. He pushed past branches, leaped over creeks, and ran for all he was worth. A river lay before him. He splashed through it. The water rose to his armpits, and he thrashed against the current, stumbled, and slipped, remembering at the last second to hold the gun high over his head to keep it dry. He struggled up out of the water and pressed on to the other side. The sounds of men yelling and German shepherds barking pushed closer with each ragged breath Samson took.

He raced past a flock of grazing sheep. The animals bleated loudly, giving away his position. He was sprinting now, running at full tilt, sweating, gasping, his heels not touching the ground. Behind him he could make out voices, shouts, swearing in German. He slowed momentarily and cocked his ear. The voices came from the left and right as well. They had divided the group and were flanking him.

Samson pushed himself harder, dashing ahead and up a hill. His heart pounded. His wet clothes caught and pulled at his arms and legs, slowing him down. Overhead, the crack of a gunshot rang out. A bullet zipped by Samson's ear. Another shot. Another bullet whizzed by. He scrambled uphill over rocks, climbing on all fours to reach the top. The barking, yelling, and shooting were gaining on him.

At the top of the hill, Samson stopped short. To the front lay the edge of a cliff. The bottom was hundreds of feet down. A complete dead end. Samson glanced back. He spotted a glint of Nazi steel less than a hundred yards away. They were closing in fast.

There was still one direction unused.

Samson looked up into the trees.

Dogs sniffed Samson's tracks around the cliff's edge while soldiers looked out and over the steep embankment. Their faces told Samson everything he needed to know. *It was a sheer drop to the bottom—no way could he have gone down.*

The German shepherds turned, sniffing, panting, tracing his footsteps back down the dirt hill that ended at the precipice. The scent wafted around a tree, apparently disappearing. The dogs continued circling, barking incessantly. A dozen soldiers milled about, searched the lower foliage, and waited for an order, unsure of their next direction. They weren't leaving. With those dogs around, they never would. Samson decided to take the fight to them.

Thump! Samson dropped down from high in the tree, tackled a surprised soldier, and knocked him to the ground. In the span of a heartbeat, soldiers all around him aimed their guns. Samson yanked the soldier to his feet and put the revolver to the man's head, using the soldier's body as a human shield.

"Noch ein Schritt und ich erschiess' ihn!"[2] Samson shouted.

An *Untersturmführer*—second lieutenant—stepped forward.

Samson pressed his pistol harder against his Nazi captive's head.

The *Untersturmführer* raised his gun and pointed it at Samson's face.

Samson gritted his teeth and moved his thumb, ready to pull the trigger on his weapon.

"For the greater good," the *Untersturmführer* said in a kindly voice. He moved his hand slightly and fired his gun. *Bang!*

Samson froze. The bullet sailed directly through the forehead of the soldier in his grip. The man's head snapped back onto Samson's shoulder, blood spattering them both.

The second lieutenant had just murdered his own man "for the greater good."

Samson's body was black and blue. One of his eyes was completely swollen shut. They'd beaten him with the butts of their weapons first. Then with their fists, after the lieutenant had yelled at them not to damage their weapons.

They marched Samson back into Auschwitz-Birkenau with his arms bound behind his back, completely stripped of any clothes. A sign hung around his neck reading *"Hurra, ich bin zurück!"*[3] The long march of shame was standard procedure, the *Untersturmführer* had explained, for any escaped Jewish dog who was found and

---

2. "One step and I'll kill him!"
3. "Hooray, I'm back!"

captured—and, he hastened to add with a swell of pride in his chest, sooner or later, *all were caught.*

In his mind, Samson spit on all of it. The march was a show of Nazi dominance, and he could take it. What wracked him more than physical pain was despair. He had failed. He was not a bird outside the wall after all. He was a helpless pigeon in their trap.

All the prisoners of the camp stood at attention. They were tired and sweating. They'd been lined up for hours again, a standard practice when escape was detected. Thousands of pairs of eyes watched as a naked, bloody Samson was marched back into the camp. The women were forced into lines at their barracks' fence.

When Rebecca saw her husband, she broke down, collapsing to her knees, sobbing from the depths of her soul. Sarah and Esther turned their faces, stunned silent at first, then they looked to Rebecca, wishing they could console her through rows of other prisoners while trying to shake off their own fear and horror.

Crying, the thirteen-year-old Yeshua stared at Samson. This wasn't the first march back into camp they'd seen, and the boy knew all too well that the man who had saved his life was about to be hanged.

Kolbe and Zach lowered their heads in prayer. Kolbe prayed in Polish. Zach prayed in Hebrew. Both men whispered so as not to be heard by any of the Nazi guards.

They watched as Dr. Mengele walked casually by them. The Angel of Death headed directly toward Samson, who was surrounded by guards now, standing at the public gallows, awaiting his hanging.

THIRTEEN

THE *UNTERSTURMFÜHRER* STOOD WATCH AT THE bottom of the gallows while a guard led Samson up the short metal stairs leading to the top. Dr. Mengele followed up the stairs a few steps behind.

The gallows' platform creaked and groaned under the weight of the men. The contraption looked to be hastily constructed out of old rail yard parts. The guard acting as executioner wrapped a noose around Samson's neck, tightened it, and motioned for Samson to stand on a chair. The other end of the rope was tied around a metal beam above. The guard pulled up the slack and secured the rope. Dr. Mengele stood alongside the executioner, smiling as he spoke to Samson.

"They often put a burlap sack over a man's head before he is hung. The sight of a man's eyes popping out of his face is said to frighten children. But I do not think we will need any head covering today—will we?"

Samson stayed silent. His eyes frantically scanned the crowd of prisoners below, searching for the one face he wanted most to gaze upon as his last image on earth.

"I might also ask if you have any last words." Mengele examined his fingernails, clearly unfazed. "You might beg for my forgiveness. Or pledge your allegiance to the Führer. What say you then, pig? Anything you want to get off your chest?"

Samson gave his head a slight shake—no.

"I didn't think so." Mengele turned to the guard and spoke in a loud voice for the crowd to hear. "Count down from five!"

The guard positioned his foot toward the chair, gauging the distance to kick it away. He rechecked the noose and nodded to Mengele.

"Five! . . . ," called out the guard. "Four! . . ."

In the center of the crowd, Samson spotted the face. Rebecca. She was weeping. He braced himself for the impending impact.

"Three! . . . Two! . . ."

An open-topped German military vehicle roared through the front gate. Commandant Höss stood in the passenger seat, waving his arms. The vehicle screeched to a halt. Höss jumped out, angry as a hornet. He grabbed the *Untersturmführer* by the coat.

"Did you not get my message?!" Höss roared. "Get him down from there immediately!"

The *Untersturmführer* stumbled backward, barking orders to his underlings. The confused guards quickly removed the noose from Samson's neck and helped him off the chair.

Dr. Mengele climbed down the steps and strolled up to Höss, shaking his head. "My dear sir, had I known this prisoner meant so much to you, these actions would have never escalated to this. But surely we cannot allow a prisoner to escape and leave such a man unpunished?"

"Are you telling me how to run my camp, Doctor?" Höss's face grew red.

"Of course not, Commandant. Just a reminder of the obvious need for order. This man escaped. For the sake of the other prisoners, he cannot be allowed to return to the barracks unpunished."

Höss eyed Samson's bruised body warily. "It looks to me as if the guards who caught him have already dispensed sufficient punishment." The guard led Samson off the gallows and stood next to him, some ten yards away from where the commandant and doctor talked. Samson's feelings leaped from numb to spinning. He strained to hear their conversation.

"A man of his strength will undoubtedly heal soon." Mengele smiled knowingly. "In fact, he will most likely be ready for this weekend's boxing match."

"That's exactly the idea, Doctor." Höss kept his voice low. His teeth were gritted.

Mengele chuckled. "So, you don't want to part with your prized American Jew. You're willing to risk the decorum of discipline for the sake of a few reichsmarks?"

"A few reichsmarks?" Höss practically spat out the words. "Do you realize I made more money on that fight than I've made in the last six months working here in this filth? Take a good look at history, Dr. Mengele. This war will soon end, and with it the need for well-qualified officers. But the need for money will not end. Jewish swine or not, this man lives, and he will fight until he loses. Have I made myself perfectly clear?"

"Your orders are understood perfectly, Commandant. Yet it would seem a camp commander would be a fool to risk putting his job on the line for the sake of this performing monkey. No—we must still insist that the escaped prisoner be punished, and punished publically. He will not be harmed greatly. I promise you that."

Höss looked Mengele square in the eye. The two men stood

staring at each other, both unmoving. Steel will against steel will. Höss held the rank, but the doctor's words were getting to him.

At last, Höss sighed. He motioned the *Untersturmführer* over and spoke to the lieutenant. "See that the prisoner is appropriately whipped for all to see. Make sure it is a normal whip. Not a nine-tail . . . and not that one with metal and glass attachments either. Then bring him to the infirmary and make sure all his wounds are tended to. I want him ready to fight by this Saturday. Clear?"

The *Untersturmführer* nodded. "Number of lashes, sir?"

"Forty," Mengele interrupted, speaking the answer on the commandant's behalf.

"No," Höss answered. "Forty is too much. I can't risk my 'performing monkey' being out of commission."

Mengele frowned. "Well, we can't have word of that getting around. What would your wife say at such laxness? Prisoners will think we've all gone . . . *soft*." The doctor overtly tapped the commander's biceps as he spoke the word *soft*.

Höss sighed again, clearly exasperated. "What is your recommendation then, Dr. Mengele?"

"The prisoner has family members here. The Jews are always talking about being their brother's keepers. Let them share the forty lashes. Twenty for Samson Abrams and twenty for his nearest kin."

"Fine. Share the lashes. Go find his brother."

"No," Mengele said. "Not his brother."

Höss gave the doctor a stern, questioning look.

"This needs to be a whipping the rest of the prisoners won't soon forget." Mengele turned to the officer, his voice as hard as flint. "Go find his sister."

Sarah and Samson were both tied to a whipping post. Two guards stood next to them. Both guards held whips. A guard ripped open the length of Sarah's prison shirt to bare her back.

"Begin," Mengele said simply. "Alternate blows. The sister first. Then the brother."

The sound of a whip cut the air. *Crack!*

Sarah recoiled and cried out.

Crack! Samson was hit next. He could use his fury-driven will to fight the pain, to stay silent, but seeing his sister being whipped nearly drove him insane.

Crack!

The whip landed on Sarah's back.

Crack!

The whip landed on Samson's back.

"Consider this a lesson in nature versus nurture," Mengele called out, addressing the rows of prisoners forced to watch. "It's similar to the training of a dog or the gentling of a colt. No matter how much love and generosity is provided by one's environment, and much has been given to many of you . . . some are born with a spirit of rebellion."

The guard reared back—*crack*—and laid another blow onto Sarah's back. She screamed. Samson could see the welts rising on her skin. The blood desperately near the surface.

"Strong discipline will decide for us if a rebellious spirit can be broken and therefore healed. Or if nature is indeed too powerful," announced Mengele.

The guard wiped the sweat from his brow. *Crack!* A blow to Samson's back. He pulled hard on the shackles binding him to the post, a method he used to stifle his own urge to scream.

Crack! Another blow to Sarah.

Crack! Another blow to Samson.

"Are we at two or three yet?" Mengele chuckled. "I seem to have lost count."

"This next lash will be five each," one of the guards said. He hurled the whip down on Sarah. *Crack!* Samson's guard followed closely behind. *Crack!*

"Ah, scarcely begun then."

Through Samson's mind flashed an image of his sister when she was just ten years old. She'd been a pretty child, though small and skinny—the gangly Jewish girl in an anti-Semitic neighborhood when they lived in America. Samson had always stood up for her, helping fight her battles, just like he'd fought for Zach, just like he'd fought for each member of his family. But that was long ago. Now he felt helpless. Helpless and hopeless.

Crack! Crack! Crack! The blows continued. Sarah was on her knees now, screaming, still tied to the post by her wrists. She turned to him with pleading eyes, silently crying out—*help me.* One blow right after another. *Crack! Crack! Crack!* Samson struggled to stay on his feet. He gritted his teeth, breathing hard, imagining this as just another fight in the ring, a fight gone horribly wrong. As painful as it was, it was easier for him to take the blows on his own back than to see his baby sister whipped and bleeding beside him.

Out of the corner of his eye, Samson caught a glimpse of the crowd of prisoners. Their faces were pained. All were silent. He wanted to find Rebecca again in the sea of faces. To reassure her somehow. To apologize. To beg her and his entire family's forgiveness for unwittingly bringing them into this hell. But he could find only one recognizable face. Samson gasped after a particularly ferocious blow, then stared hard at that one familiar face.

Kolbe.

The priest's eyes were full of tears. He was moving his lips, praying fervently, begging God to stop the beating, pleading with God to give Samson and Sarah grace and strength in the midst of this evil. Kolbe seemed to be enunciating each word as if wanting the words to be lip-read, and Samson could just make out the words on Kolbe's lips—*"The prayer of a righteous person is powerful and effective . . ."*[1] Samson recognized it as a quote from the Bible that Kolbe had spoken to Samson of several times before. It was one of Kolbe's favorite scriptures. Then, over and over, the priest seemed to mouth the same words—

Stop the whipping. The whip struck Sarah . . .

Stop the whipping. The whip struck Samson . . .

Stop the whipping. And the whip stopped.

The *Untersturmführer* stepped forward, uncomfortable. "That's forty lashings, sir."

Both guards had stopped in midstroke.

"Is it really?" Mengele asked. "You're not turning charitable on me, are you? I could have sworn I counted only fifteen for each."

"It is the sun today," the *Untersturmführer* said. "It casts a confusing shadow on the prisoners. The guards will both confirm the correct number has been reached."

The guard who whipped Samson opened his mouth, looking like he might say something, but the guard who'd beaten Sarah spoke first. *"Ja, mein Untersturmführer.* You are correct." He lowered his whip to his side.

"Well, then." Mengele glared suspiciously at the lieutenant. "It must have been the sun all right." He smiled at the officer, looked him squarely in the eyes, then called to the guards. "Take them

---

1. James 5:16 NIV.

both to the infirmary. We are not without mercy here. Tend to their wounds."

The guards untied Sarah first and carried her away. Her back was bloody and her face was stained with tears. Seeing her beaten like this nearly broke Samson's will. He had vowed that neither Mengele nor any Nazi would ever see his tears, but it was nearly impossible to hold his emotions back after seeing his sister whipped and beaten like this.

Mengele strolled over to Samson, still bound, and whispered to him with a smile as the guard began working on freeing Samson's wrists. "Of course I was counting—just like you were. And of course you each only received fifteen lashes. I only conceded the point to the *Untersturmführer* because he was mistaken, and I didn't want him to lose face. It doesn't matter." The doctor's eyes turned cold. "Know that my punishment of your family has just begun."

Deep in the infirmary, Samson lay facedown. He twisted and turned on a table. Sarah was nowhere to be seen. Familiar hands dabbed at his back with a clean cloth.

"Why are you here?" Samson asked.

"Dr. Mengele singled me out of the crowd," Kolbe said. "Asked me if I knew you. When I said yes, he said he wasn't going to waste the time of valuable medical personnel on a criminal Jew like you."

"Weren't you afraid to admit you knew me?"

"I am not afraid for myself," Kolbe said. "And I wasn't going to lie and say I didn't know you."

"Have you seen Sarah, my sister? How is she?"

"I glimpsed her on a table as I came in. She's a few wards over. They wouldn't let me tend to her wounds. I'm sorry." Kolbe opened a bottle of rubbing alcohol and held Samson down with one arm. "Brace yourself—this will sting."

Slowly, Kolbe poured the alcohol onto Samson's back. The fluid seared his skin, cleansing and burning at the same time. Samson gripped the table.

"I was almost free, Kolbe. Almost. We were all almost free."

Kolbe nodded. A tear brimmed out of the corner of his eye and splashed on the table in front of Samson. "I know you tried to escape for the good of your family. Someday, I hope you will be truly free indeed."

"Do you think that time will ever come, Kolbe?" Sweat had broken out on Samson's brow.

Kolbe laid gauze over a wound on Samson's back and taped it down. "Do you want to know a secret, my friend?"

Samson nodded.

"I'm free right now. Even behind these walls, I am free."

Samson grimaced. "I think you're as delirious as I am."

Kolbe smiled kindly. "If a man's spirit is in communion with God, he is free no matter what type of infirmary his body lies in. When the Son has set you free, you are free indeed."[2]

"Yeah, well, you Christians have an odd definition of freedom."

Kolbe brushed off the comment. He gathered some hydrogen peroxide and cotton balls and held Samson down on the table again. The priest moved gently, pressing the soaked cotton balls into the worst areas on Samson's back. Kolbe winced at Samson's pain. He had helped many Polish soldiers wounded in war, and he

---

2. John 8:36, paraphrase.

had secretly helped many of the Jews he'd hidden with medical care as well.

"Kolbe, let me ask you this. Do you truly believe a man can be free in this place? Even here in this camp? The Nazis have control of us, holding us here with guns, guards, and barbed wire."

"Yes, we are held in body, true. But God did not intend men to enslave one another."

"Then why are we in this place?"

"Because man has gone mad with war." Kolbe pulled fresh bandages from the supply cabinet as he answered.

"You blame man, then, for this evil—not God?"

"Look around us, Samson. Did God cause the Nazis to turn against the Jews? Did God construct this camp of murder and hate that you so aptly described a minute ago? The evil that you see is not God's doing. At the beginning of time, God told man to take dominion over the earth—not dominion over each other. Man has ignored God, and man has been seeking the wrong kind of dominion ever since."

"So man is at the root of all evil, not God—is that what you're saying?"

"No, I'm saying man is responsible for his own evil actions," Kolbe said. "The devil is actually the source of all evil. Do you believe in the devil?"

"Sure," Samson said, "he's running Germany right now."

Kolbe smiled, amazed that Samson was capable of any humor given what he was going through. His pain threshold was unlike anyone's that Kolbe had ever encountered. Carefully and slowly, Kolbe covered Samson's wounds with fresh gauze.

"The devil is an unoriginal sort of fellow," Kolbe went on. "He cannot create anything, but he can pervert it. So Satan attempts to change love to hate, faith to fear, and hope to despair. It's up to man to pick which sphere he will operate in—God's pathway or Satan's perversion. You cast the deciding vote which way you'll go."

"I don't believe in God anymore," Samson said. "I haven't for years. If there is a God, he might not have caused all this evil, but he could still do something about it. What does your faith say about that?"

"It is not an easy question to answer." Kolbe paused for a moment before speaking further. "All I ask is that you hear me out. I'm sure it will come as no surprise to you that pain does not seem to move God to action. Need does not seem to move God to action. Tears do not seem to move God to action. If it was so, everyone in tears or pain or need would get their prayers answered, but we know that isn't so. Therefore, if we're going to be truly honest with ourselves, the fact is that these things obviously do not seem to cause God to act. But faith moves God to action.

"Let me tell you a small story. Once there was a woman, the Scriptures say, who was in much pain. She had been bleeding constantly for twelve years. When she was just centimeters away from Jesus, she was not healed. Jesus had not noticed her. He was not observing her. He was not pursuing her to help her. He was not reaching for her; in fact he was headed the other way. It was her decision to reach out to him. She was the reacher; she reached out and grabbed the hem of his garment, and she was healed. Jesus stopped and said, 'Somebody touched Me, for I perceived power going out from Me.'[3] You see, she reached out and connected with his power by faith. That's why Jesus told her, 'Your faith has made you well.'[4] So I say again, pain and need

---

3. Luke 8:46 NKJV.
4. Matthew 9:22 NKJV.

and tears do not seem to move God to action . . . but great faith will move God to great action. That's where the answer begins, Samson. With strong faith you can reach out and connect with the power of God. Pain and evil still exist, but strong faith can get you through anything."

"Well, I wish I had that kind of faith. We could use a little more help in getting through this hell."

"Samson, when one is going through hell, one should not stop," Kolbe said. "Give your faith time. And pray. God knows you are searching for a strong faith. And he rewards all who seek him."

A scuffling sound could be heard from down the hallway, interrupting their conversation.

"Lie still. That doesn't sound good." Kolbe stuck his head outside the hallway, glanced left and right, then returned to Samson. "Eight soldiers. They're all going into the room where Sarah lies. Dr. Mengele was with them."

"Eight soldiers? Why would they need eight to guard a female prisoner?"

Kolbe inhaled sharply. "This will only result in harm, I'm afraid."

Samson rose to his feet, wincing from the painful wounds on his back. His face was drawn. "I need to get to that room."

"No. I was ordered to keep you here and tend to your wounds. It is a suicide mission to move out of this room. Just let me think." The priest shook his head, thinking hard for a moment, then pointed outside. "I'll climb out the window. Stay low. Look in the next window, find out what's happening. Then I'll return."

The scuffling sounds could still be heard.

"Good plan," Samson said. "Except for one thing."

"What's that?"

"I'm going. Not you."

Kolbe raised a hand in protest, but Samson quickly stepped to the window and slipped out. He slunk along the ground. Kolbe stayed inside by the window's edge, acting as a lookout. Samson scanned the perimeter for any guards. Suddenly, he heard Sarah scream. He raced to the window of the ward where she was kept and peered inside.

Four soldiers held Sarah down, one soldier restraining each of her limbs. The other four soldiers ringed the room, machine guns in hand. Sarah screamed, kicking, fighting hard, pulling and twisting with all her strength. Samson froze. From the shadows of the room, Dr. Mengele stepped forward, unzipping his pants. Sarah fought harder. Mengele leaned over and punched her in the face, no hint of remorse. Her body went slack, half conscious, mouth bloody.

Shaken out of his fog, Samson launched into immediate reaction. His hands were on the window, but a strong hand gripped his shoulder at the same time.

"Don't do it," came a voice from behind him.

"That's my sister in there!" Samson hissed. Frantically, he searched for something to break through the window.

"It's certain death to intervene," Kolbe said. "You cannot help your sister."

"You pray all you want," Samson said. "But I'm going to stop them." Samson turned away, his face ashen, and continued to scramble on the ground, desperately looking for a rock. He spotted a fist-sized rock a few feet away. Samson grabbed the rock, hauled off, and hurled it through the window. Glass shattered all around.

For a split second, Kolbe and Samson stared in mute silence.

"Run!" Samson hissed at the priest. "Save yourself. If they catch anybody, let it be me."

"Think!" Kolbe said. "They don't know it was us."

Guards rushed to the window, but Samson and Kolbe had

already slipped back through their window into their own ward. Breathless, they strained to hear the next sounds. Samson lay on the table facedown, same as before. Kolbe dabbed at his back with soaked cotton balls.

They could hear the voice down the hallway. It bellowed in fury. "Whoever did this—find him!" Mengele shouted.

Shortly after roll call the next morning, Dr. Mengele calmly walked by the rows of prisoners, observing them carefully before coming to a halt a few feet in front of Samson and Kolbe. Samson's swollen eye had opened, but he was still sore and bruised all over, the whipping wounds on his back throbbing. Kolbe had changed the dressings on his back once more late at night before returning Samson to the barracks. Guards holding machine guns stood in a row a few yards away from the prisoners.

"So . . . no one wants to confess to last night's crime." Mengele nodded to himself as if answering his own question. "Very well . . ." He motioned to two women standing near Samson. One was older, the other younger. "You two, step forward."

The women's faces fell, fear-stricken. They stepped forward.

"You are mother and daughter, yes?" Mengele said.

"Yes, sir," the older woman said.

"How old are you?" Mengele asked the daughter. "Sixteen?"

"Fifteen, sir." The girl looked at the ground.

"Open your mouth," Mengele said to the girl.

Samson started to speak but involuntarily stopped, unable to get any words out. Kolbe's face was grim, apparently unsure how to proceed. Petrified, the teenager did not move.

Mengele gave her one of his famous smiles. "It's okay, my dear, this won't hurt."

Tentatively, the girl opened her mouth.

Mengele nodded, smiled again, pulled out his revolver, and gently inserted the barrel into her mouth. "There . . . are you comfortable?"

The girl murmured something. Her eyes round with fear.

Mengele called out so the prisoners could hear. "Let me ask you all again. Somebody broke a window in the infirmary last night. It happened at the most inconvenient of times, and I want to know who did it. I need to know now. So I will count backward from five to one, and before I reach one and pull the trigger, the perpetrator of the crime will step forward and confess. Is everyone ready? Good. Five . . . !"

"Stop," Samson said.

Mengele gave Samson a long look. He kept the revolver in the girl's mouth.

"Let her go," Samson said.

Dead silence.

"Are you confessing to the crime?" Mengele asked.

"You know it was me," replied Samson.

Bam! Mengele pulled the trigger.

"No-o-o!" Samson screamed as he stumbled backward, aghast. The girl lay dead at her mother's feet. Her mother shrieked, fell to her knees, and sobbed over her murdered child. Kolbe wrung his hands, horrified.

"Why?" Samson yelled. "Why?" His fists were clenched at his sides.

Mengele turned slightly, pointed his revolver at Samson, held it there, then turned to the guards. The girl's mother was still screaming. "Get her out of here," Mengele ordered. "And take the body with you."

Two guards pulled the mother off her murdered daughter and led her away. Two others gathered up the body as best they could, not bothering with the bone fragments, and headed for the crematorium.

"Samson, take a step closer," Mengele said. Slowly, Samson complied, his fists still clenched. "Good. Now, take another." Mengele and Samson stood just a few feet apart. The doctor lowered his revolver and placed it back in its holster. His voice was calm, strangely unnerving, and he spoke softly so only Samson could hear him.

"Run at me now, and a row of machine guns will mow you down, but you already know that, don't you—that's why you're not attacking. You see, Samson, even with Commandant Höss protecting you, I have no fear of you at all. I never have, and I never will."

"I could kill you in two seconds with my bare hands." Samson's voice was equally calm, although it trembled with anger.

"Perhaps. But I don't know why you're so angry with *me* about all this. You killed that girl. Not me. It was your crime last night, not mine."

"You have a twisted way of looking at things."

"Do I?" The doctor sighed. "The girl's death doesn't matter. The average prisoner lasts twelve weeks here, and the poor wretch nearly made it that long. But why am I explaining things to you? The only thing you need to know"—the doctor slowed his words and spoke precisely—"is that you . . . and every member of your family . . . will die here. Rest assured . . . I will see to it myself."

"You're a coward, hiding behind your weapons, doing what you do to women and children. Any time you want to face me man-to-man, I'll be glad to oblige."

"Man-to-man?" Mengele chuckled. "Oh, I think not. Why would a man fight a crocodile? Or a grizzly bear? Certainly your displays of strength are notable, but a doctor is not taunted into taking imprudent actions. A doctor is usually only curious. But now, a doctor is angry. It's not a good combination, curiosity and anger." Mengele sighed, then chuckled again. "In regard to your comment about being a coward . . . any action I take toward a female Jewish prisoner is purely scientific research. Honestly, Samson, I didn't imagine your sister would experience such pleasure yesterday to the degree she did. She certainly cried out with joy."

A vein bulged on the side of Samson's forehead. His mind reeled. His rage tunneled to new depths.

"Oh, don't tell me you're actually angry with me," Mengele said, his voice still impeccably calm. "Forced prostitution happens in many instances of warfare. Surely you Jews studied that in your schoolbooks as children. You shouldn't even think of it as prostitution, Samson. Prostitutes get paid, and I assure you, I would never degrade your sister by paying for it."

Samson locked gazes with Mengele. "You will not win," Samson said, his voice immovable.

"Win?" Mengele asked. "Is that actually a challenge? Truly, you are the most thickheaded of swine I have ever encountered. Surely, I accept your challenge—if that's how you see things. And to prove I'm a sporting man," the doctor cleared his throat, "I'll reassign you to a new work detail: cleaning in Block 10. My block. That way you and I can see much more of each other, which I'm sure we will both enjoy."

Mengele didn't wait for an answer. He turned on his heel. "Come," Mengele called over his shoulder to a guard. "See to it that this prisoner is cleaned up, then brought to Block 10 in . . . oh, two or three hours from now. I have many intriguing things to show him there. Fascinating sights and sounds I'm sure he will never forget."

FOURTEEN[1]

THE GUARD WAS YOUNG, NO MORE THAN NINETEEN, with blond hair and a wide Aryan jaw. He looked kindhearted, out of place in the grim surroundings of Auschwitz. He led Samson across the camp in silence, then undid a series of dead-bolt locks before opening wide the door and leading Samson into Block 10. Four other guards milled about on the other side of the entryway, as if awaiting Samson's arrival. When they saw the prisoner step through the door, they snapped into place. All carried machine

---

1. The descriptions of the events presented in this chapter are all based on fact. For more information about Mengele's treatment of twins, see Robert J. Lifton, "What Made This Man? Mengele," *New York Times*, July 21, 1985, http://www. wellesley.edu/Polisci/wj/100/mengle.htm; and Laurence Rees, "Raped by their saviours: How the survivors of Auschwitz escaped one nightmare only to face another unimaginable ordeal," *Mail Online*, February 2, 2010, http://www .dailymail.co.uk/news/article-1247157/How-survivors-Auschwitz-escaped -nightmare-faced-unimaginable-ordeal.html. For more about forced prostitution of prisoners, see Alexandra Hudson, "Secrets of Nazi camp brothels emerge decades on," Reuters, July 11, 2007, http://www.reuters.com/article /2007/07/11/idUSL01447993; and "BBC TWO unravels the secrets of Auschwitz," press release, BBC Home, March 12, 2004, http://www.bbc.co.uk /pressoffice/pressreleases/stories/2004/12_december/03/auschwitz_facts.shtml.

guns except the guard leading Samson. He carried a revolver, and it was holstered.

"You may call me Hanz," the first guard said in perfect Polish. He did not introduce the other guards, and none of them offered their names. The introduction surprised Samson, particularly hearing it in a familiar language. Guards were not in the habit of offering their names to prisoners, and although plenty of Germans knew more than one language, few ever spoke to prisoners in a language they readily understood, except to give an order or a threat. It dawned on Samson that the guard was using Polish as a courtesy.

"My name is Samson Abrams," he answered simply. He glanced about the entryway.

"The matter of your name is already known," the guard said. "I've been assigned to watch over you as you work. And these other guards are to assist. It's a new detail for me as well, and I am not sure why Dr. Mengele assigned me to you. All he said was, 'Make sure he cleans the facility well.' So those are your orders. You are to use that mop and pail over there." Hanz motioned toward a small broom closet.

Samson walked over to the closet and took the mop and pail. He found a bottle of bleach to use as a disinfectant. A sink stood nearby, and he filled the pail with warm water and added bleach.

"Ready," Samson said. "Is the doctor here?"

"Dr. Mengele is often in this facility," Hanz said, "but I don't know where." He led Samson into a central hallway and motioned to a side door. "You may begin cleaning in that room first."

Samson carried the mop and pail into the first room. Hanz and the other guards followed, the other guards' weapons still drawn. A strong smell of formaldehyde wafted up from the floor. The walls were concrete and cold, lined with specimen bottles, beakers, and containers of solution, as one might see in a laboratory. Samson started in the far corner, mopping the floor. It wasn't hard work. Definitely easier than digging ditches. He worked in silence, and after a while he noticed that the four guards and even Hanz were not eyeing him very closely.

Samson stole glances at the specimens in the jars, which were meticulously arranged, most with odd letterings on the outside. He assumed they were labeled by Mengele. The handwriting was scrawled, like a doctor's prescription, and written in German. Most jars contained animal tissue of some sort. Little strips of raw meat carefully preserved in formaldehyde.

"Finished?" Hanz asked. "Okay, on to the next room then."

Samson followed Hanz out the door, down the hallway, and into the next room. Again, it contained row after row of specimen jars. Samson got to work on the floor.

"You were originally from Kraków," Hanz said. It was more a statement than a question.

"Yes," Samson replied.

"I knew a man once who lived in Kraków. We were friends as boys, then he studied at the seminary and took his vows. He was assigned to St. Mary's Basilica, the church adjacent to market square. My friend used to write to me about the hourly trumpet signal, about how beautiful it was. Do you know it, even though you are Jewish?"

"The *Hejnał Mariacki*," Samson said. "'Saint Mary's Dawn' is well known throughout the city."

"Funny about the tune. My friend wrote to me about how the melody breaks off in midstream, although he never explained why. After the war began, we stopped corresponding, and I've often wondered about the song's odd sudden halt. Do you know its meaning?"

Samson finished mopping an area of the floor and paused, eyeing the guard. He nodded. "It's an ancient legend," Samson said.
"Thirteenth century, maybe fourteenth. Mongols attacked the
city. A famed trumpeter sounded the alarm by playing *Hejnał,* and
the city gates were closed before the army could take the city by
surprise, but the trumpeter took an arrow through the throat. He
couldn't finish playing the tune. That's all I know."

"Ah, a life cut short. I am Lutheran myself. I have always
found it a shame when courageous actions are cut short by the
ravages of war."

Samson mopped another section, then stopped momentarily.
"Let me ask you—I've been in this camp for several weeks now"—
Samson eyed the other four guards warily, thick-necked oafs; they
were yawning, looking over their machine guns—"and you don't fit
the surroundings."

"I answered the call to champion the Motherland," Hanz said
with a shrug. "I am proud to serve the Nazi Party, and, despite my
lack of years, I do my duty as well as the next soldier. Be assured
that if you get out of line while under my watch, or if you try to
escape like you did before, I will not hesitate to bring you down."

"No disrespect intended."

"None taken," Hanz said. "There are seven thousand guards at
Auschwitz.[2] I'm sure that in the eyes of a Jewish prisoner, all guards
are evil. But rest assured they are not. Even in a camp such as this."

---

2. The guarding and day-to-day operations of a concentration camp as large
   as Auschwitz required some 7,000 guards total, with about 170 of those
   being female staff. After the war was over, about 750 Auschwitz guards
   were prosecuted and punished (Ian Traynor, "Survivors and leaders travel to
   Auschwitz to mark anniversary of its liberation," *The Guardian,* January 26,
   2005, http://www.guardian.co.uk/world/2005/jan/26/secondworldwar
   .germany1).

He cleared his throat and noticed Samson was finished mopping. "Finished? Okay, next room then."

Again, Hanz led the way. Samson followed. The four guards trailed Samson as he looked down at his mop pail, being careful not to spill the water. He glanced up, saw Hanz stop abruptly, and heard him gasp. It was another specimen room, just like the other ones, but this room contained a long wooden table.

On the table were eyeballs.

They were clearly human, all laid out in neat rows. The whites of all the eyes were colored a pale, sickly yellow. The irises were blues, greens, and browns. All specimens were tagged with numbers and notes. Syringes were stacked in open boxes. Vats of dye stood near the wall.

Hanz stared at the table in front of him. For some time, the young guard didn't move. Then he unholstered his revolver and pointed it at the floor, as if for added security. "I am sorry to have to show you this room," he said to Samson. "Now I know why Dr. Mengele ordered me to guard you. He told me recently that he wants to turn me into a more hardened soldier. Now I understand better his definition of duty." The young guard cleared his throat. "Please disregard the contents of the table . . . and continue with your cleaning work."

Samson stared at the table, mop in hand. He could not pull his gaze away. The implications of the experiment were clear. Someone was medically trying to change the color of people's eyes. Samson could only guess what had happened to the prisoners who had their eyes removed. It had been no accident that Dr. Mengele wanted Samson to clean Block 10. Clearly, the doctor wanted Samson to see this. Samson cleaned the room as quickly as he could. He noticed the water in his pail sloshed with grime.

He went back, still under the watchful eyes of the guard, to the closet and sink, rinsed out his mop, changed the water in his pail, and added more bleach.

Hanz led Samson to the next room but stopped when he got to the door without opening it. The door had a glass window in it with three steel bars in front of the window. "Dr. Mengele indicated that this room is not to be cleaned," Hanz said. "Nevertheless, you are also ordered to see all rooms. Do not open this door. Only look through the window." His voice fell, as if anticipating some sort of painful scene inside. The revolver was still in his hands. "Again, I am sorry."

Samson gripped the mop tighter and went to the window. It was a bigger room than the others, with draperies on the walls and carpets on the floor. About twenty-five women were inside. They braided their hair or lay about on the floor. Some sat in small groups and seemed to be speaking with one another in low voices. The women wore prison garb, although it looked cleaner and less grimy than the prisoners wore outside. All the women were fine featured and comely, although some sported black eyes and cut lips.

"These women . . . why are they here?" Samson asked.

Hanz cleared his throat and coughed. "Doctor Mengele calls this the 'light duty' room. The women have been, uh . . . ," he cleared his throat again, "pressed into service."

Samson's eyes fell. Then a sudden thought hit him, and his gaze darted throughout the room, looking for one woman in particular. He suspected the worst. Sure enough, Sarah sat on the far side of the room with her back to the door. A compress had been placed over the wounds on her back from her whipping. Samson instantly recognized her, and he rapped on the glass with his knuckles. Nothing. Quickly, he tapped again. He placed a hand on the glass.

"Please, no contact," Hanz said. It was an order, but it didn't come with much force.

Sarah turned. One eye was blacked. Her face was bruised. She gazed through the window at her brother in sad recognition. Sarah looked alone and desperate. Slowly, she covered her face with her hands.

Samson's heart broke for her. He felt sure that she blamed him for what had happened to her and to their family. He wanted to talk to her, but he knew that pressing the matter would greatly increase the risk of punishment for them both.

Suddenly, a scream pierced the dank air.

Hanz jumped. "This way," he said, clearly ruffled by the scream. He motioned toward the next room. The scream came again, followed by a scuffling sound, a long moan, and another scream. "I have been ordered to show you every room." Hanz pointed to the room where the noise of the scream came from. "Again, this is an area I was told not to let you into. Only to make sure you looked inside."

Samson peered through the window.

A pregnant woman lay on an operating table. She was tied down. Two guards flanked her, weapons in hand. Dr. Mengele stood near the women's abdomen, a scalpel poised in the air. He wore no surgical mask and paused when Samson's figure came across the door's barred window. The doctor looked up, smiled at Samson, and continued slicing into the woman's belly. The woman screamed again. Samson could see every move. He wanted to look away from the horror, but he found himself frozen, his feet unmoving, his body totally immobile.

Dr. Mengele reached inside the woman via the crude Cesarean section and pulled out a newborn baby. He cut the umbilical cord, then handed the baby to a male nurse. The mother screamed again, moaning, her forehead soaked with perspiration. Dr. Mengele drew out a long needle and filled it with bluish fluid. The male nurse held the infant tightly against his chest and thrust its eyes open. Mengele lowered the needle toward the eyes of the newborn.

Horrified, Samson's gaze shot to the wall behind the operating table. He took in every detail, trying to understand the full implications of what was going on in Block 10. Row after row of half-liter jars lined the shelves. He recognized with a jolt for the first time that inside the jars were tiny body parts—hearts, spleens, livers, kidneys. He wanted to run, to charge against the door and beat down the doctor. But the four guards behind him had stepped closer. They held their machine guns steady.

"I'm sorry," Hanz said. "I didn't know." His voice trembled.

Mengele waved his hands toward the infant. The nurse took it out through a side door. Another wave, and the mother was wheeled out on the gurney. Mengele motioned toward the window in the door.

"He wants you to come inside," Hanz said.

Samson nodded assent through gritted teeth.

"While I do not condone all of the doctor's medical experiments, I should warn you not to try anything foolish."

"Just open the door," Samson said.

Hanz unlocked the door from the outside, held his revolver on Samson, and pushed him through the door.

"Ah! Samson Abrams," Dr. Mengele said with a flourish of his hands. "You came to view my laboratory."

Samson clenched his fists. "You'll burn in hell for this."

Mengele's grin faded. He motioned to four of the guards. "You, you, you, and you," he said. "Handcuff the prisoner's legs and wrists. Set him on the floor. Hold your weapons on him, and make sure he is properly restrained. Only leave his eyes open."

There was no use in struggling. Three guards held their machine guns on Samson's head, while Hanz and another guard obeyed orders, cuffed Samson, and forced him to sit.

Mengele disappeared out a side door and called out, "Is the prisoner secured?"

"Yes, Doctor," Hanz said.

"Can he still see?"

"Yes, Doctor."

"Good. I wanted him to view one of my favorite recent experiments." The doctor reappeared, glancing to see that Samson was well restrained, and walked over to a table about three feet away. He placed two glass containers on the table.

Inside the jars were two small heads, each severed at the neck. The faces were recognizable to Samson in an instant. The eyes stared vacant. The heads were shaved bald. Samson convulsed as if his soul was ripped apart, screaming, "No! No-o-o-o-o-o! No-o-o-o-o!" He lurched, straining against the bonds that held him.

It was Rachel and Leah.

"Such an interesting experiment," Dr. Mengele said. "You would not believe how similar their internal organs were."

The soldiers tried to pull Samson back, but he exploded against the hand and leg cuffs with blind rage, the metal actually beginning to bend under the pressure of Samson's force. Samson screamed, "No-o-o-o-o-o!" over and over. He shook uncontrollably, struggling against his restraints. The guards hit him, trying to pull him back and subdue him as he raged forward, unyielding, unwilling to believe his eyes, desperately trying to reach out to his little girls, wanting to kill Mengele with his bare hands. Like a lion gone mad, Samson screamed and fought, the metal shackles bending under his force, cutting into his wrists and ankles as he surged forward with every ounce of his strength.

They continued to beat Samson. Finally, he was unable to fight anymore. There was no use. He had bent the metal shackles but they would not break, and the guards had pinned him to his knees. He stared at the faces of his murdered twin daughters, all breath in his lungs taken away. Nothing felt real. He was caught in the middle of a horrible nightmare and could not awake.

"My babies . . . ," he said simply. "My little girls . . ."

The guards slowly released their pressure. They could see that Samson's mind was far away. He had ceased struggling, and his eyes stared at a corner of the ceiling, unmoving, fixed in a vacant stare.

"No will to fight anymore, eh?" Dr. Mengele said. "Well . . . that sounds like most Jews I know. You're a whipped man, Samson Abrams. And I never even climbed into the ring with you." Mengele laughed to himself.

Samson gathered himself into a ball on the floor. He continued to stare silently at the ceiling. Through Samson's mind flashed images of Rachel and Leah . . . Their birthdays. A thousand hugs from their tiny arms. Kissing their sweet faces before bedtime.

Mengele smiled again. "Of course, you seeing all these things here today was no accident. I wanted you to know exactly who is in control and what will happen to you and the rest of your family soon. You cannot fight me, Samson. You cannot win. You are my prisoner. And you are hopeless and helpless, no matter what you do."

FIFTEEN

COMMANDANT HÖSS STOOD FROM THE CHAIR IN his office and slammed a shot glass of whiskey down on the desk in front of him. "Bring Samson here!" he ordered Dr. Mengele. "Let me see for myself."

Mengele smiled casually. "You asked for a detailed report of the day, sir. And I gave it to you."

"I did not want that man destroyed. My orders were clear."

"The Jew has not been destroyed, Commandant. Samson Abrams still breathes and moves, and he will be willing and able to perform for your next fight. I guarantee it." Mengele clapped his hands in the direction of a guard. "Bring the prisoner here. Make sure he is well restrained."

Höss's face was bright red with fury. "If someone asked me right now which I hated more—Jews or the sight of your face, Dr. Mengele—it may very well be a toss-up."

"That hardly seems a fair comparison, sir."

"Don't try my patience!" The commandant leveled his finger at the doctor. "And you are to remain at attention in my presence."

155

Mengele sighed and stood at attention. Höss strode to the table nearest the window and poured himself another shot of whiskey. He downed it in one gulp. He poured himself another and downed it. Nothing more was said for five minutes. Finally, two guards entered the room. Between them, they pulled Samson, handcuffed.

Höss looked at the prisoner, at the vacant look in his eyes, then glared at Mengele and snarled in his direction. "You are dismissed, Doctor."

Mengele saluted and turned on his heel.

"Whiskey?" The commander faced Samson.

Samson shook his head.

"Water?"

Another shake. No.

Höss exhaled loudly. "Sit down then." He motioned to a chair.

Samson stayed standing.

Höss exhaled again.

"The commandant ordered you to sit, dog!" one of the guards shouted. He clubbed Samson on the back of the neck.

"Enough!" Höss yelled at the guard. "Leave this man be. You guards will both stand outside the door with your weapons drawn." The guards both glared at Samson, then left the room. Samson stood alone before the commander. Höss pulled out his revolver and set it within an easy reach on the desk in front of him.

"Dr. Mengele has informed me of the day's events," Höss said. "Rest assured, that was his plan, not mine. Nevertheless, it is all behind us now. What matters now is what lies ahead. And that,

Mr. Abrams, should be of interest to us both. You want more food. I want a good fight. That is all we must talk about now."

"I don't think so."

"You don't think so? Well, that is an amusing response, Samson. But that's not what I had in mind."

"I will not fight again."

"Of course you will fight. You will fight, and you will win, and it will be this coming weekend. That's the bargain." Höss smiled, but it was an exasperated smile, not a friendly one.

"No."

"What do you mean . . . *no?*"

"It's time for a new bargain."

"I'm not in the habit of making new bargains."

"The new bargain is this—" Samson looked directly at the commander. "I will continue to fight for you. And I will win every fight. And I will make you more money than you have ever seen."

"I like these ideas very much, Samson. Yet I sense by your tone there is more to this new bargain of yours."

"I will fight on one condition—each time I win, you will free one member of my family. Each and every time. That is the new bargain."

Höss laughed. "I'm not in the habit of negotiating with prisoners." His voice took on a fatherly air. "Look, I understand you're emotional, Samson. Don't blame yourself for what happened to your girls. It was inevitable. Dr. Mengele is a slave to science. He performs *Zwillingsforschung*—experiments with twins—on nearly every pair that enters this camp. There's some sort of special secrets in their organs, he claims." Höss shook his head, his distaste for Mengele unhidden. "The truth is, your girls should have been disposed of in a more judicious manner."

Samson seethed. Höss may have intended to soothe Samson's anger, but the commander's true Nazi ideology had slipped out by accident. Clearly, the commandant did not care about two little Jewish girls who would have died in the gas chambers anyway. He just wanted Samson to feel like he was on his side in order to milk a few more good fights out of him. Samson clenched his fists. He could see right through the man.

Höss frowned, evidently recognizing his mistake, and switched gears quickly.

"You misunderstand me, Samson. Personally, I have no problem setting your family free. Of what consequence are a few Jews to me? But what you are asking is next to impossible. It has only been done for the servant staff of one or two *Obersturmbannführer*—lieutenant colonels—and even the top brass no longer receive favors such as this. No—an action such as freeing a prisoner could land me in some very hot water."

"Then I will not fight," Samson said. "Not this weekend. Not ever again."

Höss took a deep breath, held it in for a long moment, then puffed his cheeks out, pushing the air through his lips. "You think you hold some kind of leverage, do you? A real negotiator, eh?"

Samson stayed silent.

"Clearly you can handle pain well—we've all seen that before. So I see the point you're trying to make. As camp commander, I might be able to force you into the ring, but I can't guarantee you will fight with everything you have. You might get in there and throw the fight, for instance, just so I'd lose a lot of money. No, I wouldn't put a dastardly move like that past a grieving father such as yourself. So . . . fine, I'll concede your point. You do hold some leverage in this agreement in some small way."

Again Samson stayed silent.

"Here's where I'm coming from in this arrangement," Höss said, as if sorting out the ramifications in his own mind. "I made more money on you in that last fight than I have in the last six months. I won't deny it. Your win brought me a real financial windfall, Samson, and if you keep this up, I'll be out of the red and into the black well before the end of the year. So, you and I must both find a way to ensure our interests in this bargain. We must both be confident of what actions the other man is threatening. It's just that what you're asking is so difficult . . ." Höss seemed to drift off, pondering the possibilities.

"I do not need to know *how* you will do it," Samson said. "I just need to have your word that you *will* do it. That's the arrangement. Free one of my family members every time I win, or you will not make one more reichsmark on my gloves."

Höss clasped his hands together. "Well, okay then, Samson, it's all agreed. I'm a flexible individual, and I like to see good negotiating skills in a man. Tell me again—your new terms were what exactly?"

"Okay, I'll say it once again: each time I fight and win, one of my family members goes free."

"Oh, of course. Done. It will be extremely difficult for me to do, but you have my word as an officer. Your new deal stands."

Samson shifted his weight on his legs. He swallowed, wanting to smile in uneasy triumph, but something held him back. The commander had agreed to his new terms too readily. Samson didn't trust the man.

"You don't believe me?" Höss asked, incredulous, as if reading Samson's mind. "You need more of a guarantee?"

Samson weighed his words carefully. He wasn't sure how to answer the question and keep his life.

Höss exhaled, frustrated. "Why must all Jews need to have it in writing? Look, the bottom line is that I need you to fight this weekend, Samson, and I need you to give it your all. Simply put, you *must* win. That's how I make money, and that's the only reason you're still standing before me today. If you say you won't fight unless a family member is freed with each win, then so be it—I'll try my best to facilitate your request. But look at it from my perspective. If you are requiring something more from me, then I need to require something more from you. That's my fear with this new arrangement: I can't have you climb in the ring and lose the match." The commander shuddered. "It pains me to say it, Samson, but I fear you don't trust me . . . so let me say it again. I absolutely need you to win. You must understand that. You must not lose. And because of that, I've just decided I will help you in the ring."

"Help me? How?"

"By giving you a gift," Höss said. "Yes, I want to show you exactly what's at the root of this deal. Why? To ensure you and I both get what we want." The commander's voice turned cold. "My gift is this, Samson . . . it's a picture."

"A picture?"

"Yes, a picture can be a powerful incentive, and I believe the picture I will give you will help you fight with everything you have. It will give you proper perspective of what is really at stake here. Am I understood?"

Samson stayed silent.

"You are to say 'yes, sir' when you are in my presence." The commander's voice rose.

Samson thought a moment. "Yes, sir," he said slowly.

"Good." Höss beamed. His voice was still cold.

The commander clapped his hands together twice. The guards entered the room again, weapons still drawn. Höss put away his revolver. "Let's go," Höss announced to the guards. They flanked Samson and began to lead him out of the room.

Höss led the way down the corridor out of his office. Behind him, Samson stared at the hairs on the back of the commandant's neck. They bristled with excitement. Far more excitement than Samson was comfortable with.

Something huge was undeniably churning in Höss's mind, and Samson sensed it was not going to be to his advantage.

Höss led Samson across the camp and into another brick building, then unlocked a smaller side room inside the larger building. One of the guards closed the door behind them and locked it. Inside the smaller room, the commandant pointed toward the wall, to a small, dual-paned window about the size of a ship's porthole. It provided a clear view into the larger room on the other side of the wall.

"You've heard rumors, yes?" Höss said.

Warily, Samson nodded. He eyed the commander.

"Well, we do not have long to wait." Höss looked at his watch. "Yes, it's just about time. Go ahead, Samson, position yourself so you can see through the porthole. There is nothing new for me to see on the other side, only for you."

Samson looked at the commandant, then shook his head no. Samson had a hunch about what went on in the other room, and even in the interest of studying his enemy, it was nothing he wanted to view.

Höss pulled out his revolver and pointed it at Samson's head.

"Come now, my good man, play along. As I mentioned, this will put things into perspective for you."

One of the guards shoved Samson toward the tiny window. Samson peered through the porthole-style glass. On the other side was a large and dimly lit shower room, like one might find in an old gymnasium.

"Ah, it's time." Höss's voice was throaty. "They are arriving. Look closely, Samson. This is my gift: I want you to see exactly what I am saving you from."

Hundreds of people began to file into the room. They were naked, and they came in every age, shape, and height. Men, women, boys, and girls. They walked placidly. Some looked at the floors. Others gazed at the showerheads on the walls. Others simply stared straight ahead.

The entry door closed behind them. They were locked into the shower room.

"Pull the switch." They heard the order coming from a guard in an adjacent room, followed by a loud bang of metal on metal. Samson heard a muffled humming noise.

"I am an honorable man, Samson." Höss's eyes were glassy, like a man possessed. "I keep my word. I told you once that if you won a boxing match, you'd get more food. And you received it. I also told you that if you lost, you'd lose your life. Look closely, Samson. Burn this image into your mind. Let this picture fuel your next fight with anger and hatred and fear. This, my good man, is exactly what I'm talking about. This is where the losers go."

Samson peered closer into the window. There was a faint hissing sound. Something discharged from overhead vents. Samson's stomach turned, instinctively knowing something horrible was happening. He had seen the results, but he had never seen the actual event. It was as if a poisonous cobra's venom hung overhead and then suddenly descended on all those below. Those closest to the induction vent collapsed almost instantly, their bodies falling on top of each other like dropping dominoes. Other people staggered about, twitching, struggling for air, silently screaming, clawing at the walls, climbing over each other, trying to escape.

"Such an effective killing tool," Höss said, his chest puffed with pride. "When one of my subordinates, Captain Karl Fritzsch, first used Zyklon B gas to dispose of some Russian POWs, I was there watching, taking notes. The gas is powerful stuff, really humane in my opinion. The prisoners' suffering is quite short, relative to other methods."

A boy about Simon's age climbed on a pile of dead bodies, trying to get away. He was crying and choking, his eyes bulging, his mouth shrieking. Finally, the boy collapsed. Dead. His eyes stayed open, staring at the porthole Samson stood behind.

Samson was aghast. The sight of innocent men, women, and children dying before his eyes was more than he could bear. He wanted to strike out, to lash out at the commandant. But the handcuffs bit into his wrists. Two machine guns, as well as Höss's revolver, were aimed at him. There was nothing he could do.

"Why?" Samson said, his tone stunned. "What have these people ever done to you?"

"What have they done?" Höss looked surprised. "It's sheer pragmatics, Samson—survival of the fittest. Each lunatic, cripple, and epileptic costs Germany four reichsmarks per day. There are at least three hundred thousand total in those three groups alone. That's 1.2 million reichsmarks a day. Think, Samson, just think! All of the taxpayer money we're saving by getting rid of them along with any other undesirables."

"None of those people looked insane, crippled, or epileptic," Samson said. "Even if they were, what would it matter? How can you put a price on a life?"

"Well, I wouldn't expect a Jew to understand," Höss replied. "You people are the worst. You're all communists, Bolshevists, robbers, and conspirators. The Jews bought all our property and lent their money at exorbitant interest. Every son of Abraham is a cunning, arrogant, financial manipulator."

"My father was a teacher," Samson said. "My mother was a musician. That doesn't sound like what you just described, does it? So which is it? Dr. Mengele believes we Jews are all unintelligent subhumans. You believe we're all clever crooks. The Nazis can't have it both ways."

Höss's face turned red with anger. He thrust a finger in Samson's face. "Look—if it was up to Dr. Mengele, he would already be studying the insides of your body for the benefit of science. He has an inquiring mind, and he can't understand how a smaller Jew beat a larger Pole. He wouldn't do the dissection kindly, you know. He'd take his time and carve you up in pieces while you're still alive, wanting each organ to be as fresh as possible before beginning his study."

Samson turned his back on Höss, taking one more look at the boy in the room full of dead bodies. He turned back to Höss and motioned toward the room. "How do you sleep at night?"

"Only a child loses sleep to a nightmare. Soldiering requires the discipline to do the unthinkable. And repetition of the unthinkable breeds placation of the mind."

Hatred settled over Samson like a thick fog. He hated the commander for all he was worth. He hated every inch and fiber of the man's being. He hated his own position of powerlessness, and he hated the thought that his fighting again would line Höss's pockets with more money. He wanted to break the neck of the man in front of him, not make a deal with him.

"I have been far too good to you, Samson. But if you keep fighting, and—absolutely—if you keep winning, then you and your family will not come to these chambers." Höss nodded, extending his hand for Samson to shake. "You have my word."

Samson stared at the commander's hand. *He must have forgotten himself.* Commandants did not shake hands with prisoners. For a moment, Samson thought of how many lives must have been taken by a mere gesture from that hand, how many had been killed by the first finger of that hand pulling a trigger, how many signatures from that hand had been put on paper, authorizing the killings of tens of thousands of innocent men, women, and children.

Samson swallowed his pride and shook the hand of this murderer who had just pledged to free his family, one by one, for every victory achieved. Samson had his doubts regarding Höss's honor, but he did not doubt his love of money. Höss squeezed Samson's hand powerfully. Samson squeezed Höss's hand back firmly, not yielding to the show of strength. He took a deep breath and released the commander's clasp.

It felt like he'd just shaken hands with the devil.

Four nights later at Solahütte, the officers' parlor was packed.

Samson stood alone in one corner of the ring, waiting for his opponent to arrive. He hated the thought of sending another man to the gas chambers, but he was ready to fight with a new resolve.

I will not fight for myself tonight, he thought. *I will fight for the blood of my daughters . . . I will fight for the blood of my parents . . . I will fight with a strength the Nazis have not yet seen in any man . . . ever.*

Commandant Höss was smoking an enormous cigar. He was already seated ringside next to his wife, Hedwig. On his other side sat Dr. Mengele. Höss took another puff, left his seat, and stood at the edge of the ring, blowing smoke from behind Samson.

"There was no inmate here healthy enough to give you a real fight," Höss said, chuckling. "So we decided to give you a bit of a challenge. The tougher the opponent, the greater the odds, the more money I make when you win. But don't worry, you will not be killed if you triumph over this man."

Samson flashed Höss a questioning look. "Why would I get killed if I won?"

"Take a look for yourself." Höss motioned to the side door. A tall, blond, muscular SS officer wearing boxing gloves was working his way through the crowd. The officer had at least seventy pounds on Samson. He warmed up, shuffling, shadowboxing through the crowd until reaching the stage. The officer stepped into the ring to the loud cheers of his peers.

This was not a fair fight on several levels, Samson knew. He eyed the German heavyweight loosening up in the ring. At least he would not feel guilty this time for sending a man to the gas chambers. This Aryan soldier would not be killed if he lost; embarrassed and ridiculed by his peers, yes, but killed . . . no.

"He looks like a worthy opponent," Samson said to Höss.

"The worthiest we could find."

"So who's your money on tonight?"

The commander took a deep puff, blew out the smoke, and grinned at Samson. "It's all on you, you dirty Jew. I love a long shot."

Ding! Ding! The bell sounded. Höss returned to his seat.

Samson kissed the Star of David tattoo beneath his Auschwitz numbers and came out of his corner.

The officer emerged, keyed up but calm. He did not run in like the last boxer, although Samson noticed the officer did come in a bit flatfooted. That meant he was probably not a professional fighter. But clearly he was not a beginner either, and he had a large height and reach advantage in addition to his weight advantage.

Pop! The officer hit Samson with a left jab, then another, working his extensive advantage in arm length.

Samson threw a lunging left and missed. He was running on adrenaline instead of using smart boxing skills. Samson followed his miss with an uphill combination, but the far taller man easily deflected the blows with his gloves.

Thump! The officer nailed Samson directly in his eyebrow, still hurt from Samson's last fight. The scab split. The crowd roared at the sight of blood running down Samson's face. The blood running into his eye momentarily blurred his vision, and the tall officer immediately took advantage of Samson's marred eyesight, throwing another combination: a vicious hook, a swift right. But Samson, wounded and half blind, was still too fast. He ducked the blows, bobbing and weaving, until—

Crack! Samson's eye trouble cost him. The officer hammered Samson with a shot to the stomach, knocking the wind out of him. Hurt, Samson covered up, his gloves and forearms over his head and face. Unable to score clean punches, the officer hit Samson with "rabbit punches," illegal punches landing on Samson's lower back. The officer rained punches on Samson's kidneys.

The crowd went berserk, howling, "Crush the Jew!" Samson twisted and turned, trying to avoid the punches to his whip-scarred lower back while covering his face and head. Finally, Samson was able to twist around and tie up the bigger man in a clinch. He took a couple of deep breaths, then shot a glance ringside.

Mengele was laughing.

Laughing heartily . . .

The doctor was pointing at Samson and laughing with sheer, evil joy radiating from the man's face.

That look snapped something inside Samson.

Samson broke the clinch and threw the bigger officer backward, then charged at the man. The officer bounded forward, but instead of punching, Samson ducked low and grabbed the man by his legs. He lifted the officer off his feet, screamed like a madman, and drove the boxer into the corner of the ring. *Crack!* The officer's spine crashed into the corner. He breathed heavily, out of wind.

Samson unleashed a barrage of punches—devastating hooks to the body, left uppercuts, right crosses. The officer struggled to break free, but Samson muscled him back into the ring ropes. A lightning-fast right hook to the ribs was followed by a crushing left to the head. Samson let loose a hailstorm. Fury poured out of him. He was no longer boxing. He was crazed, raging, unstoppable, slugging it out in an all-out attack. He pounded the massive Nazi. One crushing punch followed another. The pain of his daughters' murders had sent Samson into a frenzy.

All the officer could do was cover up, trying to deflect the punches with his arms and gloves and not his head. But Samson was too fast, strong, and experienced to be slowed by that type of defense.

Crack! A punishing uppercut sent the officer to his knees. The referee struggled to push Samson to a neutral corner. The officer rose. Samson threw the referee backward and belted the fighter in the face. The sound of breaking facial bones rippled across the parlor. The big man went down hard.

Several officers in the crowd drew guns, taking aim at Samson.

Höss jumped to his feet, revolver in his hand. "Do not shoot that man!" he screamed above the melee. "Honor for the ring!"

The officers reluctantly obeyed the commandant and held their guns without firing.

Samson stood back, panting.

The Nazi was on the mat, bloodied, unconscious. Out like a light.

"When a man wins, he is to be congratulated! That is the way of sport," Höss shouted, slowly holstering his gun as he eyed Samson. Höss gathered a large handful of reichsmarks, tucked his winnings into his jacket pocket, then started clapping.

No one joined in.

Samson walked across the ring toward where Mengele sat. He pointed his glove at the doctor and shouted with fury, "He is a Nazi. I am a Jew. Who's superior now?"

A thin, dry silence quieted the room.

Mengele stood from his chair with a start. He shook, then went for his revolver. Soldiers sprang from their chairs, hands on triggers, pointing their guns at Samson for his deliberate insolence.

Höss slid through the ropes and stood next to Samson. He held his palm out to the crowd, telling them to stop. The sight of the commandant standing next to Samson made the guards lower their weapons. "It was a fair fight, gentlemen," Höss called out. "Sometimes even an SS officer has an off night." He turned to Samson and hissed in a low voice, "I can't hold back these drunken brutes forever. It's time you went back to the changing room."

Samson stood, unmoving. He continued to glare at Mengele.

Mengele glared back.

"*Goret'v adu!*" Samson spoke in the doctor's direction. It was a language he knew Mengele would understand.

Samson turned his back on Mengele and walked out of the ring unguarded. He strode through the crowd untouched, heading for the changing area.

Höss knew the meaning of the phrase, but he decided to feign ignorance. Wearing a sly grin, he sidled up to Mengele. "I don't suppose you'll translate?"

"It was Russian," Mengele said.

"Yes, but what does it mean, my good man?"

"It is what is said only when Nazi officers are too lax on Jewish prisoners."

"You will not harm the man any further," Höss said firmly, then chuckled, patting a wad of bills in his pocket. "Certainly not while he continues to make me this kind of profit. Now, tell me, Doctor, and tell me precisely—what does the saying mean?"

Mengele turned to Höss, his eyes like jagged glass.

"It means . . . 'burn in hell.'"

SIXTEEN

THE CEMENT WALLS OF THE BATHROOM STALL
were cold and damp. The light overhead was dim. Samson stood
over the toilet bowl, grimacing in pain. The burn shot through his
internal organs with such ferocity that his knees went weak and he
nearly buckled. He braced one hand against the wall while shaking
badly. When he finished, the bowl of the toilet was red with blood.

He'd been in similar predicaments in previous boxing matches.
Even a strong man's kidneys can only handle so much abuse from
rabbit punches being thrown to the lower back. Samson knew it
would take at least two days for the blood to stop flowing inter-
nally. Until then, he'd be in agony every time he urinated. Samson
flushed, stepped out of the stall, and let the door bang behind him.
A nearby guard adjusted his machine gun and nodded.

"Change into your regular prison clothes," the guard said. "And
be quick about it. The truck is waiting to take you back to camp."

From the shadows another figure moved.

"I'd like a moment with the prisoner." The voice was clear
and confident, although quiet. A figure moved into the dim light.

Hedwig. She held a large loaf of bread and a cord of salami, as well as a dinner plate filled with cooked meat, mashed potatoes, and vegetables. She held out the food to Samson.

"Your winnings," Hedwig said. "My husband said to make sure you received them."

Samson glanced at the woman, nodded slowly, and took the food from her. He wiped the blood off his mouth and scooped up a finger full of the mashed potatoes from the plate.

"It was my husband's dinner tonight," Hedwig said, glancing at the plate. "Steak. Forgive me for not being able to get a fresh plate for you. He only ate one bite of the meat before being called away. I thought you might welcome the extra sustenance."

Samson bit into the steak and chewed gingerly, his jaw aching. The dinner may have once belonged to Höss, but there was no way Samson would let it waste. The steak was still hot, charbroiled on the outside, juicy and tender on the inside. How long had it been since he'd tasted meat of this quality? The bread and salami he would save, but he knew he wouldn't be allowed to carry a Nazi dinner plate with him, so he ate the other food as quickly as his jaw permitted.

"You know . . . my maid was Jewish." Hedwig brushed a strand of blond hair behind her ear. "She was my best friend. She always knew what to say and how best to listen."

Hedwig's words confused Samson. Why was the commandant's wife telling him this? And why did she keep staring at him? Samson met her steady gaze with a questioning look.

"*Frau* Höss," the guard said. "The prisoner must leave."

"Give me one moment!" Hedwig's tone turned sharp. Her gaze circled back on Samson and her voice softened. "You're still bleeding badly. Your eye. Your face."

"I'm okay." Samson kept eating.

"I wish I'd brought some iodine. Next time I'll bring some with me. They will give you some in camp tonight, won't they?"

Samson considered his words carefully. He wiped some blood away from his mouth again. "Perhaps . . . the infirmary is stocked with such items."

"Well, I insist that you receive medical care." Hedwig looked at the guard. "You will make sure he is transported straight to the infirmary, yes?"

The guard stifled a smirk, quickly noticing that Hedwig looked sincere. "Of course, *Frau* Höss," he said, swallowing stiffly.

Samson kept eating. He finished the dinner and held the empty plate out to Hedwig but stopped short. "Sorry, I didn't want to take the plate with me," Samson said, on the verge of a stammer. "But . . . uh . . . I don't know if you are allowed to . . ."

"If I can take a plate back after a Jew ate from it?" Hedwig asked, her voice matter-of-fact. "It is true that I am not a military woman, but even so, I am not unaware of what goes on in this camp. Or what has gone on in this war, for that matter. They killed her last month, you know—my maid." Hedwig's voice cracked. "I miss her greatly. She was much more than an excellent maid to me. She was a true friend, and a woman in my position does not have many true friends. I will never understand why they do what they do." Her voice dropped. "Sometimes I wish I could run away from all this horror."

It was at that moment when Samson looked at the woman through different eyes. She was grieving, it was apparent, and he understood that even a woman married to someone as powerful as the camp commander had limitations placed on her. Samson wanted to say something more, something in consolation, but noticed the guard tapping his foot. He handed the plate to Hedwig with a polite nod and headed for the door. From a nail behind the door, his prison garb hung; he grabbed his striped clothes and pulled them on quickly on top of the boxing trunks. On the way out, Samson stopped and quickly wheeled around on one foot. The guard raised his rifle. Samson shook his head.

"Relax," Samson said to the guard. "I mean the woman no harm." He swung his attention to Hedwig. "If I am allowed a question, *Frau* Höss, tell me this: Does your husband plan on killing me?"

The words hung in the air.

"You mean no disrespect by the question," Hedwig said. "I can see that. Only that you seek a straightforward answer. I will tell what I have surmised. There are only two *things* Rudolf Höss loves—honor and money—and the former is usually more important than the latter." The word *things* seemed weighted, as if the woman knew she did not make the list.

"Honor is more important than money—so what does that mean in relation to my question?" Samson asked.

"It means be cautioned." Hedwig cleared her throat. "No man—not even a skilled fighter such as yourself—can keep winning forever. And although my husband greatly values the large sums he makes on you, his allegiances to the party run even deeper."

Samson nodded. "Tell your husband I need to see him tonight." He grimly wiped his mouth, which was still trickling blood from the corner, and walked away.

"Stop!" came a booming voice.

It was Höss. He had appeared silently and now stood behind Hedwig. Two guards stood on either side of him. "You've got something you want to say to me?" the commander asked.

Samson nodded.

"Good," Höss said. "I've got something I want to say to you too."

Samson followed Höss back through the changing area, through the officer's parlor, down a corridor, and into a small, private office. Guards flanked Samson on all sides. Hedwig disappeared. When they reached Höss's office, he turned to his guards abruptly. "Stay outside," he ordered.

Höss sat behind a desk in the office, reached into his jacket pocket, and pulled out another of his ever-present enormous cigars. Samson stayed standing in front of him. Höss clipped off the end of his cigar, lit it with a silver lighter, and blew a cloud of blue smoke toward Samson.

"I'll begin," the commander said. "Dr. Mengele is no personal friend of mine, yet he is a colleague and a Nazi officer, and you are our prisoner. As much as I find it amusing, every time you holler insults at the man like you did tonight, you make us all look bad, which does not bode well for me in the long term. Understand what I'm saying? I should have you whipped again."

"Are you going to keep your word?" Samson asked, trying to suppress his outrage, sensing that Höss was setting up a chess move against him.

"What are you talking about, my good man? You got your food. I saw by the empty plate that you even ate my dinner tonight." The commander laughed ruefully. "I should have Hedwig whipped for that."

"We had a new bargain."

"Oh that." Höss took another puff of his cigar. "Look, I said I would set them free. I did not say when."

Samson clenched his fists and took a step forward.

Höss quickly pulled his gun and aimed it at Samson's face.

Samson stopped. Höss smiled and set his gun down casually on his desk.

"Simmer down." Höss pointed a finger at Samson. "Letting a Jew go in such a way as to protect him or her from being quickly caught and killed is a tricky matter. Do you want me to free your wife only to have her whipped and back in the camp the next day? What good would that do? Trust me, I'll free a family member whenever I can . . . Now, so there is no mistake, how many in your family are left?"

Samson wanted to fly across the desk and tear Höss's lungs out. He felt sure this was just a stall tactic from Höss, and Samson had a gut-wrenching feeling that he was being lied to. But he bit his tongue, swallowed, and answered, "My wife, my son, my sister, my brother, and his fiancée . . . and a teenage boy . . . his name is Yeshua. I was going to ask for my sister's infant son, but I've heard the small children and infants are killed immediately."

Höss nodded. "So six left? Good. We'll keep a fair tally. That means six more fights, eh?"

"Five."

"Five?"

"I won one tonight."

"Ah yes," Höss said. "One tonight, five more family members to go, and then one more fight to top it all off . . . perhaps for your friend the priest. Or maybe even one to free yourself. I count six." The commander smiled, patted his jacket pocket twice, the one where Samson assumed his pocketbook was kept, and blew another enormous cloud of cigar smoke in Samson's direction.

"All right," Samson said. "Six." There was no use arguing with the man, not this night anyway, when the commander's mind was so near to his newly fattened wallet.

"Sometimes my generosity surprises even me, Samson. I'm a man of my word. Every fight you win will yield the freedom of one of your family members. I'll begin work on this right away. Who would you like freed first? Your brother? Your son?"

"My wife."

"Ah, the love of a spouse. Not every man knows such pleasure. But a fine choice, Samson. A fine choice."

"When exactly will you begin work on this?" Samson eyed Höss distrustfully.

Höss eyed Samson back. Face now placid, he looked at Samson and said two words that Samson could have sworn he'd heard before at Auschwitz.

"Tomorrow morning."

Nearing Hut 57, the *Kapo* happily munched on half of Samson's bread and salami as the two men made their way back to the barracks. The night was bitterly cold for early spring. The air held frost, like it might even snow at any moment.

"We heard you fought well tonight," the *Kapo* said, licking his fingers. "Impressive. To hear the guard tell the story, it sounds like the officer had you beat, but you turned it around. How long do you think you can keep this up, anyway?" The *Kapo* bit off another mouthful of bread.

"Why? Are you afraid your supply train will stop?"

"Look—we have a deal." The *Kapo*'s breath blew out frosty air. "Any time you want to back out of the bargain, be my guest."

"No, you look—" Samson said fiercely, speaking to the man in Hebrew. "You're not the one taking beatings in the ring, and you're not the one in danger of being sent to the gas chambers if you lose. And you have not lost what I have already lost. So do not ask me any more of your pathetic questions."

"It was merely a question."

"No it wasn't, and you know it. You *Kapos*, you're all alike. You're Germans in Jewish skin doing Hitler's bidding. You know how much we hate you? You're traitors, beating and killing your own people the way you do. You sell out your brothers to save your own hides."

The *Kapo* bristled and raised his truncheon. The two men stopped walking and stood face-to-face in the dark. Both were breathing heavily in the cold air. The *Kapo* spoke first. "I'll ask you whatever I want. I'm a survivor, that's what I am. Before the war I was a man of great importance. Wealthy and respected. So don't tell me you've suffered like you're the only one who's suffered. We've all suffered. You're no different than me."

"You might have suffered." Samson glared at the man. "But you and I are not alike. I'll survive this war by strength and integrity. You'll survive by cunning and deception."

The *Kapo* snapped and swung his truncheon. Samson easily ducked and raised his fist, ready to slug the man in the jaw.

"Do it!" the *Kapo* said, his voice a hissed whisper. "Hit me and see how long you'll live. I'll yell, and guards will come running, and that will be the last time either of us sees any of your precious bread again. I'm the one who'll live through this war—you will not. How does your integrity chew on that?"

Samson held his fist in midair. Each man glared at the other. Slowly the breath went out of Samson. He let his fist fall to his side. The *Kapo* lowered his club.

"You know I'm not going to hit you," Samson said.

The *Kapo* nodded and sighed. "We're not far off in our views, you and I. I'm no friend of the Nazis. I'm just another man, trying to survive like you."

The *Kapo*'s words stayed in the crisp air, and the two men began walking slowly, this time in silence.

At the corner of the hut, the *Kapo* paused. "Between you and me, I'm rooting for you, Samson—and it's about more than the food. But just so we're clear . . . when we go inside the barrack, it's all business again, understood?"

"If you never fight back," said Samson, "you won't be able to live with yourself when this war is over."

"I'm not strong like you. You've got to fight your way. I have to fight mine."

"You think you're fighting? Really?"

The *Kapo* nodded. "I got food to your children last week, didn't I?"

Samson inhaled sharply, as if struck. "Yes . . ." He mulled his words, still not knowing how much he trusted the *Kapo*. "When you saw them . . . can I ask you how they were?"

The *Kapo* nodded. "Your boy ate his food all at once. The girls too . . . and I'm sorry, Samson. It took me a day before I could even reach them—Mengele hovered around them like a vulture. But I gave them all the food allotted them—I truly did. Your girls ate one last good meal, I promise you that."

Samson's gaze fell. "Did . . . my daughters say anything to you? Anything you remember? Anything at all?"

"One of them said something, yes. But I couldn't tell you which girl it was."

"What did she say?"

"Well, I had less than ten seconds when I handed off the food.

I told them they were to eat all the food right away, that the food was a gift from their daddy, and that there would be more to come. Then I heard someone coming down the hall, and I needed to run."

"What was it? Do you remember the words my daughter spoke?"

"It was at the mention of the word *daddy*," the *Kapo* said. "Your little girl simply smiled and said, 'I love my daddy. My daddy always gives us good gifts.'"

From left: Joseph Levi, Yosef Alcana, and two other young men sit on a fence with a young child in a park. Yosef and Joseph were both deported to Auschwitz. Alcana perished, but Levi, a champion boxer, survived and emigrated to Israel.

United States Holocaust Memorial Museum, courtesy of Miru Alcana

View of the Kraków gate.

Public domain

Jews move their belongings into the Kraków ghetto in horse-drawn wagons.

United States Holocaust Memorial Museum,
courtesy of Archiwum Panstwowe w Krakowie

A German officer checks the papers of Jews moving into the Kraków ghetto.

United States Holocaust Memorial Museum,
courtesy of Archiwum Panstwowe w Krakowie

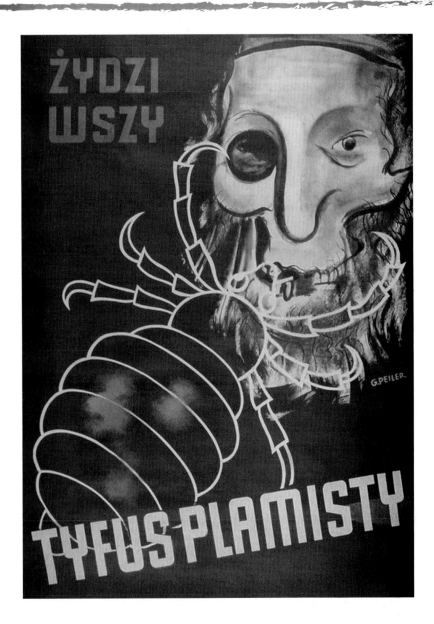

A Nazi propaganda poster associates Jews with lice and typhoid.

Public domain

A poster advertising the anti-Semitic propaganda film Der ewige Jude (The Eternal Jew) *hangs on the side of a Dutch building.*

United States Holocaust Memorial Museum, courtesy of Samuel (Schrijver) Schryver

Arbeit Macht Frei *("Work Makes Freedom," or "Work Makes [One] Free")—Main camp entrance to Auschwitz.*

Logaritmo, via Wikimedia Commons

View of a section of the barbed wire fence and barracks at Auschwitz at the time of the liberation of the camp.

United States Holocaust Memorial Museum, courtesy of Philip Vock

Newly arrived Jews from Subcarpathian Russia get off the train in Auschwitz-Birkenau.

A view of the Auschwitz II camp showing the barracks of the camp.

Children taken from Eastern Europe during the SS Heuaktion (Hay Action) and temporarily imprisoned in Auschwitz, awaiting their transfer to Germany, look out from behind the barbed wire fence.

United States Holocaust Memorial Museum, courtesy of
Belarusian State Archive of Documentary Film and Photography

Maximilian Kolbe.

Public domain

A warehouse full of shoes and clothing confiscated from the prisoners and deportees gassed upon their arrival.

United States Holocaust Memorial Museum,
courtesy of Institute Contemporary History Paris

A warehouse in Auschwitz overflows with clothes confiscated from prisoners.

United States Holocaust Memorial Museum, courtesy of
National Archives and Records Administration, College Park

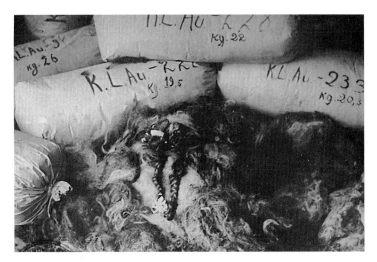

Bales of the hair of female prisoners found in the warehouses of Auschwitz at the liberation.

United States Holocaust Memorial Museum, courtesy of
National Archives and Records Administration, College Park

*View of the execution wall between Block 10 and
Block 11 in the Auschwitz I camp.*

United States Holocaust Memorial Museum, courtesy of
National Archives and Records Administration, College Park

A sign on the electric fence in Aushwitz. The sign reads, "Caution, danger."

United States Holocaust Memorial Museum, courtesy of
National Archives and Records Administration, College Park

Roll call at Auschwitz. A scene from the film The Last Stage.

United States Holocaust Memorial Museum, courtesy of
National Museum of American Jewish History

The SS parlor and retreat, Solahütte, and its surrounding grounds just outside of Auschwitz.

SS officer Karl Hoecker relaxes with women in lounge chairs on the deck of the Solahütte retreat.

*An accordionist leads a sing-along for SS officers at
the Solahütte retreat just outside Auschwitz.*

United States Holocaust Memorial Museum, courtesy of Anonymous Donor

SS officers Dr. Josef Mengele and Rudolf Höss socialize on the grounds of the SS retreat Solahütte just outside of Auschwitz.

United States Holocaust Memorial Museum, courtesy of Anonymous Donor

A survivor stokes smoldering human remains in
a crematorium oven that is still lit.

United States Holocaust Memorial Museum, courtesy of Francis Robert Arzt

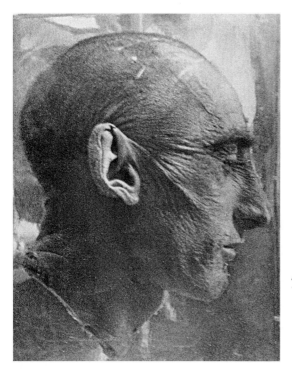

A victim of Nazi medical experiments. The severed head was all that remained intact.

United States Holocaust Memorial Museum

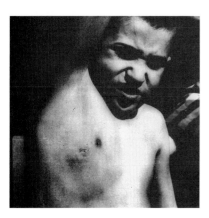

A Jewish child is forced to show the scar left after SS physicians removed his lymph nodes. This child was one of twenty Jewish children injected with tuberculosis germs as part of a medical experiment. All the children were murdered on April 20, 1945. More pictures of children who were victims of medical experiments were not included herein due to their graphic nature.

United States Holocaust Memorial Museum

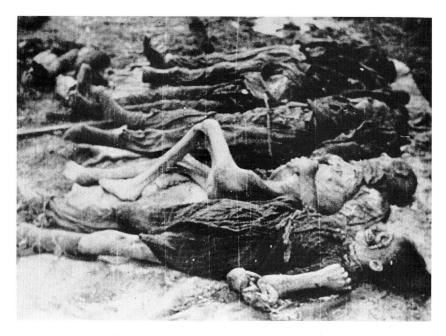

Corpses of murdered victims in Auschwitz.

United States Holocaust Memorial Museum,
courtesy of Leopold Page Photographic Collection

SEVENTEEN

SAMSON FOLLOWED THE *KAPO* INTO THEIR barrack for the night. The *Kapo* paused just inside the door and held his finger to his lips. Both men froze, not from fear, but from quiet surprise.

The soft, melodic sound of Hebrew singing drifted to their ears. Shadows danced on the wall. Zach sat toward the far end of the barrack. He held a single candle and was encircled by a small group of prisoners. Zach looked gaunt, his cheeks hollow, and there were strange, sickly splotches of purple on his face and neck. Yet there was a renewed, confident glow about him, one that Samson hadn't seen in his brother for months. Zach lifted a bent tin cup in the midst of the group and murmured the beginning of the traditional Passover prayer: *"I lift up the cup of deliverance and call upon the name of the Lord our God."*

The Jewish prisoners around Zach answered quietly, in unison: *"We will praise the Lord our God forever."*

Kolbe sat in the group as well. *A remarkable sight,* Samson thought, *to see a Catholic priest in the middle of Auschwitz taking part in a Jewish ceremony.* As angry at God as Samson felt, there was a part of him that clung to his faith, part of him that was flooded with comfort by the Passover prayer. He knew he should not blame God for the evil that men did, but he could not help feeling that God should have shown up by now and stopped this insanity.

"'Out of the depths, I called upon God, who answered me with great deliverance,'" continued Zach, reciting his family's special Passover prayer he had spoken for his people so many times before.

"'We will not die, but live,'" Kolbe and the group responded.

"'I shall walk before the Lord in the land of the living,'" said Zach, his voice rising a bit.

"'We will not die, but live,'" recited the group.

"'The stone which the builders rejected has become the chief cornerstone,'" prayed Zach in a singsong tone.

"'We will not die, but live,'" prayed the group in response.[1]

Zach opened his eyes and abruptly stopped the prayer. He locked gazes with his brother and stood to his feet. Spotting Samson, the group jostled one another, quickly rushing to surround him. Zach and Kolbe reached Samson first and embraced him while the others murmured congratulations and patted him on the back.

"Don't stop a Passover prayer on my behalf," Samson said. "If there is a God . . . I don't want to answer for that."

"We're so proud of you," Zach said. "Other *Kapos* have already passed along the details of the fight. Good news travels fast—even in a hellish place like this."

---

1. This call-and-response can be found in the Haggadah, the traditional Passover Seder text. See, for example, *A Passover Haggadah*, edited by Harold Bronstein (New York: Central Conference of American Rabbis, 1974; repr. 1994), 74–75. See also Psalms 116:13; 118:17; 130:1; 116:9; and 118:22.

"How's your eye?" Kolbe said, noticing the blood. "Please, sit down, let's have a look at those wounds. How do you feel?"

"Well . . . I've felt better," Samson said with a grin, not wanting to alarm his friends. He sat.

Kolbe examined Samson's head. "Here—bring that candle over here," he said to one of the group's members.

Slam! The *Kapo* thumped his truncheon against the frame of the building. The group flinched and cringed. That sound usually meant a beating was coming.

"Enough of this!" the *Kapo* ordered. "Everyone to your bunk, now! Last thing we want is for some guard to stroll by on a routine check and find you all up and about with candles and celebrations." He turned to Kolbe and Zach hovering over Samson. "You have ten minutes to clean him up. And no more noise." He brandished his truncheon.

Reluctantly, everyone pulled away from Samson, shaking his hand and smiling as they separated, waving at him as they headed for their bunks.

"Well done tonight," said one older man. "Every time you beat them, you give us hope."

Samson shook his head as the man walked away. *How could his victories in the ring bring hope to his fellow prisoners?* He turned to Zach who was, for some reason, staring at the small candle. "Where'd you get that candle, Zach?"

"It was stolen from a supply closet," Zach said.

"That's dangerous. It could get us all killed."

"Don't talk to me about danger, Samson. You've said yourself that some things are worth risking your life for—family, tradition, trying to escape from this camp . . ."

Kolbe ripped a strip from his shirt, dipped it in "holy" water from the cup Zach had used in the prayer, and gently placed the rag over Samson's eye, stemming the blood flow. The pressure on the wound caused Samson to grimace in pain.

"You are their champion," Kolbe said. "Every time you win, you give them hope. This celebration tonight—your victory prompted this."

Samson grabbed Kolbe's arm. "I am no champion. If they think I can save them, they're wrong."

"I understand the weight of that burden on you, Samson," Kolbe said, continuing to clean his wounds. "But you must understand that your triumphs may be far more important than you realize. Sometimes when hope is renewed, faith is renewed . . . and that can be far more important than saving a person's flesh."

Samson did not know what to think of this monk. At times Kolbe's faith inspired him. At times it baffled him. He decided to press the matter further. Samson eyed the priest and grinned. "Maximilian Kolbe . . . what would your fellow monks think of a Catholic participating in a Jewish Passover prayer?"

"You think I'm going to get in trouble with my order for this?" Kolbe chuckled.

"No, just genuinely curious."

"Every Christian should celebrate Passover. God freeing his people from slavery in Egypt was a foreshadowing of Christ freeing us from the power of sin and giving us eternal life. Passover is a miracle worth remembering—even for a Catholic priest." Kolbe poured water slowly from the Passover cup onto Samson's face, trying to cleanse the wound.

Samson looked at Kolbe and Zach, these men of two different faiths, and stifled a smirk. "You know, both of you believe in a God you have never seen, in a heaven you have never been to, and in a

Bible written by people you have never met. Some would call you *foolish fanatics.*"

"'The just shall live by faith,'" Kolbe said. "The prophet Habakkuk said that in the Hebrew Scriptures. The apostle Paul said exactly the same thing in the New Testament.[2] Tell me this, Samson. You don't think it's possible—not the mere hundredth of a chance—that there might be things that are real even though we can't see them?"

"Sure . . . ," Samson said slowly, squirming a bit under the priest's hands. "A God might exist somewhere out there, even an unseen God. But that doesn't change the fact that I'm still not happy with him." Samson's long-simmering doubts were rising to the surface. He grabbed Kolbe's hand that was pressed against his forehead gash and pushed it away.

"So you're not happy with God because you believe he is not at work," Kolbe said. "You want God to swoop down and save you, do it quickly, and do it in the manner you prescribe?"

"It's not like that," Samson said. "God could stop this war, end this suffering. Plenty of people are praying for that. So where is he when we need him?"

Zach flushed and jumped into the discussion. His present physical weakness didn't stop him from feistily interrupting. "Well, I've got an answer to that," Zach said. "I believe it is simple, Samson, but it's a hard pill to swallow."

Samson gave his younger brother an inquisitive look, wondering where he was going with this.

"All this pain is our punishment," Zach said. "That's what I believe. It's for our disobedience as a people, for not being good Jews and not keeping the Orthodox law."

---

2. Hebrews 10:38. See also Habakkuk 2:4: "The just shall live by his faith."

Samson stared at his younger brother, stunned. "I've always suspected your faith revolves mostly around tradition," Samson said. "But you actually believe God is deliberately inflicting harm on us?"

"I certainly do," Zach said, unwavering.

"I don't," responded Kolbe, pressing on one of Samson's shoulder gashes. "God might discipline his children for going astray, but God's discipline is more like guidance and always done in love. Discipline and punishment are not the same, and God does not punish his children with wrath—he's not an evil father who would break his child's legs for not jumping high enough. No, Zach . . . that can't be the answer. God chastens us with his Word—the Scriptures convict us of what is right and wrong. God would not commit the mass murder of his own people as a punishment. He is not the source of this evil."

"Then what is?" asked Zach. "I'm a fair man, Kolbe, and as they teach us at yeshiva—Hebrew school—I'll give your full opinion a fair hearing." Zach leaned against the bunk, arms crossed, listening.

Encouraged, Kolbe continued. "Jesus said in the book of John that Satan comes for only three reasons: to steal, to kill, and to destroy.[3] Everywhere you see killing, stealing, and destruction, Satan is at the root of it. Satan is real, and he can influence humans to do evil."

"You're saying that this is all ultimately the work of the devil—or of mankind doing the devil's bidding?" Samson retorted. "Then my same question still stands: God is supposed to be more powerful than Satan, so why doesn't God intervene? That sure seems like something a good God would—and *should*—do."

Kolbe dabbed more water onto Samson's forehead, the rag already blood soaked from his wounds.

---

3. John 10:10, paraphrase.

"Well, we've skirted around this question before," Kolbe finally responded. "A fuller answer takes some time to explain."

"Go ahead." Zach looked around the barrack and shrugged. "We're not going anywhere."

Samson nodded.

"There are two schools of thought," Kolbe continued. "The first goes like this: God gave man dominion and authority over the earth, like a lease on a property, and free will to do as he pleased. Man turned that dominion, that lease, over to Satan in the garden of Eden by trusting Satan's word over God's word, by disobeying God's simple command not to partake of one thing, the tree's fruit, and believing Satan's lies. By trusting Satan's word instead of God's word, man made, in a sense, Satan his master, and therefore what belonged to man then belonged to Satan. That is why Satan had the right to tempt Jesus with the world's riches and kingdoms in the fourth chapter of Matthew—they were his to offer. Now God only intervenes when asked because God keeps his word, and he gave dominion on this earth to Adam and Eve's descendants. And even though Jesus has redeemed us from the law of sin and eternal death, we still must apply our faith to connect with God's power. The bigger the mountain, the problem, the stronger our faith must be to move it."

"So you believe in an all-powerful God who by his own rules, so to speak, requires us to have faith, strong faith, before he will intervene?" Zach asked.

"I told you there were two major schools of thought," Kolbe said. "In this first school of thought, although God owns everything, he's put it into man's hands, allowing mankind to do with it what he will for the duration of this 'lease.'"

"But still, why doesn't God answer our prayers for intervention?" asked Zach, pacing as he contemplated his own question.

Kolbe took a deep breath. "Well, some say God never answers prayer above the level of faith that is used."

"What do you mean by 'level of faith'?" Samson asked.

"I mean if you pray for a hundred zlotys to pay your rent with, then you'll get it if you truly believe," answered Kolbe. "But if you have enough faith to ask for ten thousand zlotys to pay for rent, food, water, a horse, a field to farm, toys for your children, and the other things your family may need, as well as extra to bless others with, then you will get that—if you believe. Jesus said in Mark 11:24 that 'whatever things you ask when you pray, believe that you receive them, and you will have them.'[4] In the first chapter of James, Jesus' brother wrote, 'Let him ask in faith, with no doubting, for he who doubts is like a wave of the sea driven and tossed by the wind. For let not that man suppose that he will receive anything from the Lord; he is a double-minded man.'[5] God wants us to come to him with strong faith, so we must feed our faith and starve our doubts."

Samson and Zach traded a look with each other—*an unusual monk to say the least.*

"You haven't answered our question. Why doesn't God get us out?" asked Samson.

Kolbe stopped applying pressure to Samson's wound for a moment. "What is your level of faith? Jesus said in Matthew 18:19 that 'if two of you agree on earth concerning anything . . . anything that they ask . . . it will be done for them by my Father in heaven.'[6] So I ask you, do you honestly believe God will stop all this, the whole war, this slaughter of your people along with so many others, right now, just because we three pray?"

---

4. Mark 11:24 NKJV.
5. James 1:6-8 NKJV.
6. Matthew 18:19 NKJV.

The question hung in the air. "I believe God could end all this in a second," Zach said, a bit defiantly.

"I did not ask you if you believed he *could*," Kolbe said. "I asked you if you truly believed God *would*, right now, end all this, just because we prayed and asked him to."

"I don't know," responded Zach. "I don't know if my faith is so strong that I could honestly say I knew beyond a shadow of a doubt that God would do that just because we three prayed."

"And that is our challenge," stated Kolbe. "When enough believers pray with real, mountain-moving faith, believing not that God *can* stop this . . . but that he *will* immediately stop this . . . then he will. Not praying in hope, mind you, but praying in faith and power, praying with the knowledge that God will end all this just because we ask. Until that moment, this war, this slaughter, will go on. Faith is the connection to God's power. Without faith, there is no way to tap into God's unlimited power."

"So you're saying, in a way, that much evil enters the world because of a lack of faith." Samson thought for a moment, turning slightly as his wounds shot sharp pain through his back. "I don't know if I will ever have the kind of 'mountain-moving' faith that you speak of, Kolbe. I don't know if I have ever met anyone with faith that strong. It seems . . . unattainable."

"You said there was a second school of thought," Zach said, intrigued.

"Yes," said Kolbe. "There is. The Scriptures also teach that God is sovereign. That means that God is all-powerful, all the time. Yet God can't do everything, if the 'thing' is contrary to God's nature. For instance, God cannot sin. God cannot lie. God cannot do evil. So, in a sense, it's true that God is paradoxically 'limited' by the very nature of being God."

"Go on," Samson said, caught up in the thought, momentarily forgetting the sting of his wounds.

Kolbe knit his brow, concentrating while cleaning Samson's wounds. "Within sovereignty, God has set up regulations as to how our earth is run. He ordained and energized rules that pertain to moral and physical realms, and mankind has to reckon with these rules or else suffer the consequences. For instance, God set into motion the law of gravity. If you don't heed this rule, then you'll pay a painful price."

Zach and Samson both began talking at once, but Kolbe held up his hand. "Think of it this way: If a man holding a baby in his arms decides to jump off a steep cliff, both of them will need to reckon with gravity. Even if the man and the baby fall to their deaths, God is still good. God won't change his rule of gravity just to do what we think he should."

"Fine," Zach said, as the candle sputtered and flickered over his face. "You're saying that mankind has chosen to do evil by engaging in this war. We understand that. Mankind must reckon with the natural consequences of war, namely that war causes death, suffering, and pain, even for innocent people—we understand that too. That's why we're all suffering in this camp. It's a natural consequence of man's decision to choose evil actions. But that still doesn't answer the question of where God is in the midst of this suffering."

"The answer is that God is still present, still engaged, and still active within the lives of people," Kolbe said, standing up. "Picture God at the top of the cliff, warning the man with the baby not to jump. The man jumps anyway. God is with the man and the baby on the way down, offering love, grace, and reconciliation even as the man and baby are bound by the law of gravity and plummet to their deaths. And God is at the bottom of the cliff, offering comfort to the families as they grieve."

"That doesn't seem good enough," Samson said slowly, thoughtfully. "Why didn't God just save the man or the baby in the first place? It still sounds like God is just sitting idly by."

"Although we're discussing faith, try to think of it logically," Kolbe said. "God respects man's free will, even if the man chooses to mock God's rule—just like jumping off a cliff mocks the law of gravity. You asked: How can a good God allow people to suffer, particularly innocent people? First, don't blame God for the suffering. Blame Satan, for being the father of lies, and then blame mankind, for making choices that mock God. The fuller answer is that sometimes we don't know why God acts as he does, to the extent that he does. God gives us answers, but sometimes we don't want to listen. It might seem like God is sitting idly by, but rest assured, he is not."

"That still doesn't sound good enough for me," Zach said, frustrated, shaking his head and absent-mindedly fidgeting his hands. "Why isn't God doing more?"

"Maybe he is and we just don't know it," Kolbe said, raising one eyebrow. "Again, that's where faith enters in—no matter what school of thought you hold to. God always invites us to faith—faith that God is good, faith that evil can be defeated, and faith that God has his reasons why he must allow certain things to happen."

"I still can't say I'm in agreement," Zach said.

"Faith is always God's invitation to us—as well as God's requirement of us," Kolbe said. "Without faith, life overwhelms us. We need faith against all odds to survive this war."

"So," Zach asked, "are you saying that if we have faith, it will guarantee our survival?"

Kolbe exhaled slowly. "Jesus always marvels at great faith. And if we have great faith, we will see him in heaven. We will have that ultimate victory no matter what happens to these tents of flesh we call bodies. But you have both admitted that none of us here right now can honestly say that we believe beyond a shadow of a doubt that God himself would stop this war just because we prayed. And I admit I can't say that my faith is so strong that I could, with my faith alone, pray such a powerful prayer as to call down God himself and end this war in a heartbeat. But I do believe this concentration camp will eventually be brought down, along with the Nazis, and that God's chosen people, the Jews, and God's adopted children, the Christians, will be triumphant in this war."

Samson listened respectfully, at times nodding, but often remaining still, sometimes closing his eyes to focus on fighting the pain wracking his body.

"I believe God's hand is already moving the world toward the victory of good and the defeat of evil. So the faith that's required of us sometimes allows God to perform miracles that free us from our suffering, but sometimes it's a faith that simply trusts that God is good and knows what he's doing, even though God doesn't always explain it all to us."

"So you're saying faith is still the answer, even if we all die in these camps?" asked Zach.

"Faith is always the answer." Kolbe exhaled again, pondering the difficulty of the words. "How can a good God allow suffering? It all comes back to faith in the face of adversity. Faith, courage, and hard work will open the door to victory in this war. I'm certain of it. Remember also that God works through people, just as Satan, I believe, is working through Hitler. And in due time, God's working through men and women all over the world will bring us victory in this war." Kolbe stared up at the ceiling of their barrack as if looking up to God at that moment. "Yes, I pray every day, sometimes by the hour, that the Allied troops will be victorious and the war will end. Millions around the world are praying, and I believe with all my heart that God will answer them. Mark my words: the Nazis will not win. Meanwhile, we must have faith regardless of horrible circumstances. The only way for us to survive is through unshakeable faith."

The *Kapo* leaned off his bunk. "Time's up. If he bleeds, he bleeds."

Samson turned to Kolbe as the three slowly rose. "If there is a God," said Samson, "and he is the loving and powerful God you say he is . . . then I want to believe. But in all honesty, I can't say I do. Not yet, anyway."

Kolbe handed over the bloody rag to Samson. "Keep applying pressure. It should stop bleeding in a few more minutes." Kolbe gently patted Samson and Zach on their shoulders and walked away.

Zach spoke quietly to Samson. "He's an odd monk, isn't he?"

Samson nodded, heading for his bunk, but Zach suddenly stopped him, his tone dead serious.

"I need to talk to you, Samson. Alone. When the *Kapo* falls asleep, slip outside and meet me around back of the barracks."

His manner was so dour, so sober, it took Samson aback. He knew Zach better than anyone. Whenever Zach used that tone, it had always meant he wanted Samson to help him do something dangerous.

"What is it?" Samson asked, desperately wanting to lay his bloody, aching body down on a bunk.

Zach's eyes were pleading. "I need your help, Samson. I know you're hurt right now, but I fear if I don't do this tonight, the chance will never come again."

Slowly Samson nodded. "As soon as the *Kapo* is asleep. I'll meet you there."

EIGHTEEN

THE BACK OF THE BARRACKS WAS CLOAKED IN darkness. Far away the pale glow of one light shone in the otherwise black sky. The night had turned bitterly cold. The wind had picked up, and small, hard flakes of snow gusted about. The ground was already covered by a thin, white iciness.

"I thought we were nearing spring," Samson said, his face grim.

"This is what they call 'spring at Auschwitz,'" Zach said, shaking his head.

"It's dangerous for us to be out like this, little brother." Samson's whisper was hoarse. "Be quick. What's your plan?"

"On Saturday nights, security is at a minimum. They're all still back at Solahütte smoking and drinking, and they will be for at least a few more hours."

"Go on."

"Esther and I are still unmarried, Samson. We have never . . . been together, as man and wife . . . I have never been with a woman, Samson. Ever . . ."

Samson gave Zach that knowing look brothers give each other

when they should know better. Sure, he grasped what his brother was asking, and he understood the passion behind it, but he had already been through enough pain for one night—he desperately needed rest. He turned away, but Zach grabbed him, stopping him from leaving. Samson slowly turned back, trying to have patience. "I'm tired and still bleeding, little brother," pleaded Samson. "What you're asking for can wait."

"There is another selection coming up," Zach said, shivering. "The rumor is all around camp. Look at me, brother—I'm fading. I don't have your vigor. At the next selection I will be chosen, I know it . . . and then I will go to the gas chambers. You know it, and so do I."

Samson stared at Zach. His brother had not been robust to begin with. He'd lost far too much weight since arriving at Auschwitz. The strange sickly purple splotches on his face and neck had emerged and grown worse over time. Samson knew Zach's assessment of his fate was reasonable, looking as poorly as the young man now did. But Samson still shook his head. "Little brother, I would do anything for you. But I know what you are thinking, and any plan of that kind is suicide."

Zach grabbed him, desperate. The fire in his eyes blazed. "We're all going to die here anyway. It's just a matter of time. But we don't need to die tonight—not if we're smart. I know I have asked you favors in the past, but this request means more to me than my own life. Please, Samson, I'm begging you. Please."

A memory flashed through Samson's mind. When Zach had been a little boy and Samson a teenager, Zach used to plead for Samson to play hide-and-seek with him. Life had been so different then. He could see Zach as a little boy, a mane of curly hair, his bright smile, and his skinny little frame. Samson had always loved Zach, and he never could say no to him for long.

Outside the *Frauenabteilung*,[1] Samson and Zach crouched by a fence. The night sky was starless, and snow fell continuously. Shivering, Samson and Zach crawled around a corner of the women's barrack on their elbows and knees. They eyed a single guard and moved stealthily out of his sight line.

"If this works, I expect you to name your firstborn after me," Samson said wryly, attempting to lift his brother's spirits.

"What if it's a girl?" Zach asked.

"What if it is?" Samson responded, a faint smile on his face. His eyes stayed pinned on the guard in the distance.

Zach gave a faint smile in return. "As soon as he rounds that corner, we'll have about one minute to make it over the fence and into the women's barrack. I've timed him before."

"You've been planning this for a while then, little brother."

"I've been planning for it my whole life."

"Okay, there goes the guard."

"It's time. Go!"

Samson and Zach took off running. Both kept as low as possible. When they reached the fence, Samson hoisted Zach up. In Zach's weakened condition, he struggled to the top, and by sheer force of will he slung his legs up and over the fence, quickly dropping to the ground. Samson followed, scaling the fence quickly, then dropped down next to Zach. The guard rounded the corner on his way back. The brothers took off again, staying out of sight, and headed straight into the *Frauenabteilung*.

It was pitch black in Hut 17. Inside the front door, Zach lit his

---

1. Women's barrack.

Passover candle with one of the few matches he had managed to pilfer. He whispered into the darkness beyond the small pool of light his candle provided. "Esther . . . Esther . . ."

"I'm here." A quiet voice came out of the darkness as Esther stepped forward into the light. She wore her prison garb with an improvised belt made of ripped cloth pulled tight around her waist. Her hair had grown out just enough to hold a small headpiece made from scraps she had found around the camp, bits of cloth and torn fabric that she had woven together. Rebecca had placed the small flower Samson gave her into the headpiece, and Esther beamed like every bride beams on her wedding day. She glided across the rough wooden floor toward Zach. He gently took her thin hands in his and pulled her close, resting his forehead against hers.

On the outer edges of the candlelight, Samson saw that Esther was surrounded by a dozen women.

"Samson," came a familiar whisper. "Samson—is that you?"

Samson burst forward, grabbed Rebecca in a hug, and lifted her off the ground. They'd been married for a long time and did not need to speak. Samson held on to his wife as if he would never hug her again. He kissed her on the cheek and wiped the tears from her eyes.

"We don't have much time," Zach said.

Samson stepped back from Rebecca, still holding her hand, and turned to Zach. "You're right, little brother. Let's get you married."

***

Samson stood in one corner of the hut. Several women lined up as bridesmaids. Rebecca stood beside Esther as the matron of honor.

In a low voice, Samson recited the *ketubah*[2] in Hebrew, roughly working his way through the ancient marriage ritual as best he could remember, occasionally stopping to wipe the blood that still dripped down his forehead into his eye. Zach and Esther's hands were still tightly intertwined.

At the same moment, two hands shook in the Nazis' Solahütte parlor. Höss and Mengele sat down around a card table. The adjutant,[3] the *Obersturmbannführer*, and an *Untersturmbannführer* sat with them. Hedwig sat some distance away at a side table with two other officers' wives.

Beer and whiskey were poured. Höss and the rest of the men tossed back their drinks and began a card game. They smoked cigars and placed their bets and laughed and bragged, drowning their thoughts in alcohol and revelry.

The more they drank, the more they forgot, and the more their laughter grew.

Soft laughter grew inside the women's barrack of Hut 17 as Samson and the others gently, quietly danced while Esther circled Zach seven times, smiling broadly, all of them very softly singing *"Hava Nagila."*

---

2. The *ketubah* is in essence an agreement that formalizes the various requirements by Halakha (Jewish law) of a Jewish husband to his wife.
3. The first assistant to the commandant. He was the superior of all noncommissioned officers and men of the commandant's staff.

Inside the officers' parlor, Höss and his men belted out their *Trinklieder*, boisterous German drinking songs. All except Mengele. The other officers slapped each other on the back and continued singing, but Mengele quietly slipped away outside, headed for a waiting truck.

As a guard drove the doctor back to camp, Mengele pulled out his truncheon and twirled it in the truck's cab, watching the darkened forests out the window. The guard drove slowly due to the snow on the road, and as Mengele twirled his club, he looked forward to using it later that evening.

Smash!

Inside Block 10, Mengele's truncheon slammed down on the legs of Simon.

The boy screamed, instantly awake with extreme pain. He shot out of bed, ducked Mengele's grasp, and limped away as quickly as he could to a corner of the room, where he cowered in fright.

Mengele smiled cruelly, lunged for the boy, caught him by the shirt collar, and threw him to the floor.

Simon screamed and kicked.

Mengele lifted his foot over Simon's chest; Simon twisted away as Mengele stomped down hard.

Stomp!

Inside Hut 17, Zach's foot shattered a lightbulb. It was all they could find, but they wanted to stay as true as possible to the ceremonial breaking of the glass.[4] There were "congratulations" and "mazel tovs" from all who were present. Zach hugged Esther like he was hugging her for the last time, running his hand through her short, dark hair, remembering how long it once was.

Höss ran his hand through Hedwig's long blond hair in the midst of the officers' parlor. The commandant was drunk. He slurred his words and clumsily drew his wife to him. The other officers cheered him on, enjoying the public display of affection.

Gently—but firmly—Hedwig pushed her husband away, gripping both his hands with hers.

Esther gripped both of Zach's hands tightly. Then they relaxed. The new husband and wife consummated their marriage in a tiny corner bunk. Other prisoners had draped blankets around the bunk to offer some privacy in the dark and had gathered at the other end of the barrack, several rows away.

The piercing scream was sudden and came from outside.

Samson stood with Rebecca in the shadows at the far end of the barrack, both momentarily stunned. The scream sounded painfully

---

4. In Jewish tradition this part of the ceremony is normally done with a wine glass to signify the consummation of a marriage.

familiar. Too familiar. They hurriedly exchanged glances, and Samson bolted out the door. Zach came along seconds later, putting on his shirt. He charged out the door behind his brother. Zach had immediately recognized the sound of the scream.

The freezing night air hit both Samson and Zach like a punch to the gut. Snow pelted them in the face. Wind kicked a white flurry around them. They stopped dead in their tracks, each staring at the sickening sight outside Block 10.

On the other side of the fence, strapped to a post, Simon twisted and turned. The boy was naked, freezing in the night air, crying.[5]

"Simon!" Samson shouted in desperation. He sprinted toward his son. Zach trailed, trying to keep up. Samson reached the fence and scaled it quickly. Zach was close behind him, struggling up and over.

The boy's eyes were closed. He was sobbing. His frail ten-year-old body shivered in the snow. Black and blue marks abounded on his torso.

Samson reached the boy in a flash, took off his own shirt, and wrapped his son in it.

Simon's eyes popped open. "Daddy . . . I'm so cold. Daddy . . . hold me." Simon's teeth chattered.

"Everything will be okay, son," Samson murmured. "Papa's here." He tied the shirt around his son and went to work on the

---

5. Nazi doctors would test people to see how cold the human body would need to be before hypothermia and death (Telford Taylor, "Opening Statement of the Prosecution [of the Doctors' Trial at Nuremburg], December 9, 1946," in George J. Annas and Michael A. Grodin, *The Nazi Doctors and the Nuremburg Code: Human Rights in Human Experimentation* [New York: Oxford University Press, 1992], 74–75; Peter Tyson, "The Experiments," NOVA Online, October 2000, http://www.pbs.org/wgbh/nova/holocaust/experiside.html#free).

leather straps that held Simon's wrists. The straps were tied so tightly, they cut into Simon's skin, slowing circulation to his nearly numb hands. As soon as Zach caught up, he immediately started helping to try to loosen the straps.

"Daddy . . . that man . . . he put something in me. He called it 'an experiment' but it hurts, Daddy. I'm bleeding . . ."

Simon's words stuck like daggers in Samson's heart. "What did he put into you, Simon?"

Simon shook his head, not answering. His face fell in shame.

"Where is it, Simon, where?"

Simon sobbed and looked down, indicating his backside.

Confused, Samson looked to Zach for an answer.

"I heard about this," Zach whispered painfully, barely able to speak as he kept working on Simon's bindings. "Mengele puts rectal temperature gauges inside to check how cold a body is before it dies."

Horrified, Samson looked at his son's face. He shook off the shock, reached down behind Simon, gently pulled the gauge out, and ground it underneath his boot. In a fit of rage, he pulled at one of Simon's straps with such force that he ripped the leather binding loose, tearing it in half. One of Simon's arms was now free. Samson went to work on the other bound hand. The strap was almost off, but a voice from the darkness made Samson's blood freeze.

"I believe the phrase was *Goret'v adu*, wasn't it?" Mengele said. "'Burn in hell' . . . a favorite Russian phrase. What an interesting choice of languages, Samson." The doctor laughed. "You're easier to bait than a common mouse."

Samson and Zach whipped around. Mengele stood in the snow, his arms folded. Next to him were five SS officers, machine guns pointed in the prisoners' direction.

"Take the boy back into Block 10," Mengele called out. "And wake all the prisoners in the ten closest barracks, every single one of them. I want them to see what kind of pain is inflicted on Jews who dare to interrupt my medical experiments."

NINETEEN

It looked to Samson like more than a thousand prisoners were lined up outside Block 10. It was past midnight, the snow had turned to a cold rain, and Samson was tied to the same whipping post as he had been once before. Zach was marched out and tied with leather straps to another post beside Simon's. Mengele set a mysterious glass jar down on the ground, but Samson could not make out what was inside.

Mengele wound up a whip, quietly and calmly, apparently unaware that Samson was loosening the binding on his left wrist. Samson's fury burned in him, fury that any man would ever touch his son in that manner—the same man who had killed his daughters.

A moment for revenge was coming.

Samson subtly pulled at the binding. Blood trickled from his wrist and hand from the force he was exerting. Mengele approached the two bound prisoners. Samson stopped straining. "Höss may be able to stop me from killing you for now," whispered Mengele in Samson's ear. The near-freezing rain dripped off both men. "But since you and your little brother felt you had the right to stop my experiment, I think it's only fitting that your brother takes Simon's place."

Samson grinned faintly. Mengele was in striking range. Wrath still ruled Samson's mind, but he could tell that his calm demeanor surprised Mengele and even unnerved the doctor a bit. Still tied, arms locked in front of him around the post, Samson loosened the leather straps just enough to pivot and move. *Crack!* Samson swung his left elbow directly into Mengele's jaw, knocking him to the ground.

Three guards rushed forward, truncheons raised. Mengele, dazed from the powerful blow, raised a hand to stop them. "No! Leave him to me." Mengele wiped the blood from his lip. "Just tie him *tightly* this time."

The guards tied Samson again as the rain fell harder. Mengele got up, brushed off his heavy coat, composed himself, and walked a few steps away to where Zach was bound. He pulled out a heavy metal rectal gauge from his pocket and moved toward the prisoner. "Relax, and it will hurt less."

Zach closed his eyes.

When he was through, Mengele wiped his hand on his knee, paced back toward Samson, and unraveled the whip.

Samson stole a glance at the whip. It wasn't the same weapon Mengele had used before. This whip had nine heavy leather strands with jagged pieces of metal and broken glass bound into each.

"What would Commandant Höss say about you using that nine-tail whip?" Samson asked, his teeth gritted.

"He'd say you're a filthy Jew." Mengele reared back.

Samson took a deep breath.

Crack! On the downstroke, the metal pieces and glass shards sunk into the skin on Samson's back. On the upstroke, the whip caught and tore open his flesh. He recoiled and wanted to shout in pain, but he had vowed not to give Mengele the satisfaction.

Crack! Mengele let loose with another blow. Again Samson recoiled. *Crack! Crack! Crack!* Again and again, the doctor unleashed the whip, throwing all his weight and force into each lash. Out of the corner of his eye, Samson noticed a prisoner faint, hitting the ground hard. The whip crashed down again—*crack!*—and Samson saw a spurt of blood rise over his left shoulder. *Crack! Crack! Crack!* The whipping continued. Nine lashings so far. Samson thought he himself might collapse at any moment, but he steeled his will and kept his breathing under control as best he could.

He had learned from years of boxing in the ring and fighting on the street that when taking a pummeling, if you can control your breathing, it increases your stamina to ride out almost any storm. Now he rode out each lashing as it came down and tore into his skin. He had no doubt Mengele would go all the way to forty lashes. Maybe more, if he was in a particularly foul mood.

Crack!

Ten. The pain was almost unbearable. Samson felt his knees losing their strength.

Crack!

Eleven. He bit the inside of his cheek to keep from screaming.

Crack!

Twelve. Samson saw a piece of his skin fly off and land in the dirt. An image of Rebecca shot through his mind. Was she in the crowd, watching, praying, cringing? Undoubtedly she was, but he couldn't see her anywhere. Samson searched for a familiar face. Someone. Anyone. Any compassionate visage to take his mind off the horrible whipping and give him a moment of respite from the searing pain.

Crack!

Thirteen. Samson let out a gasp.

At the far side of the crowd, near the front, Samson spotted what he'd been looking for. A grimy, downturned face, but it was familiar. The face belonged to a boy, a little older than Simon. The boy was sobbing uncontrollably.

Yeshua.

Crack! Fourteen. The pain reached a new level.

Samson stared at the boy's face. He could feel his body beginning to go into shock, starting to shut down. He wasn't sure he could cope with much more. *Crack!* Fifteen. Yeshua looked so innocent, a pure countenance so out of place in the brutal surroundings, like a tender shoot growing out of dry ground. He was despised and forsaken, a boy of suffering all too familiar with pain, despite his few years.

Crack! Sixteen. Samson gasped. The boy raised his face. His lips were moving as if in prayer. The pain was so mind-numbing that Samson was slipping in and out of the seen world, barely holding on to consciousness. One moment in Auschwitz. One moment far away.

Crack!

Mengele was sweating. Winded. Samson could smell alcohol on him. He snapped back to reality and shot a glance at the doctor. Mengele actually needed to rest between lashings. Wincing, Samson could barely stifle a smirk. He decided to hit the doctor where it hurt.

"You're not much of an example for German superiority, are you?" Samson called out, deliberately loud enough for the prisoners and guards to hear. "I mean, being so weak with the whip!" The exertion of calling out in a loud voice nearly caused him to fall down. Samson felt it was worth it because the insult sent Mengele into a boil. But Mengele reared back, raging, laying into Samson even harder. *Crack! Crack! Crack! Crack!*

Twenty-one total.

Blood spattered the ground.

Crack! Samson saw a guard flinch. *Crack!* Another guard turned his head. The crowd of prisoners in front of Samson grew blurry and dark. The unseen world was becoming visible again.

"Stop!"

A voice called out from a distance. It was loud and angry, the enemy's voice, but it warmed Samson at the hope it held out.

Höss had appeared from nowhere. The commander was surrounded by the adjutant, the *Obersturmbannführer*, and an *Untersturmbannführer*. He strode to the doctor and thrust his finger into Mengele's chest. "What exactly do you think you're doing?" The strong smell of whiskey wafted off all the men.

"Commandant, I caught this Jew trying to—" Mengele said, but Höss cut him short.

"I expressly told you not to use the nine-tailed whip on that prisoner!" Höss belted out his words in a slur, but he held himself upright, his face rigid as a board.

"Commandant, I must protest," Mengele said. "This prisoner interrupted one of my experiments."

"Save it!" Höss barked at the doctor. His cheeks were fiery red. "He's had enough. Take him to the infirmary." The commandant waved his hand at the crowd. "And send all these prisoners to bed. There are lots of ditches to be dug tomorrow." Höss clapped his hands twice, and the guards nearest him untied Samson from the whipping post. Samson collapsed to his hands and knees.

"As you wish," Mengele said to the commandant, clearly irritated. "You have my word your command will be done."

"I expected nothing less," Höss said, annoyed.

The commandant wheeled slowly and walked away. His entourage walked with him. The rest of the guards began to corral the prisoners and herd them back to their barracks.

Samson's mind was coming back to him. He heard Höss walk around the corner of a building and out of sight. Samson's back heaved in pain. He heard the doctor above him, exhaling loudly, working the lid off the mysterious glass jar.

"Some salve for your back," Mengele said with a leer. He poured some of the jar's contents into his palm and smeared it into Samson's back.

Samson gasped in agony and began to shake. "What . . . what is . . . that?"

"Oh, just a little mixture I like to call *broken glass and sawdust.*" The doctor gave Samson another hard pat on the back.

Facedown on a table in the infirmary, Samson looked about his surroundings as best he could. The room was empty of guards, but his legs and arms had been firmly handcuffed to the table. His back throbbed with fire. There was no one tending his wounds this time. No Kolbe. No nurse. Blood dripped onto the floor. He could hear Zach calling out, still chained to the pole in the freezing rain. Every scream from his little brother was a knife to his soul. Samson could not help a wave of guilt hitting him. Had he not chosen to interfere and save Yeshua, perhaps none of them would be in this hellish place.

The door to the ward opened. Samson heard footsteps and glanced in their direction. It was Mengele surrounded by a cadre of

guards. By the hand, the doctor held a boy who looked to be offering no resistance—it was Simon.

"Your brother cries out like a little girl," Mengele said to
Samson. "Apparently, he does not share your same resolve." From
outside they heard Zach scream again.

Samson's head snapped up. Simon was clad in medical-patient
garb. Samson couldn't figure out why he was not struggling against
the doctor's grip.

"Daddy! You're alive," Simon said excitedly to his father.

"Simon, are you alright?" Samson's protective parental instincts
were immediately on alert.

"I'm okay, Daddy," Simon said, strangely relaxed. "The doctor
gave me a chocolate bar."

Samson's mind reeled. His reflex told him to shout at Simon
to spit it out, to make himself throw up. But he'd heard rumors of
the doctor giving chocolate and candy to his preferred children. It
was the sick action of a depraved man, but the food was real at least.
Samson decided to risk it.

"You must want something," Samson said to the doctor. "Tell
me what it is, and I'll do it. Just don't hurt my son again."

"Oh ho!" Mengele grinned. "So now you're pleading with me,
are you? It wasn't that way outside, now was it?"

"Why is my son here?"

"I'm helping him out," Mengele said. "Your son grew very cold
outside."

"He wouldn't have been outside in the first place if it wasn't
for you."

"Tsk, tsk, Samson," Mengele said. "We can't suppress the
progress of science, can we?" The doctor smiled as he leisurely
pulled back the cover of a set of surgical tools. He squeezed on

surgical gloves and tenderly lifted up a handsaw as if lifting a baby. He examined the saw's edges, admiring them, and nodded to a guard.

The guard snapped to work and brought over another table. He hefted Simon onto the table and slipped restraints over his limbs. The boy cried out, more in surprise than alarm.

"Daddy, what's happening?" said Simon, beginning to cry.

"What do you want?" Samson roared. "You must want something. I will do what you ask. Take my life for my son's!"

"It's not your life I'm after tonight, Samson," Mengele said. "You see, I've spent my life studying nature versus nurture. My entire thesis rests on predisposed genetics. You're either born with intelligence, strength, and talent, or you're not." The doctor's tone had become like a schoolteacher's, but then he lowered his voice and spoke into Samson's ear so the guards couldn't hear. "Every time you win in that ring, you suggest a flaw in my hypothesis concerning Jews. And we absolutely cannot have that, can we?" Mengele gave the surgical saw another close inspection.

"I will lose then," Samson whispered quickly. "And you could bet against me. I'll double your earnings!"

"It's not money I'm after," Mengele said.

"I'll guarantee I'll lose the next time I fight," Samson repeated, his voice still low. "I promise it. Your theory will be flawless. Just leave my son alone."

"You know, Samson—you don't look all that Jewish." Mengele walked toward the table of surgical tools and gave them another close look. "Are you sure you're a full-blooded Jew? If you weren't full blooded, that would explain your winnings, wouldn't it?"

Samson strained against the metal bindings that pinned him facedown.

"Relax!" Mengele ordered Samson. "You'll ruin the experiment again."

The words hung in the air. Mengele sighed loudly, as if speaking to the guards. "One would not expect a Jew to protect its young with such vehemence. But then again, even rats often protect their young." He turned back to Samson and spoke low again. "I'm very interested to see just exactly how you will respond when your young suffers right before your eyes. Be assured, I will document all this for the good of science."

The doctor paused for a moment as if lost in thought, then added, "By the way, I'm sorry, but I don't want you to promise you'll lose in the ring. I can't make that deal with you because I can't risk you breaking your word to me, and besides—I actually don't want you to lose in the ring, Samson. You know what happens to the losing boxer." Mengele paused and gave Samson a long, cruel stare. "I want that pleasure all for myself."

The doctor straightened up and ordered the guards nearest Simon. "Hold the boy steady. I expect there will be quite a bit of movement." Mengele leaned toward Simon and added in a kind voice, "I've decided you must keep your arms. I like the way you play the violin. But just to prevent any frostbite from spreading, I'm going to remove your right leg."

Simon screamed and thrashed against his bindings. A guard swatted him across the mouth.

"No!" Samson shouted. "The boy doesn't have frostbite! He was only outside for a few minutes. You know that! Simon—tell the doctor you can feel your leg."

Confused, Simon cried harder. "I can feel my leg," he said through tears. "My leg is fine!"

Mengele looked directly at Simon's leg. It was indeed healthy, no marks, no blotches. Mengele raised the handsaw. "Hold him steady," he ordered the guards. "Lots of pressure now." Mengele stopped for a moment and stroked the boy's forehead. "Look on the bright side, my boy . . . Tomorrow morning all of this will be over."

One middle-aged guard chuckled at the inside joke. "Perhaps we should use anesthesia?" the guard suggested.

Mengele shot him a glare.

"I don't care about the boy, Dr. Mengele," the guard said. "I just don't want to have to hold him down through all that sawing. It has been a long day, and it's so much work holding the children down for these forced amputations."

Mengele lifted the saw to just below Simon's hip joint. "We are not going to waste perfectly good anesthesia on a Jew," Mengele responded.

"No!" Samson shouted.

Simon writhed. Down came the handsaw. It slid once roughly across Simon's upper leg, ripping the top layer of flesh and drawing blood.

The door burst open.

Commandant Höss stood before them, hands on his hips. Two guards stood with him, machine guns in their hands. Mengele stopped cutting. He and the rest of the guards snapped to attention.

"How can I sleep with all this incessant screaming?" Höss yelled, furious.

The guards pulled back from holding Simon and froze.

"Your quarters are some distance from here," Mengele said suspiciously. "The noise shouldn't have awoken you."

"I'm referring to the skinny Jew still chained outside in the rain," Höss said. "His constant screaming is giving me a headache." Höss surveyed the horror in progress. Simon's leg was intact but bleeding. Mengele held the handsaw, its blade tinged with blood at the edge. Samson was pinned down on his front; his back was a freshly bloodied mess. Höss shook his head in disgust. He stepped directly in front of Mengele, six inches from his nose, and shouted so his spit flew in the doctor's face. "Too far!"

"I have no idea what you mean," Mengele said calmly and took a step back.

"It means I am too tired and too drunk to waste time with formalities." The commandant's voice was flat. "I run Auschwitz, and at least for this evening, I am finished with any semblance of patience. Let Samson and the boy go. And take down that Jew from the post outside. His yelling and screaming is worse than a woman's." Höss turned to leave but then stopped, a look of reconsideration on his face. "If you are going to torture Jews, Dr. Mengele, that's fine . . . just don't torture *my* Jews. Am I clearly understood?"

"Understood," Mengele said.

"Good," Höss said. "Call that priest back in. Have him give Samson the proper medical care. Give him a ration of bread, and send him back to his barrack. If there's ever a man who needs to heal quickly, it's that man on the table, Doctor, so see that it happens. And now"—the commandant cleared his throat and looked directly at the doctor—"if I am woken one more time because of your actions, I will show you firsthand who has the power in Auschwitz."

Inside the Hut 57 barrack, water streamed onto Samson's bloody, shredded back. Kolbe cleaned the gashes with a damp rag soaked in rubbing alcohol that Höss gave him to treat Samson's wounds.

Samson lay facedown on his bunk as the alcohol burned his raw skin of impurities and potential infections.

"You're going to get yourself killed," scolded Kolbe.

Samson offered no reaction. He simply lay on the bunk, fighting to control his pain.

"Mengele would have gone easier on you if you had only cried out in the whipping," Kolbe said. "That's what he wanted. Elbowing him in the face and insulting him surely didn't help matters."

Samson tried to rise on one arm but could not. He was beyond exhaustion and in too much pain.

"What happened to your son is horrible," Kolbe said. "There are no words for it, and I ache for the horror he has been through. But I'm also deeply concerned about you, Samson. I'm still worried that you are blaming God for the sins of men." The monk laid fresh gauze and medicine on Samson's wounds.

"I'm not," Samson said, but added in a mocking tone, "but you said it wasn't men. You said it was Satan, the root of evil himself, that was causing all this."

"Mock me if you wish." Kolbe spoke his words carefully. "Satan's greatest accomplishment is convincing the modern world he doesn't exist."

Samson bit down in a grimace as another wave of rubbing alcohol hit his back.

"Do you see all those stars out there?" Kolbe motioned out the barred window. Samson followed his gesture and in his periphery vision saw a strip of night sky and its uncountable millions of stars. "God put them all out there for us," Kolbe added, wonderment in his voice.

"Why does any of this even matter?" Samson asked. "We're all going to die soon."

"You're right. We are all going to die—either in this camp or somewhere else when we're ninety-five and toothless. But where we go after we die is up to us. That's what's at stake, Samson—your eternity."

"I don't believe in heaven or hell," Samson said, defiantly.

"You will after you die," Kolbe said. "Everyone will arrive at one of those two destinations."

"Well, just so long as I'm no longer in this place," Samson said with a pained grimace.

Even Kolbe laughed. "True. I'd say Auschwitz is one of the closest things to hell we'll ever experience on earth. But as bad as Auschwitz is, the real hell is even worse."

Samson thought a moment. "Answer me this, Kolbe. Isn't our being here, even in Auschwitz, all part of God's will? That's what you Christians believe, isn't it? That everything—even this horror— is all part of God's will being done?"

"God has permitted horror to exist on earth, that is true," Kolbe said. "But Jesus told us to pray that the will of God would be 'done on earth as it is in heaven.'[1] Why would Jesus ask us to pray for God's perfect will to be done, if God's will was always automatically done on earth? If it were automatic, then there would be no reason to spend time praying for it, because it would happen whether we prayed or not. No, what's happening here is not the perfect will of God, Samson. God's will is never for men, women, and children to be raped, tortured, and murdered. Mankind needs to cooperate with God in order for God's perfect will to be done here on earth as it is in heaven."

Samson was listening, and the logic seemed sound to him. But

---

1. Matthew 6:10 NKJV.

he responded obstinately, not wanting to admit that Kolbe was making solid sense. "You Christians amaze me. You talk about God's actions as if they were all fact."

"If I knew for a fact, I wouldn't need to believe." Kolbe grabbed the chair he was sitting in. "I do not believe this chair is holding me up. I know it is. You only need faith for the things you cannot know for certain. You cannot see the wind, but you know it's real because you can see its effects. The writer of the letter to the Hebrews wisely wrote, 'Faith is the substance of things hoped for, the evidence of things not seen.'[2] That kind of faith chases out the fear of death."

Kolbe helped Samson into a sitting position so he could check him for additional wounds and remove some shards of glass still embedded in his back. Samson looked him square in the eye, trying to determine if Kolbe himself really had no fear of death because of his faith. "Everyone is afraid of death," challenged Samson. "Even me. I am afraid of death. And you are afraid of it too. If you aren't, then why don't you walk into the gas chambers right now?"

"Because I don't believe it's my time to die yet. I believe God is keeping me alive for a certain purpose."

"Well, I think you're lying," Samson said. "I'm not ashamed to admit I am afraid to die. But if you truly are not afraid, then I envy you."

"When a man walks with God, fear cannot beat him. Nothing can," said Kolbe. "Faith is a fierce enemy to anyone who stands in our way."

Samson was still unmoved. "Fury makes for a tough opponent as well. Mengele will see that the next time I step in the ring."

---

2. Hebrews 11:1.

TWENTY

Inside Solahütte's parlor, Samson stepped into the ring. Boos and hisses erupted from the crowd.

Although Samson's wounds were no longer open and bloody from the second whipping, the scar tissue was still in the process of forming on his back. Some of the stitches Kolbe put in were still imbedded in Samson's skin although they should have been removed within ten days. Mengele wanted to make sure the scars lasted, so he would not allow Kolbe to remove the stitches at that time. Samson's body was becoming a crisscrossed maze of rips, tears, and zippered seams.

On the off weeks, Höss had sent word to Samson that he was giving him extra time to heal. A *Kapo* snuck word to Samson that one week the commander had brought in a women's musical troop for the officers' entertainment instead of boxing. Höss was, reportedly, extremely unhappy about losing a week's winnings, but the commander sent Samson a small amount of extra meat and bread that week anyway, all with an urgent order to "get healed."

Now the boxing was back on, and the crowd was eager for the

main event to begin. A seething fury etched into Samson's scowl. He'd looked into a mirror in the changing area when he suited up. The face in the reflection startled him. Staring back at Samson was a half-starved, beaten, caged animal. He determined to use the image to further fuel his fury and hoped it would strike fear into his opponent. But when Samson climbed into the ring, the fear was his own.

He paced to and fro, waiting for the battle to start. He scolded himself for his nerves and told himself to settle down. Samson knew he was acting far too skittish, fearing what might be lurking behind him. He glanced around the room. It seemed a normal-enough night. Bets were being made. Drinks were being gulped down. Backs were being slapped as officers joked and laughed, enjoying their camaraderie.

Near the front, Höss lit a cigar, one arm around Hedwig. Out of the corner of Samson's eye, he noticed Hedwig staring at him. He looked at the German officer's wife. Her eyes locked on him. Samson held her gaze for a moment, wondering what went through the woman's mind, this woman so close to power yet so caged herself. Then he glanced away. In the far corner of the room he spotted Mengele. The doctor was sitting alone at a table sipping wine. Samson secretly wished Mengele was in the ring tonight with him. He imagined going toe-to-toe with the man, beating Mengele to death with blow after blow of pure, unbridled hate. But that could never happen.

There was no sign of the other fighter anywhere. Samson hated the thought of defeating another inmate in the ring, but after beating the Nazi officer in his last bout, what kind of opponent would they pit him against?

Three tall, heavily muscled German soldiers in boxing trunks suddenly stepped up from behind Samson and surrounded the ring's opposite corner. Cheering arose, and Samson turned around, eyeing the three boxers for a moment, dumbfounded. The ref-guard stepped into the ring.

"What's going on?" Samson shouted above the din. "I thought I was fighting next."

"They didn't tell you?" asked the ref-guard, puzzled.

Samson stared at him, waiting for an answer.

The ref-guard chuckled. "This is your fight, Jew. You fight all three, one at a time, one right after the other . . . until you lose."

Samson's mind reeled. He glanced at his opponents. All looked powerfully built, well rested, well fed, with at least a fifty-pound weight advantage each. On a good day he could handle one . . . maybe two . . . But three? Samson lowered his head, anger boiling as the truth dawned on him. Tonight's fight was never intended to be fair. It was a battle designed to wear Samson down and send him to the gas chambers.

Deep in Samson's heart, this deliberately unfair, imbalanced match tapped something visceral. A memory flashed in his mind. Samson had been twelve years old, walking home from school, and surrounded by bullies. They pushed him, shoved him, kicked him, punched him. The scar in his psyche unleashed something savage. He'd fought the whole gang of thugs back then. He'd do the same tonight.

Ding! Ding!

The bell echoed through the room. The crowd rose to its feet in unison, shouting insults at Samson and cheering on the first Nazi boxer. Samson stayed near his corner a moment, shuffling his footwork, studying his opponent for a few seconds. He was a tough-looking Aryan with a scar below his right eye. Samson knew the intelligent, composed technique would be to keep away from his opponent's longer reach, wear him down by making himself a hard target to connect with, and force the taller man to miss as often as possible until he was too tired to properly defend himself.

Not this time, Samson thought. Like a hungry lion, Samson roared and charged at the other fighter, unleashing a barrage of punches. *Crack! Crack! Crack!* Two body shots were followed by a left hook to the Nazi's head. The first fighter was driven back into his corner. Samson stayed right on him.

The fighter tried to cover up, ducking, but Samson pummeled him in the ribs, head, face, and then back to the ribs. It wasn't even boxing anymore. It was an all-out slugfest. Samson didn't even bother to cover up and protect himself. *Crack!* He caught the fighter with a violent right uppercut—*snap*—and broke the Nazi's jaw.

Thud.

The man hit the canvas.

It was all over in a matter of seconds. The crowd went quiet momentarily, stunned at the viciously swift onslaught.

The ref-guard motioned for Samson to go back to his corner, but Samson waved him off, refusing to back away. Frustrated by Samson's obstinacy, the ref-guard began the ten-count. Samson stood over his opponent. "Come on, get up!" Samson yelled. He was calling to the crowd more than the fighter on the mat. "Get up and beat the Jew! Let's see you beat the filthy Jew! Come on—let's see it!"

"Four . . . five . . . six . . . ," The ref-guard continued his count.

The first fighter rose to one knee on the count of nine. At ten, he stood.

"You should have stayed down," Samson called out. *Crack!* Samson hit the Nazi so hard, the Aryan's head snapped sideways.

Blood sprayed the first row. The opponent stumbled backward and fell through the ring ropes onto the floor. Out cold.

A surge of victory welled up in Samson. *One down*, he thought. He turned and shouted in German at the next two boxers, "Come on, get in the ring, you cowards! I'll crush your hearts and make you watch me do it! Come and get the weak, filthy Jew!"

Stunned and infuriated by Samson's insolence, several soldiers drew their guns, pointing at Samson; they looked to Höss for the command to shoot. Samson shouted to the soldiers, "Yes, shoot me! Go ahead, prove you are cowards! You're too scared to get in the ring with me, so shoot me! Come on!" Samson sensed he had gone berserk, but he didn't care. This was no traditional boxing match. The rules had all changed, and he was going to beat the bullies at their own game.

Höss stood. Other soldiers clamored about him, weapons drawn. Samson didn't know exactly what they were all saying, but Höss wasn't taking their advice. The commander pushed them aside and shouted, "Bets have been laid! Honor will preside here! The fights will go on!" He pointed at Samson and shouted even louder, "Samson! Shut your mouth and box!"

The soldiers lowered their guns. Samson remembered his goal. He was here to save his family. He silently vowed to make the next fight equally severe.

The ref-guard motioned for the next fighter. Boxer number two stepped into the ring. He looked younger, more cautious than the first man, with a tall, athletic build and an unmarked face. Samson sized him up as someone more used to exhibition boxing than street fighting. Yet from the way his opponent stood near the ropes and continued his warm-up, Samson knew he was nobody to be trifled with. This fighter was experienced in the ring.

Ding! Ding!

The bell sounded. Samson charged straight in, same as before, and nailed the second Nazi with a hard right, then a crushing left. His all-out blitz style was powerful, but it had no inherent defense and left Samson wide open. The fighter had learned from the first opponent's mistakes. He rammed a left jab into Samson's face, followed by a right cross to his head and a left uppercut to Samson's chin. Samson stumbled back, paying for his sloppy attack.

The second boxer soon proved to be a smarter and more experienced boxer than the first opponent. He tagged Samson with another combination, using his lengthy reach advantage. Samson covered up for a moment, his years of boxing training returning to him out of habit. But then, running on pure rage, he let loose. Samson ducked the Nazi's right hook and sunk a glove deep into the man's stomach, hammering him with devastating power. The fighter bent double, knees hitting the canvas. He vomited, spewing brown bile all over the ring, then rolled to his side, twisting in pain, gasping for air.

Two down, Samson thought. He raised his arms in victory, looked right at Mengele, and yelled in German: *"Deutsche überlegenheit? Ist das, was das ist?"*[1]

Again, soldiers looked to Höss for a command to shoot, but Höss waved them off and gathered another stack of money. The crowd grew frenzied, some clapping, some booing, some shouting insults toward the ring. A chant began. In unison, the crowd clapped in anticipation of the last of the three fighters while an attendant mopped the ring and dried it with a towel.

The third Nazi boxer climbed into the ring, raised both arms

---

1. "German superiority? Is that what this is?"

above his head in a clasp, and pumped his hands in early victory. He was a gorilla of a man with armchair-sized shoulders and a crooked nose that looked to have been repeatedly broken. The crowd went wild even though the fighter lingered near the ropes. Samson wondered at the delay until he eyed Mengele walking toward the ring and motioning toward the fighter. When Mengele reached the ring, he pulled a vial from his pocket and whispered something to the third boxer. The boxer turned his back to Samson to give a show of hiding his actions, but Samson could still see the bulk of the moves. Surreptitiously, Mengele poured the contents of a vial onto the outstretched gloves of the third fighter. The boxer nodded a thank-you to Mengele, then turned toward Samson with a subtle smirk on his face.

The crowd erupted in cheers, yelling for their champion. The third boxer bounded forward into the center of the ring. He smashed his gloves together, urging the crowd on. It was clear he couldn't care less about the first two fighters' losses. Samson used the delay to take stock of his condition. He'd already taken a number of hard shots to his head and body. He was winded from fighting the first two bouts without strategy, as a hard charger. His back and facial wounds had already been reopened, and he could see blood dripping down on his trunks, as well as taste blood in his mouth.

"Come, little Jew-rat," the third Nazi yelled, taunting Samson. "I will teach you Aryan superiority."

"You don't scare me," Samson answered in German. "Not even with Mengele whispering in your ear."

"You might be afraid if you knew what he told me," the Nazi said.

"What's that?"

"That you once had two daughters. And that your son is next."

Samson snapped.

Ding! Ding!

The final bell sounded. Samson and the third Nazi charged right at each other and clashed in the middle of the ring. Toe-to-toe, the two boxers pummeled away. Neither man was fighting with a smart, cagey, or educated style. Both swung wildly, both landing hard hooks and haymakers. Their defense was nonexistent. It was a brawl. *Thud!* Samson got caught with a blistering right, again ripping the stitches over his eye. Blood flew. Samson fought back with two hard body shots. The heavyweight answered with a short counterpunch to Samson's neck. Samson gasped and staggered back, choking, surprised by the unusually dirty punch.

The Nazi rushed in quickly to take advantage of Samson's loss of wind. He hauled off for a huge right hook, rearing back as far as his arm would reach for maximum power, but Samson, being lighter and quicker, struck with a hard, fast left jab followed by a powerful right uppercut in the man's gut.

Pained and choking for air, the Nazi tied Samson up in a clinch to prevent further damage. Both men gasped for air—Samson from the throat punch, and the Nazi from Samson's stomach punch. Clinching, the Nazi could only hit Samson with a couple of light punches to the back, but those wounds were fresh and bloody, having already been reopened and torn. The Nazi leaned on Samson, using his weight advantage to tire his smaller opponent. Samson fought to get his arms free. His eyes burned . . . Whatever liquid Mengele put on the Nazi's gloves had found its way to Samson's eyes from the punches. His eyeballs felt as if they were on fire. Vainly, Samson tried to wipe his eyes on his upper arm.

He broke free from the clinch, threw a wild right, and missed, his vision blurred by the chemical agent. The Nazi slipped behind Samson and nailed him with two hard hooks to Samson's back.

Samson hollered in pain, several stitches ripping, and turned, ready to kill. In came Samson, ducking through the Nazi's offense, blinking the toxin-induced tears out of his eyes, driven by the pain in his back from the torn stitches. *Crack!* Samson sent a crushing hook into the Nazi's side. Ribs broke on impact. Samson followed with a ferocious left uppercut. After that it was one relentless punch after another.

Crash! Samson hit the Nazi so hard he reeled into the corner of the ring, grasping at the ropes, struggling to stay up. Samson grabbed the Aryan's neck with his left gloved hand, pinned him against the corner, and landed four quick bone-crushing rights to the nose. *Crack! Crack! Crack! Crack!* Blood flew. The Nazi remained on his feet, completely unconscious but unable to fall to the mat as Samson held him in place. The ref-guard jumped in, trying to stop the slaughter, but he was not strong enough to pull Samson back. *Crack, crack, crack!* Samson continued the pummeling. Blow after blow landed squarely on the Nazi's face.

A squad of soldiers jumped into the ring. Six men struggled to pull Samson off. Three pulled their guns. From the far side of the room, two gunshots shattered the melee—an overhead light fixture crashed to the floor. Samson froze, momentarily distracted from his rage. He backed off. The Nazi fighter slumped and fell face-first to the mat. The whole room quieted, turning to see Mengele slowly lower his revolver, wisps of gun smoke trailing from the barrel. Samson wiped blood and sweat from his eyes.

"The Jew has been bred with a bull," Mengele called out. "Or his genetics have been mutated. It is not a fair fight if the man is a crossbreed."

Several soldiers shrugged in confusion—*What's he talking about?* A few others nodded. Still others took out their sidearms.

Höss slowly stood, clapped a few times, then stopped. "Nonsense, Dr. Mengele," Höss called out. "You are an educated scientist, but the Jew is simply an anomaly—the highest of his species. The fight was fair. All bets will stand." Höss gathered his pile of money and motioned toward the ring. "The guards will escort the prisoner to the changing area and then back to camp." The commander waved around at the crowd and smiled broadly. He knew how to defuse them. "Now, more refreshment, everyone. The next round is on me!"

Samson stared at the Nazi on the mat. The fighter's face was a pool of blood. His thick neck was bent at a strange angle. A medic stood over the Aryan, checking the carotid artery for a pulse. Slowly, the medic rose to his feet and turned to Samson.

"You killed him," he said simply, and climbed out of the ring.

TWENTY-ONE

Later that night when Samson stepped inside the barrack of Hut 57, every prisoner stood to his feet and started quietly clapping. Samson was stunned, completely taken off guard. He was never the kind of man who dealt well with emotional outpouring. But he did his best to appear at ease with the admiration. Höss had insisted that a medic clean and sew up Samson's wounds, stitching his forehead back together, sewing up the broken stitches in his back. Most of the blood had been washed away, but Samson still looked like he had been through a war.

"We heard what happened tonight," Kolbe said, beaming a big smile. "No small accomplishment."

An older man stepped forward, tears in his eyes. "First they took my wife," he said. "Then they took my son. Soon they will take my life. But you give to me hope, Samson. You give back to me my pride for being a Jew, one of God's chosen people. I shall carry my head high until I can carry it no longer." He turned to the

229

rest of the room. "Our champion has won a victory, just like the Samson of the Tanakh[1] resurrected for us."

Several prisoners nodded. They surrounded Samson and shook his hand, thanking him with tears in their eyes. Caught up in the moment, several forgot about his wounds and patted him on the back. Samson winced, blistering pain shooting through him from the friendly pats. One inmate was so elated, he actually offered Samson a piece of bread, the man's only food rations. Samson declined, insisting that the man keep his sustenance. Samson had given all his winnings to the Hut 57 *Kapo* to pass along to his family, but Samson had a feeling that after the victory that night, Höss would pass along a few more scraps of food to keep him strong enough to put on a good show next time. Samson insisted that all the prisoners needed to go to bed. They needed their rest.

Once they had dispersed, Samson pulled Kolbe to the side of the barrack, out of the earshot of the rest. "Did you put them up to this?" Samson asked. "I don't like it, nor welcome it. This kind of talk is dangerous to them if the *Kapos* or guards hear it."

The priest shook his head. "You must understand . . . Hope is spreading like a vaccine. If a man can defeat three opponents in the ring, then it shows that with God anything is possible. We all prayed earlier that God would give you victory. And God answered that prayer, yes. Your victory reminds the prisoners that God has not forsaken them."

Samson lowered his head, disturbed. "There are dangers that come with being the one who is perceived as the bringer of hope. I need to think about my family and protect them from becoming

---

1. Hebrew Bible or Old Testament. *Tanakh* is derived from the Hebrew letters of its three component parts: *Torah* (Genesis through Deuteronomy), *Nevi'im* (Prophets), and *Ketuvim* (Writings).

even more of a target. Being a leader here is a very dangerous position to be in. If the Nazis see me like these men do . . ." Samson trailed off.

"They already do," said Kolbe quietly. "You won, Samson. Rejoice in that."

Samson shook his head. "Tonight it was three opponents. Next week it could be five. The week after that, if I make it, a dozen. Don't you see, Kolbe? I've run out of time. Höss will continue to make these matches more and more impossible to increase the betting odds and sweeten the pot. He sees only the money. This was the last fight I'll be able to win."

"You think *you* won the fight tonight?" The priest's face turned grave.

"What are you talking about? Of course I won. I'd be in the gas chambers right now if I didn't."

The priest patted the bunk beside him, motioning Samson to sit while he opened up the makeshift medic kit that Höss had allowed him. "You are an incredibly strong man, Samson. I've never seen anyone with your strength and resilience to keep fighting. But let me ask you this: What do you think drives you with such superhuman force?"

"You want an honest answer?"

"Of course."

"Anger, I suppose," Samson said. "Hatred of the Nazis. Adrenaline. Pure will. All those things, I guess. To tell you the truth, I don't really know. I've never been afraid to fight, and I've always used my strength to protect those who can't fight for themselves. That's what keeps me doing what I'm doing."

"So you believe you won tonight on a combination of anger, sheer muscle, and willpower?"

"What else would there be?"

Simon awoke and quickly sat on the edge of his bunk, peering into the corner of the dank, dimly lit room.

"Andrew, are you awake?" Simon whispered into the darkness.

Andrew, a short, skinny Jewish boy about Simon's age, turned over. "Yes, Simon, I keep waking up from those nightmares." Andrew sat up, rubbing the nub where his leg used to be. Mengele had recently cut off Andrew's leg at midthigh as an "experiment" to see if the Jewish boy would die if the amputation was done without anesthetic. The resilient little Andrew did not die; he had passed out from shock, pain, and blood loss and had awoken with only one leg.

"I had a good dream, the first good dream I've had in months," said Simon.

"Oh, please let me hear it. I can't remember having one good dream in so long." Andrew leaned closer to Simon.

"Well, it wasn't really a dream; it was actually a memory of my father back at home. He was reading me and my sisters the story of Samson in the scriptures, and he pointed something out that we had never noticed before. None of Samson's enemies, the Philistines, could figure out what the source of his great strength was, so Samson must not have been very big. I mean, if he was a huge man with giant muscles, everyone would have known that his strength came from his immense size. So Samson must have looked pretty normal on the outside because no one could figure out why he was strong. But then my dad showed me that when the *Ruach Hakodesh*, the Holy Spirit, would come upon Samson, he had supernatural strength."

"I remember when my parents used to read me stories from the Tanakh," Andrew said sadly. His eyes fell. "Before they were taken from me."

"So then my dad tells me that if I have strong faith in God and strong faith in what God can do through me, I could be like that. I told him I didn't believe I could ever have that kind of strength. He patted me on the head and smiled at me. Then he reminded me of the places in Psalms that say 'The LORD gives *strength* to his people,'[2] and 'It is God who arms me with *strength*.'[3] Then my dad walked over and grabbed a heavy cast-iron frying pan, a full-sized one. He told us that he wanted us to forever remember that real strength comes from God. So my dad picked up the big cast-iron frying pan, braced it against his legs, and he bent the frying pan with his bare hands—he rolled it up like it was bread dough. When my mother saw what he had done, she was really mad because he'd ruined her favorite frying pan, but since my dad was an ironworker he promised he'd make her a new one at work."

"That actually happened?" asked Andrew, stunned.

"Yes, that is a true story, and I will never forget seeing it with my own eyes. I just hope my dad has not forgotten that faith lesson he taught me."

"Maybe if God can give your dad that kind of strength, maybe . . . maybe there is hope for us yet," said Andrew.

Simon nodded. "Yes, Andrew, I believe there is hope for us."

"Strength from God," Kolbe said. "That is the secret."

"I used to believe that faith in God could bring about an

---

2. Psalm 29:11 NIV, emphasis added.
3. Psalm 18:32, emphasis added.

unnatural strength. But that was when my faith was strong . . . I am not so sure anymore," Samson said.

"Well, these are unusual times, Samson. In normal times, I believe God's power is typically given to help us overcome evil, to transform us so we become more Christlike, and to help us radically love people who aren't readily lovable. Yet sometimes—particularly in unusual times—God's strength is given simply to display his supremacy."

"You're really trying to tell me I won tonight because of God's strength, not mine?" Samson asked.

"I'm not positive to what degree you were aided," the priest said. "But think of it this way . . . you are a physically strong man with great skills and experience in the boxing ring. No one would doubt that. Yet you are a middleweight fighting against heavy-weights, and you're half starved and ill rested. Only a few weeks ago you received twenty-three lashes with a cat-o'-nine-tails, and a week before that you were also whipped. You're being held together by stitches over very serious wounds that would have killed most men just from blood loss and shock. Yet tonight you beat three fighters in a row. And as a result of your wins, you are bringing hope, comfort, and fresh resolve to many desperate people. So you tell me, Samson—is this your strength at work . . . or God's?"

Samson sat on the edge of the bunk in the barrack. His whole body ached. Blood still dripped from the edges of his bandages. He sat silently, contemplating the priest's words. After a long, pregnant pause, he spoke.

"I want to believe, Kolbe." Samson's voice was barely a whisper. "You know that, don't you? I honestly thank you for your prayers, and I will take any divine strength I can get. But when it comes to faith, you need to know I'm still a long way off."

The priest nodded. "What might be holding you back?"

Samson shook his head, unable to answer.

"I think I know," the priest said. "The apostle Mark recorded a story about a man who interacted with Jesus in a similar way. The man was shown miracles, great miracles that were very much in his favor. 'I do believe,' the man said, 'help me overcome my unbelief.'[4] My gut tells me that your journey of faith is much like this man's, Samson."

Samson shrugged. "Perhaps."

Kolbe patted him on the knee. "You are not far off, my son. Now, get some rest. Morning comes early for prisoners at Auschwitz."

Samson was dreaming.

At least he thought he was.

He was sitting around a dinner table with his father and mother on his right hand, his daughters on his left. Around the table were Simon, Zach, Esther, and Sarah with her baby, Elijah. Rebecca sat across the table from Samson. She lifted the cover on a steaming dish of roast lamb. Samson could smell the meat inside. Herbed and fragrant, the sort of smell that drifts out the window on a warm summer evening and spreads all over the neighborhood.

Crash!

The door to the barrack burst open.

Mengele, flanked by five armed SS guards, stormed into the barrack, guns drawn and pointed. Samson sat upright. Blood leaked out of his bandages again. It was pitch black inside the barrack, the

---

4. Mark 9:24 NIV.

middle of the night. The guards carried flashlights, shining them directly into Samson's eyes. He estimated he'd been asleep for two or three hours at the most.

"Get up, swine," Mengele said.

Guards grabbed Samson and pulled him up, snapping handcuffs on his wrists.

"Where are you taking him?" Kolbe asked. His voice stammered out of the darkness. "He won tonight—"

A guard struck the priest in the mouth.

"We're taking him wherever we want, old man," Mengele said.

Samson turned to the priest, thinking quickly. "Kolbe, if you see my wife, tell her I always loved her—"

"Save your sentiment," Mengele said with a sneer. "You won't be dying yet, Jew." The doctor walked closer to Samson and spit in his face. Mengele smiled cruelly and cocked his head to one side, studying the spit as it mixed into Samson's wounds and rolled down his face. Mengele backed up and laughed outright, adding, "No, you won't be dying tonight, Samson. You'll only wish you were."

Inside Block 10, Samson was pinned down on the same operating board where he had been held before. Metal bindings restrained each limb.

Dr. Mengele seemed oddly distracted. He searched through his operating tools for something. "My observation is that you fought with great cunning tonight," Mengele said, still looking through his tool drawers. "Which is to say, you won by craftiness and deceit."

"You're saying I won by less-than-honorable methods?" Samson asked. "I fought stronger, faster, and smarter than my opponents were able to. It was a fair fight. Was it hard to watch me beat them? Was it difficult knowing there wasn't a man in that room who could stop me tonight?"

"The words of a liar and a cheat mean nothing to me," Mengele said, turning away. He moved toward a long, sharp surgical knife.

The door burst open and a familiar figure was wheeled in on an identical operating board by four guards. Samson's face went white. Rebecca's mouth was bleeding, her lip swollen. "Samson!" Rebecca's voice was urgent. "What's going on? Why are they doing this?"

Mengele turned to Samson. The doctor's words seemed carefully measured. "You murdered a man tonight, Samson. That fighter was a valiant son of the Third Reich. For that, you must be punished."

"Murdered?" Samson said. "That was hardly murder. That beast would have done the same thing to me if he had the chance. Where would I have gone if I'd lost?"

"A moment ago you claimed it was a fair fight," Mengele said. "It was you, Samson Abrams, who chose to break the rules."

"You were the only one to break the rules," Samson said. "You put poison on that man's gloves. It nearly blinded me."

"Blinded you . . ." Mengele smiled. "You don't say? I've always been fascinated by a visually impaired animal." The doctor set down his knife, folded a medical towel, and set it on the table. He picked up the knife again.

"What's this got to do with my wife being here? Let her go! Commander Höss is aware that she's scheduled for release. Ask him. He'll tell you."

"Scheduled for release?" The doctor's smiled faded. "Oh, Samson, you are sorely mistaken. There are no prisoner-release programs here except one." The doctor giggled. "And I do not think your wife would enjoy that option very much." Mengele turned to the guards, his voice commanding. "Make sure she is well restrained. She may struggle."

Fierce, Samson turned to Mengele. "Don't you dare touch her! I swear by almighty God, I'll kill you if you do."

"Kill me, eh?" Calmly, Mengele ignored Samson. He cut open Rebecca's shirt, exposing her belly. A bump revealed her pregnancy. "Just as I thought." Mengele stared at Rebecca's abdomen with glee. "Why didn't you tell me about this earlier, Mrs. Abrams? A doctor can help in such matters, are you not aware?"

"It has just come about," Rebecca said quickly. "Samson—don't let him touch me. Please!"

"Just come about?" Mengele said. "How could that possibly be the case? There is no consensual union among prisoners in the camp. You must be lying . . . or else a whore."

Rebecca gulped and bit her lip, realizing her error.

"You're twisting her words!" Samson yelled. His mind reeled. A panicked fury was overtaking him. Desperate for more time to think of a plan, he blurted out in German, *"Glaubst du an die Hölle?"*[5]

Mengele stopped for a moment, surprised. He turned to Samson, looking at him, apparently mulling over his answer before delivering it. "No . . . I do not. Unless you mean having to live with Jews." He turned to the guards. "Is she secure?"

One of them nodded.

Mengele raised a knife over Rebecca's belly.

"No-o-o-o-o!" Samson yelled. Rebecca screamed and strained against her manacles.

---

5. "Do you believe in hell?"

Mengele paused, knife still in the air. "You want me to stop?" he said, his voice casual.

"Do not kill that baby!" Samson ordered, as if he had authority. Rebecca screamed again.

"Oh, I will get the baby," Mengele said, slowly and deliberately. "Make no mistake, it will happen. But your concern prompted me just now to think of another use for a woman. Tell me, Samson, it was your sister, was it not? What was her name again? Sarah? She rather enjoyed her time of special privileges, did she not?"

"'Special privileges . . .' Is that what you call it? Are you insane?!" Samson yelled, growing desperate.

"Well, then, perhaps this female Jew will follow a different path." Mengele turned to the guards. "Hold her tightly. I don't want any bucking." Mengele set down his knife and unzipped his pants. Rebecca twisted and writhed, fighting and straining. Mengele grabbed Rebecca's throat with one hand.

"I will kill you!" Samson shouted. "I swear it! I will kill you all."

Crack! A guard rammed Samson hard across the face with the butt of his rifle. Samson spit blood, knocked half conscious.

It was over in less than a minute.

Mengele mopped his brow with a handkerchief and pulled up his pants. He looked around at the room full of guards, then shrugged. "Anyone else want her?"

"*Ja,*" said a thick-necked guard. "I'll have a go."

Samson's mind snapped. He screamed and strained against his metal bonds. The rage inside him exploded in a burst of adrenaline. He pulled so hard on the metal latchets holding him that they began to bend. His bonds cut into his arms. Blood flowed from Samson. Suddenly, the metal rivets began to pop and break under the extraordinary strength unleashed by Samson's blind rage.

Mengele heard the pop and saw the rivets giving way. Stunned, he turned to a guard. "I've never seen such an unusual display of strength. It's unnatural. Perhaps this devil has power we could study and learn from. Something unusual . . ."

The guard nodded.

"Hit him again," Mengele said. "Harder this time."

Crack! The guard cracked Samson across the head with the butt end of the rifle. Rebecca screamed and spit at the guard on top of her. She fought against her restraints with all her strength.

Samson slipped into unconsciousness . . .

TWENTY-TWO

A CONSTANT BEATING RAIN FELL. THE *VORARBEITER* waved the prisoners over to the ditch and grunted out a single command: "Deeper!"

Samson shook his head and gripped his shovel tighter. The morning was dark and gloomy, simply another routine day in camp for most. The prisoners had been at Auschwitz long enough to understand the command's implications without further explanation. Samson headed toward the lip of a ditch that needed to be expanded. A rush of bodies would soon be headed his way. Head hung low, his mind and heart numb, Samson began to enlarge the pit, along with the other workers. Nearby stood two Jewish *Sonderkommandos* speaking at the ditch's edge.

"I heard that Samson Abrams is nearly two and a half meters tall and weighs over 140 kilograms,[1] a giant," the first *Sonderkommando* said.

"I heard he fought nine SS soldiers in the ring all at the same time," the second *Sonderkommando* replied.

---

1. Around seven and a half feet tall and well over three hundred pounds.

"Well, I heard he didn't just fight them, he killed every one of them. Hit them so hard he split their skulls wide open."

"I wouldn't doubt it." The second man's eyes were wide with awe. "He is like the Samson of old, raised from the dead by God himself."

"Maybe," the first said, "but if he keeps winning like this, eventually they'll have to kill him."

Samson paused for a moment, listening, then continued to dig. He wasn't cheered by the rumors of his strength. He wasn't even amused by them. What did it matter? Samson had no heart left. The fire had been quenched, and there was little will to live. He thrust his shovel into the ditch and lifted out the usual amount. His shoulders were soaking wet. The rain fell down the back of his collar and washed into his stitches. Samson dug and shoveled, dug and shoveled. He tried to remember better times . . . times when he held his wife and children in his arms and danced with them in his home. But the memories were fading; the pictures in his mind were blurry.

All he could think about was the digging and the lifting, the hole full of muck that needed to be enlarged, and the rush of corpses soon to be coming their way.

Samson's mind flashed back to a conversation he had with Kolbe several weeks earlier.

"How could they do these things?" Samson had asked. "Why are they trying to destroy my people? How could they believe these horrible lies about us?"

Kolbe thought for a moment before answering Samson. "I have learned that truth is not, on its own, a persuader. It never really has been, and it probably never will be. It is repetition that creates persuasion. The lies and propaganda that the Nazis have told their own people are horribly wrong, but they are powerfully persuasive because of the repetition with which they are told.

"Many heard Jesus in his day but did not believe him," Kolbe continued. "Many heard Moses but did not believe. Many have heard the pope but have not believed. Truth has often failed to persuade. In fact, error, falsehood, and lies have often been embraced. We see it in these murderers, these assassins, of Nazi Germany right now as they try to destroy your people, the chosen ones of God. The propaganda of the Nazis, likening the Jews to rats and vermin, teaching their children that Jews are less than human—by teaching these lies over and over and over, people come to believe them. And once they come to believe them, acting on them, treating others as less than human, becomes easy. Truth is rarely a persuader, Samson . . . repetition is a persuader . . . repetition creates the illusion of authority and truth. And that is why the Nazis can do these acts of horror. They have been taught lies through repetition to the point that they believe and act on these lies. The horrible truth is that truth itself does not persuade as often as repetition does." These words of Kolbe's flashed through Samson's mind in the midst of that deep death ditch, the shovel of mud slipping in his wet hands.

It was dark inside Hut 57 when a hand reached toward Samson as he slept. Samson grabbed the hand suddenly, eyes wide open and ready to strike.

"I did not mean to—I'm here to—" Hedwig stumbled over her words.

The last person Samson ever expected to see that night was

the commander's wife. His fists relaxed a bit. There was nothing aggressive about Hedwig, but Samson was still on edge. A visit from Höss's wife was not only bizarre, it was unimaginable, nothing short of mind-boggling. Samson looked around the murky barrack, searching for SS guards, but Hedwig was alone. He kept a grip on her hand, afraid that if he let go she would either scream or run.

"What do you want?" Samson hissed, still shaking from the burst of adrenaline that went along with being woken in the middle of the night. "You could get us both killed."

The nighttime clouds drifted and a faint beam of moonlight shone through the window. Hedwig held out a small, round loaf of homemade German bread with her free hand.

"I heard what they did to your wife and baby," Hedwig said. "I came to offer my sincerest, deepest apologies, Samson. Not all Germans are evil."

Samson grunted and took the loaf. "You did not have to come here in the middle of the night to bring me bread. Why are you here?"

"My husband was drunk last night. He let slip the details of your new bargain with him. I come to you simply as a mother and a wife . . ." She drifted off a moment, and Samson now peered at her closely in the dim light. "I do not think he'll do it," Hedwig continued. "He is honorable, for the most part—that's true. But I am not sure if he will be able to free your family members. The party has been greatly tightening their position on such matters lately. Honestly, I do not expect he will risk his career to keep his word to a prisoner."

Samson studied her. Hedwig's hair was the color of a wheat field in the summertime. Her eyes spoke with sincerity, pleading with Samson for understanding. This was a woman obviously tormented between her sense of duty to her husband and culture and her sense of right and wrong. Samson had met Germans like this before. They felt helpless against the Nazi regime and conscience stricken over the horrible injustices being committed.

"What if there is enough money in it for him?" Samson asked, wondering if his suspicions were true. He had hoped that if he earned Höss enough profit from the wagers, he would then let Samson go. But this supposition was based on the idea of an upper threshold. Once Höss reached a certain amount of winnings, perhaps where he could see himself retiring after the war, then Samson believed he would be willing to free his prized Jew.

"He does love the extra money," Hedwig said. "Which is why I pose your question back to you. Think, Samson—do you truly believe he will free your family knowing they are the main reason you keep fighting? Why would he remove your incentive from the equation?"

The woman's question stopped Samson cold. "You came to warn me, then? What are you trying to say?"

Hedwig took a deep breath, glanced around to make sure no one in the barrack was awake, and gathered herself carefully before she spoke. When she did, it was in an even lower whisper than before. "Honestly, I don't believe I can offer much help to you directly . . . but I think I can save what is left of your family."

It was clear to Samson that Hedwig was full of compassion. She wanted to reach out and do what she could. Samson locked gazes with her, his attention caught; for some reason this woman cared. She did not see him as the vermin that Goebbels' Nazi propaganda machine insisted he was. She saw him as a man, a human being, one of God's children.

He nodded. "Go on. I'm listening."

"On Saturday nights," Hedwig whispered, "when all the

officers are occupied at the fights, I often drive off the base and go to town. It would take two trips. In the first, I could fit in your sister, wife, and son. On the second, your brother and his fiancée."

"There is a younger boy; Yeshua is his name. And a priest."

"I know who you are referring to." Hedwig looked down. "I do not know if three trips could be managed. But I will see what I can do."

Samson paused, then looked at the woman closely. A question had been formulating in the back of his mind during their entire discussion. He did not know how to ask it without appearing ungrateful. He knew she had real compassion, but he was also suspicious. He decided to ask it directly.

"What's in this for you?"

Hedwig stood quietly, glanced about the room, then bent down again and whispered into Samson's ear, "My conscience."

The commander's wife turned and swiftly slid out the barrack's door.

Far away, Samson heard a cough. Surely it was just another prisoner rolling over in his sleep. But the sound of the cough came from a direction that unnerved Samson.

Five bunks over lay the man Samson feared most in the barrack. The man was a fellow Jew; he had struck a bargain with Samson for a share of his winnings, and he had insisted he was fighting the Nazis the only way he knew how. Yet Samson knew without a doubt, the Hut 57 *Kapo* was no one to be trifled with.

It was Saturday night, several days since Hedwig made her visit. Samson paced in the corner of the boxing ring at the center of the officers' parlor. He quickly kissed the marred Star of David on his wrist as he warmed up.

The Hut 57 *Kapo* walked briskly next to Dr. Mengele as the two men made their way through the parlor. They were flanked by guards. The parlor was business as usual. Bets were being laid. Smoke drifted through the air. Drinks were spilled. Men laughed and told jokes, despite having killed countless people earlier in the day.

Commandant Höss sat at his usual table. Dr. Mengele crossed the room with his retinue, made straight for Höss, and whispered quickly into his ear. Höss listened to the doctor for a moment. The commander's eyebrows lowered in anger. Samson saw the interchange and wondered what dark secret the two men were discussing.

Mengele departed as quickly as he arrived. Höss stood, grabbed two *Untersturmführer*, and whispered to them. The officers turned immediately, grabbed other officers, and whispered some more. Those officers turned to other officers and whispered. Whatever the news was, it was spreading like wildfire.

Höss stood straighter and raised his hand. The room quieted to pin-drop silence. Höss took a deep breath, grimaced, then nodded to the *Kapo*, who stood by the door.

"Bring them in!" bellowed Höss, his voice infuriated.

Samson eyed the door. Five SS guards climbed in the ring with him and pointed guns at his head. Panic rose in Samson's chest. He kept his gaze glued to the door. Then he gasped and sunk to one knee.

Guards marched four people through the door at gunpoint. Samson's sister, Sarah; his wife, Rebecca; his son, Simon . . . and finally Hedwig, her face lined with tears.

"Take them into the ring," ordered Höss. "Do what must be done!"

The room was still deadly silent.

Slowly the prisoners were prodded through the crowd. When they got within range of Höss, the commander yanked Hedwig out of the group, stared at her a moment, then slapped her across the face. She winced, shook off the slap, and stared coldly into the eyes of her husband. Not a guard moved. Then Rebecca, Simon, and Sarah, led by the guards, were forced through the ropes and climbed into the ring.

"You have made a mockery out of yourself," Höss said to Hedwig. His voice was low, but it filled the room.

"I could say the same for you," Hedwig said.

Höss punched his wife. He hit her square on the chin with a closed fist. The blow knocked the poor woman flat to the ground. Hedwig writhed, mouth bloody, then slowly struggled to stand, her shoulders slumped. This time, she did not look her husband in the eye.

Höss leaned into her ear. "What is about to happen is your doing, woman. This is your fault. What is about to happen is on your head. I have no choice." Höss turned to a guard. "Take the woman back to my quarters. I will deal with her later when I get home."

The guard took Hedwig by the arm, led the woman through the crowd, and out the door.

Rebecca, Simon, and Sarah stood in the center of the ring. Two guards held their rifles on them. Dr. Mengele climbed into the ring and stood behind the prisoners. In the corner, ten feet away, stood Samson, four guards' machine guns at his head.

Höss ducked under the ropes, stood on the other side from Samson, and called out to the crowd. "These prisoners were caught trying to escape! What raised the severity of their crime is that they coerced my wife into aiding them. Let this be an example to you all—our enemy is cunning and ever defiant; even a strong Aryan can be outfoxed by the slyness of a Jew. As always, an example must be set."

The crowd murmured their agreement. Höss drew out his revolver, walked closer to Samson, and brandished the weapon. His voice lowered. "You should have trusted my word . . . I would have kept it. The fact that my wife was involved makes me want to kill you." The commander turned away from Samson and raised his hand for the crowd to quiet down again.

"Dr. Mengele," Höss said. "Proceed with the prisoners' punishment."

Mengele nodded calmly and pushed Rebecca, Simon, and Sarah to their knees. The doctor drew his pistol, walked around in front of the prisoners, and called to Samson, "We are not without clemency in the camps. Not all will die for their crimes. Only one. Samson—you will make the decision. Which one will die?"

Samson's jaw fell open. He wasn't sure if he had heard the doctor correctly.

A hush fell over the crowd. Every eye was on the center of the ring.

"Come now, Samson," Mengele called again. "Which prisoner will die? Quickly now. We don't have all day."

Rebecca, Simon, and Sarah stared at the doctor in horror, then looked at each other, shaking. Samson and Rebecca quickly caught gazes with each other. Samson turned to the commander. "Commandant Höss . . . how can you ask this? Have you no pity? You can't ask a man to choose between his family—"

But Höss folded his arms and stood stone-faced as the doctor interrupted Samson. "Choose!" Mengele's tone grew angry. "Or they will all die. Now who will it be?"

Samson stared at Mengele, shot a glance back to Höss, then lunged forward, desperately trying to reach his family.

Crack! A guard clubbed Samson on the back of the head. Other guards tackled him, wrestled him down, and pounded him with their truncheons. Samson struggled powerfully, charging forward with five guards trying to beat and pull him down. He raged forward several more steps before the group of soldiers pinned him facedown. Helpless, with machine guns pointed straight at him, Samson cried out in Hebrew to his family, "I love you! . . . I'm sorry . . . I'm so sorry . . ."

Rebecca extended her hand as far as she could toward Samson. "I love you, too, Samson. I always will love you . . ."

There was something odd in her voice.

Rebecca glanced up at Mengele. The barrel of his revolver was pointed straight at her. She turned away and looked at her sister-in-law, then turned to the other side and took a long, loving look at her son. Simon was shaking, crying. The boy was living through a nightmare.

"You have one more opportunity," Mengele called out. "Pick who will die."

Samson lay pinned to the floor, unable to move, shaking his head. His mind and heart were frozen. He could not make this impossible decision. He tried to speak, to say something—anything—to buy more time. But he found his tongue thick and leaden. He could not speak.

Mengele shook his head in frustration. "If no decision is made, then I will have to choose for you."

In a split second, Rebecca turned on her knees. Her face was composed and resolved, and she reached out for Mengele's gun. Samson saw what Rebecca was doing and instantly knew the decision she had made.

"Höss!" Samson screamed. "It's my fault! Kill me, not them! Please don't kill my—"

Mengele's gun went off. Rebecca's hand was on the barrel, pointing it toward herself.

"No-o-o-o-o-o-o!" Samson screamed.

Simon and Sarah shrieked. Simon continued to scream as Sarah sat shaking violently, her mouth agape, unable to register what had just happened in front of her eyes.

Samson screamed again, reaching out toward Rebecca. The guards continued to pin him down with their body weight.

Commandant Höss shook his head in disgust.

Mengele calmly wiped the blood off his revolver.

Rebecca lay on the mat, a pool of crimson collecting around her head.

Höss motioned, and the guards let off their pressure, allowing Samson to finally break free from them. He crawled to his dead wife and hugged her close to his body, her blood running over his chest and boxing trunks.

Mengele reholstered his revolver, climbed through the ropes, and stood poised on the edge of the ring. The doctor caught sight of the *Kapo* and nodded. What transpired between them was clear: the *Kapo* had informed on Hedwig. He'd soon find his dinner plate fully laden, no doubt. Mengele cleared his throat.

"There will be no boxing this evening," Mengele called to the crowd. "I believe we've just had our entertainment. Have some more drinks, everybody." He smiled broadly. "I'm buying the next round."

TWENTY-THREE

THE CLOCK ON THE WALL OF THE OFFICERS' PARLOR struck midnight. Höss threw back the last of his whiskey, stood, and motioned for a guard to escort him to a truck so he could head back to camp. Since the death in the ring, for the rest of the evening, the commander had been boiling in his fury. He hated the thought of his wife talking to Samson about escape. He hated that Mengele had discovered the plot. He hated the idea of returning to his quarters in the camp and sleeping in a separate bedroom. Mostly, he hated his life. He longed to be elsewhere, free from the burdens of being commander in a squalid concentration camp.

When Mengele noticed Höss stand, he walked directly to the commander and motioned for the guard to leave. Mengele had bought round after round. After the hubbub of the shooting had subsided, the doctor retired to a table some distance away from Höss and slowly nursed a drink the rest of the evening.

"We need to talk," Mengele said to Höss.

"Tomorrow morning," Höss said. "Don't you think you've done enough for one night?"

"You'll want to hear what I have to say. Let's go to your office."

Höss sighed, rubbed his eyes, and nodded. The two walked to the other end of Solahütte, to Höss's office away from camp. Höss shut the door, walked around his desk, and sat. Mengele remained standing in front of him.

"I want the Jew," Mengele said. "And I want him by tomorrow."

"You can't have him," Höss said. "We've been through all this before, and I've made myself perfectly clear."

"The prisoner tried to escape again. He coaxed your wife into helping him this time. Doesn't that deserve the full extent of your wrath as company commander?"

"The part about my wife helping him is strictly confidential, at least as far as prisoners are concerned. You heard the order I gave to the officers tonight after the shooting. Any word of the escape must go no farther than the doors of Solahütte."

"Word has a tendency to get out," Mengele said. "Samson, his sister, and his boy all saw what happened, just the same as you and I did. You think those filthy Jews are going to keep their mouths shut? You'll be the laughingstock of this camp. And besides, if they don't describe the incident to others, you can be absolutely sure that one of the soldiers will."

"What do you mean 'absolutely sure'? Are you trying to tell me my officers don't follow my commands?" Höss's neck grew red with anger.

Mengele sniffed. "I'm absolutely sure, Commandant, because I'm the one who's going to tell."

"You're going to what?" Höss stood to his feet.

"You heard me. And I won't just tell the prisoners either. I've got bigger plans for this news."

"Who exactly are you going to tell, Doctor?" Höss spat the

words. "May I remind you I am your superior, and what I think you're about to say next is treason!"

"Take a seat, Commandant. You will want to catch every word of what I say." Mengele pulled a package of cigarettes out of his pocket, lit one, and inhaled deeply.

Höss remained standing. He was beginning to shake with rage.

"It's like this," Mengele continued. "You're not playing by the rules of this camp. Your superiors will not consider what I tell them treasonable based on that fact alone. The rules of this camp state that Samson needs to be executed for helping set up an attempted escape. So why are you letting this prisoner live? That's undoubtedly what your superiors will be eager to hear. And I'll tell them plainly. You're letting a prisoner live so you can make money off him." Mengele coughed loudly. "That's the same as telling your superiors you don't make enough money in your position as camp commander. It's scorning the provisions of the Third Reich, and I think Himmler will want to hear about it. If you ask me, Commandant Höss, you are the one guilty of treason."

"Enough!" Höss slammed his hand down on the desk. "I could have you killed at the smallest move of my finger. I could—"

"Save it!" Mengele's tone turned angry. "You won't have me killed, and you know it. I may not have your rank, but you'd need to drum up an awfully good excuse to get rid of a man of my standing within the party. You don't have anything against me other than suspicions that can't be proved. So I will live, and I will—indeed— go to Himmler if you don't give me the Jew immediately."

"Another life—that's your demand?"

"I want Samson on my operating table by tomorrow noon." Mengele's tone became calm again. He took another drag on his cigarette. "It's all science, you know. The Jew forces me to retest my theories. He's clearly inferior, yet he keeps on winning. I simply want to know why."

"The Jew mocks you," Höss said. "That's why you want him dead."

"The Jew mocks us all," Mengele added.

Höss glared at him. He chewed on the corners of his mouth, twisting the doctor's proposition in his mind. Finally, he exhaled sharply.

"It must be done at the gallows," Höss said. "If rumors are indeed floating around, rumors that criticize my hand of leadership, I must make a public showing of a heavy hand. You're right—we've been too soft with his attempted escapes. If a prisoner thinks all that's going to happen is a whipping, then there's little incentive for him not to try. The rest of the prisoners must all clearly see that when an escape is planned, a life will be taken. After he's dead, you can have the body for science. You will not go to Himmler, and no mention of this conversation will ever leave this office. Am I understood, Dr. Mengele?"

"Clearly." Mengele tossed the butt of his cigarette on the floor of Höss's office and walked out.

Höss slumped back against his chair. He was breathing heavily, partly from rage, partly from the prospect of losing his moneymaking machine. He mulled the doctor's proposition over in his mind again. If Samson was gone, it meant Höss could never get out of the stink hole he was in, not to mention his current financial problems. He was a trapped man.

Höss reached toward the bottom drawer of his desk, unlocked it, pulled out a bottle and a glass, and filled the glass to the brim. He brought the glass to his lips, intending to throw the alcohol back in one gulp, but stopped quickly and set the glass down, untouched.

"Guard!" he yelled.

A guard quickly appeared at Höss's door.

"You know the prisoner they call Kolbe?" Höss asked. "He's a priest—always doing good around the camp."

"I will find him, Commandant," the guard said.

"Bring him here to me now."

Kolbe stood beside Samson in the barrack of Hut 57 early the next morning. The sun was just rising. Other prisoners slept or sat on the edges of the bunks, yawning and stretching.

Samson stared out the window at a little bird in a white birch tree, just like the one he saw the day he had tried to escape. The bird sang freely while he stared at it. It sang twenty yards from where Samson stood, just on the other side of the Auschwitz fence. He could not help thinking that the bird's song and quick flight were a painfully ironic contrast of freedom to where he himself stood. They were a stone's throw from each other and yet in different worlds.

"How long before they hang me?" Samson asked, still staring away at the bird.

Kolbe had dark circles underneath his eyes, his spirit deeply pained over what had happened to his dear friend. "I heard someone say they want to make sure the entire camp sees what happens when an inmate participates in escape."

"Wasn't my wife's life enough?" Samson said. "Wasn't the life of my unborn child enough? Weren't my daughters' lives enough? Weren't my parents' lives enough? So now they want to kill me . . . Why?"

"Because those in authority in this place have turned their backs on God," Kolbe said. "Their thirst for blood knows no limit."

"Who can ever stop this, Kolbe? How can a man stand by day after day and watch his family be slaughtered, one after another? Perhaps killing me is for the best. I no longer want to live. But my son . . . my sister and brother . . . his wife . . . I will no longer be able to help them. Kolbe . . . there's nothing I can do, is there?"

"You have done so much already. Samson, I want you to think back and remember something. Do you remember when I told you there is no greater love than laying down one's life for a friend?"

Samson nodded to Kolbe.

"God did that," said Kolbe, his eyes closed as if praying, "and something more. He loved his son like you love yours, and yet God gave his son for you and me and the world."

"Then God is a heartless fool," Samson said. "No decent father would allow his child to be tortured and killed . . . not for anything in the entire world."

"God allowed his son to die to prove his love for all the rest of his children." Kolbe opened his eyes. "And all God asks of us in return is that we have faith." The priest looked at Samson with kindness in his eyes, the same kindness he had looked at him with the first day they had met. But this time Samson noticed something different in Kolbe, something ominous and out of character for the little priest.

"Kolbe, what's wrong?" Samson said. "Are you afraid . . . ?"

The priest swallowed, then fought a nervous yawn. He lowered his voice. "Forgive me, my friend, I did not sleep well. Last night I had a conversation of very real substance, although I can't disclose to you all the details of it yet. For now we wait, Samson. I don't know the future, and neither do you. Soon this morning, God willing, all will be understood."

Slam!

Two guards burst through the barrack's front door. One struck the side of the barrack with his truncheon. Another shoved a prisoner aside and kneed him in the back.

"All prisoners are to report to the commandant outside—immediately!" shouted a guard.

The other guard took a long, hard look at Samson. "Make sure you're there!" The guard spun on his heel and walked out.

The morning was already warm. Near the public gallows, thousands of prisoners lined up in rows of ten, sweating and dreading what was to come.

Kolbe followed closely behind Samson, his head bowed, deep in prayer. They stopped at the gallows where Höss and Mengele waited, and stood near the front of the crowd. Commandant Höss looked at Samson, then Kolbe, then shook his head in disgust. Ten minutes passed while more prisoners were lined up. Finally, Höss stepped forward and addressed the crowd.

"As you may have already heard, an escape from this facility was planned and foiled. From here on out, there is but one punishment for taking any part in an attempted escape. Death. And it won't be quick either. It will come in the form of one of the slowest, most painful methods you can imagine."

Höss paused, took a deep breath, and continued. "Samson Abrams and Maximilian Kolbe, step forward."

Guards surrounded Samson and Kolbe, grabbed them, and brought them in front of the commander.

"Höss—what are you doing?" Mengele asked.

Höss ignored the doctor. "Samson Abrams," Höss said. "You

are the guilty one. You had knowledge of, and acquiescence to, the attempted escape. An example must be set for the camp. But your little friend here," he motioned to the priest, "offered to take your place."

Mengele stood dumbfounded.

Höss shot a glare at the confused doctor and continued. "Under the rules of this camp, it is an acceptable proceeding. A life for a life is still a life. Therefore, the rules of this camp are being adhered to, something my superiors and yours will be content with."

"Are you joking?" Mengele said in a fierce whisper. "All so you get to keep your prized American Jew. Just for the record, I am strongly against this, Commandant."

"You would do well to mind your tongue." Höss shot the doctor a look that said *back off.* "Sacrifice is honorable," continued the commander, "and I will always honor a man of honor." He looked at a guard and motioned toward Kolbe. "Take him away."

"No . . . Kolbe, don't do this!" Samson pleaded. The thought of this kind priest giving up his life for Samson screamed of injustice. He could not just stand by and let that happen.

Guards began to carry Kolbe away. Not toward the gallows, but toward a corner of the camp near Hut 57.

From the clasp of the soldiers, Kolbe looked Samson straight in the eye and called out, "Some men must be shown what true faith is. Will you believe if I practice what I preach?"

"Kolbe, you could make it out of here alive," Samson called back. "This is insanity. Why are you doing this?"

"Sometimes a man needs to be shown faith to be reminded of what faith is and of the power of it. The Lord will give you strength when yours runs out, Samson. Don't abandon your faith in God, and save as many as you can. The Lord makes death vanish in life eternal, and he wipes away every tear."

Höss called out to the crowd, "Let it be known that this is the punishment for anyone who attempts escape!"

"Forgive them, Lord. They know not what they do," Kolbe said quietly. Rough hands pushed him to a small wooden box and shoved him inside. Kolbe turned around slowly in the cramped space and stared at Samson for a moment before the guards slammed the door shut. One eyeball could be seen looking through the small barred hole in the front of the box.

"Good-bye, my friend," Kolbe called from the box.

Several prisoners lowered their heads.

Samson stared at Kolbe in horror, momentarily at a loss to speak. "What will happen to him in there?" Samson motioned to the box.

Mengele interrupted before Höss could answer. The doctor's frustration had switched to cheerfulness. "It climbs to 120 degrees. No food. No water. No place to defecate. It's like a slow burning oven, Samson. Most don't make it more than two or three days. I will be very curious to see how long this little priest can last."

Samson squeezed his eyes shut, then opened them, staring in the direction of Kolbe.

Höss nodded to a guard who dismissed the prisoners.

Mengele walked past Samson and gave him a pleasant nod, asking him one last question before he left. "How long, Samson? How long will he suffer for your sins?"

"Twenty-one days," the inmate said as he and Samson stood in Hut 57, watching a guard walk away from Kolbe's hot box. "No

inmate has ever lasted as long as Kolbe has. Twenty-one days . . .
his faith keeps him alive." Dawn had just broken, although the sun
was not yet up.

"I've never even asked your name," Samson said, a lump in
his throat. Other prisoners in the barrack were just beginning to
stir.

"My name is Aaron. I cling to every scrap of information that
is reported about your fights. Every week you win, you continue to
bring us great hope."

"You're a *Sonderkommando*, aren't you?" Samson asked.

"Yes, why do you ask?"

"No reason—just mulling an idea," Samson said quickly. He
was still watching out the window.

"Well, if you're worried about whether or not you can trust me,
you can. We *Sonderkommandos* may work for the camp's *Vorarbeiter*,
but you know we hate the Nazis just as much as every other Jew in
this camp."

"No need to explain yourself." Samson continued watching outside. As soon as the guard disappeared around a corner,
Samson stuck his head out of the barrack and checked both ways,
as he had done every morning since Kolbe was confined. The
coast was clear. Without a word, Samson sprinted out of the hut
toward Kolbe's hot box.

"Where are you going?" Aaron called in a whisper.

Samson didn't answer. He was already nearing the box. He
dove for cover, glanced around him, and whispered near the box's
front. "Kolbe, can you hear me? I've brought you something special
today."

Quickly, Samson fished something out of his shirt and shoved
it through the tiny hole in front of the box. It was Kolbe's makeshift

cross that he had made from small sticks when they first came to Auschwitz. Samson saw the priest finger the cross as if it were a prized possession. Samson passed through the hole a torn-off corner of his shirt soaked in water. The priest took the rag, pressed it to his lips, squeezed the tiny drops of water from it, then passed it back through the hole.

"Kolbe, listen to me," Samson said. "I figured out a way to get you out of here. You just need to hang on, okay, Kolbe?"

Kolbe made no sound.

Samson peered through the hole. Kolbe was shrouded in darkness and did not appear to be moving. Samson whispered again, "Kolbe?"

Still silence.

"Greater love . . . greater love . . . ," Kolbe said in a hoarse, dry voice.

"The sun is coming up in a minute. You just hang on, my friend, hang on."

Samson sprinted back to the barrack.

The *Kapo* met him at the door. Aaron was nowhere in sight. "I should have you whipped for taking that long," the *Kapo* said. It was a new *Kapo*, not the one from before. The one who'd informed on Samson and Hedwig had been transferred to a different hut under fear of Samson's reprisal.

"And I should kill you with my bare hands," Samson said. "We've got a bargain. Part of my bread when I win my next match and you let me go out that door."

The *Kapo* grimaced. "When's that buzzard going to die, anyway?"

Samson shot the *Kapo* a fierce look. "You will speak about that man with respect—am I understood?"

The *Kapo* wrinkled his lip in disgust. "Another two mornings.

That's all I'll give you. Then we'll need to strike a new bargain . . . one where I get the food up front."

"We won't need a new bargain," Samson said. "Get word to Commandant Höss. I need to see him immediately."

TWENTY-FOUR

Inside Höss's office, surrounded by guards, Samson stayed near the door. Höss leaned forward in his chair, pulled out his gun, and set it in front of him, as was his habit, daring Samson to make a move for it. Höss motioned the guards to leave.

"I was told you have a new plan," Höss said, "a plan that will make me so rich I can retire for the rest of my life. This had better be good."

"Do you believe in the master race?" Samson asked. "In Aryan superiority?" He knew what Höss's answer would be, but posing the question was part of his strategy.

"Are you mad?" Höss said. "You're asking if I believe in the basic tenets of the Third Reich. If I didn't believe, I would never admit it to you."

Samson took a step closer to the commander, eyeing the gun on the table. "My new plan involves an experiment . . . a wager, if you will. My life to prove that your belief is wrong. The good news for you is twofold. If I lose the bet, you will be a wealthy man. But if I win, then you'll make more money than in your wildest dreams. It's a no-lose situation for you."

Höss fidgeted at the sound of large piles of cash heading his way. The commander's glance jumped around the room in agitation, unsure where to land. He stood, walked to the shelf, took a cigar out of a box, sniffed it, clipped the end, and lit it. All the time he mumbled under his breath. Finally he sat again, blew out an enormous cloud of blue smoke, and said, "Okay, I'm listening."

"Who is your best?" Samson said.

"Our best *what*?"

"Your best heavyweight in Germany?"

"A fighter such as yourself should know the answer already," Höss said. "Without a doubt, it's Max Schmeling."

"The Black Uhlan of the Rhine. The former heavyweight champion of the world," Samson said. "He beat Johnny Risko. He knocked out Joe Louis."

"Yes, and Joe Louis came back two years later to knock out Schmeling. I follow the fights. You do not need to recite his record."

"The plan is to bring him here," Samson said.

"For *what*?" Höss was losing his patience.

"To fight me."

Höss burst out laughing. "Your idea is insane." He calmed himself, then exploded again in laughter. "Are you out of your mind? Assuming he agreed to come for an exhibition bout, which is a huge assumption . . . even if I pulled every string I've got to get him here, you wouldn't stand a chance. Have you looked in a mirror lately? When you came to the camp, you were already lean from the ghettos, but probably still a healthy seventy-five kilograms when you arrived. Even with the extra food I've been feeding you, you're probably down to sixty-eight kilograms, and stitches are holding you together at the seams. Schmeling probably has thirty-five kilograms of weight advantage.[1] He may not be at his peak right now, but he's

---

1. Samson's weight had decreased from about 165 pounds to about 150 pounds; Schmeling would have outweighed him by nearly 80 pounds.

only about thirty-six years old, and he's no amateur like these pugs I have so generously been putting in the ring with you."

Höss stood and folded his arms across his chest. His intrigue had turned to annoyance, and Samson could see he would need to turn the conversation quickly. Samson took another step closer, eyeing Höss's gun.

"Your laughter is key to the plan's success, Commandant. The odds against me will be huge. Fifty to one. Maybe a hundred to one. You bet a year's salary on me. If I win . . . you easily retire."

"But you'll lose!" Höss roared the words.

Samson shook it off. "Either way, you could charge a hundred reichsmarks or more for each and every person who attends the event—your take at the door alone will be huge. Bill it as something audacious, like 'German Champion Versus Jewish Champion.' Hitler himself would come to see that. Get word out to other camps. Invite enlisted soldiers as well as officers. You could easily pack Solahütte and make it standing room only. That should be no problem with someone of your reach."

Samson could see Höss's mind churning. The commander was clearly doing the math.[2] His eyes sparked with interest, and he stared at the ceiling. He let his cigar go out.

"It's a wonderful idea," the commander said at last, his voice low.

---

2. During World War II, 1 reichsmark equaled roughly 40 cents in American currency, so admission would have been about $40, or just under a month's salary for a Nazi private and about a third of a month's salary for a Nazi captain, depending on active service allowances ("Pay of German Army Personnel in Africa," *Tactical and Technical Trends* 20, March 11, 1943, http://www.lonesentry.com/articles/ttt07/german-army-pay.html). If Höss brought in 250–350 spectators to Solahütte, he would have grossed a minimum of $10,000—about ten years' wages in the early 1940s, or about $1 million in today's money. If Höss placed a 1,000 reichsmarks bet at 100 to 1 odds and Samson won, that would equal 100,000 reichsmarks, or about $40,000 in 1940, about $4 million today (plus the $1 million gleaned from admission). Interestingly, the reichsmark was massively devalued after the war, and the special reichsmarks used in concentration camps were completely devalued after World War II.

"You could get the Führer to come, then?" Samson asked.

"Oh, he'll be here," Höss said. "Any event to prove superiority. But it will take a while for me to put the fight together. Maybe a couple of months. It won't be easy to get Schmeling here either, particularly to coincide with the Führer's schedule, but it can be done." The commander rubbed his hands together. "Indeed, it's a no-lose situation for me. But what do you want in return? Is it worth my freeing you? That is what you want, yes?"

Samson looked the commander directly in the eye, gauging him. For a moment neither of them moved. Slowly, Samson nodded yes.

"Then it's a deal," Höss said quickly.

"Wait," Samson said. "I'm not through."

Höss glared at the prisoner.

"I also need your word of honor as a man and as an officer that this is my last fight. I want you to swear your honor on a Bible. The more I fight, the more money I make for you—we both understand that. So why would you ever be motivated to set me free? It's because you won't need any more money after this fight. That's why I'm asking for your oath. And not only that, but as an added incentive for me not only to fight but win, I want a bonus."

"A bonus?" Höss chuckled. "Oh, I think not."

"If I win, you'll have more money than you could spend in a lifetime. In return, I ask for you to free my whole family immediately after the fight. The ones we originally made an agreement about. That's my brother and his wife, my sister, and my son . . . and two more prisoners: the priest, Maximilian Kolbe, and a young boy about thirteen years of age named Yeshua. All of them freed together."

Höss's eyes flew open wide. "Are you crazy? Do you have any idea how hard it would be to free them all together?"

"That's the deal I'm offering. As for your ability to free prisoners, that's as easy as you driving out of this camp in a covered army truck, and you know it. No one would ever know, and you could dump us fifteen kilometers down the road with civilian clothes from your warehouses, one hundred reichsmarks, and forged travel passes. No one would ever need to know your name was involved with the plan."

Höss picked up his gun, dallying with his weapon as he paced. "I should shoot you for even suggesting such a thing. Come to think of it, I should shoot you for implying I wouldn't keep my word, no matter how much money is involved."

Samson stepped a bit closer. "To shoot me would, perhaps, be doing me a favor . . . but you won't do it. You would say and do the same things in my circumstances."

Höss studied Samson. A long, slow burn passed between the two. Höss picked up his cigar, lit it again, and watched as the smoke twirled into the air near Samson's face. Samson did not budge, eyes staring at Höss.

"Well, it would be a great deal of money," Höss admitted. "And what you offer is honorable. You will lose, no doubt, but sacrifice is always honorable. I admire that. So . . . hmm . . . the question is simple: What are a few Jews to me? Truly, they make no difference. If you win, you all go free. And if you lose, your family will stay put, and for you . . . the former bargain still stands. You are not afraid to go to the chambers, then?"

"I am less afraid of death every day." Samson's answer was so fierce, so without hesitation, that it even took Höss by surprise. The commander played with his gun a bit more, twirling it like a boy playing army in his own backyard.

"What if I say no to the deal?" asked Höss.

"Then I'm through. No matter what you let Mengele do to me, I won't fight again. I'll get word to my family to take their own lives quickly before Mengele can reach them. We're dead one way or another here. It's just a matter of time anyway."

"Oh, ho ho." The commander laughed. "So you're laying it all on the line, then? Let me ask you this, Samson—as much as I want you to win for my sake, I sincerely don't think you'll be able to beat Schmeling. So, is this all to be a martyr? Or is it to prove Mengele wrong to his face?"

"I have never desired to be a martyr," Samson said. "I will leave that to better men than me."

Höss nodded, opened a drawer, and pulled out a Bible. He knocked the dust off it and tossed it on his desk. Samson eyed the Bible, and Höss smiled as he laid his hand on it.

Mengele stood by a horizontal chalk line about five feet above the ground near a wall.[3] A line of children was heading his way, straight off the train car. Samson was being led back from the commandant's office. As Samson walked, flanked by guards, he watched the dark parade.

"Now children," Mengele said, "if you are shorter than the line, then you get to take a shower . . . a nice, hot shower, won't that be nice?" The doctor's tone was cordial, almost jovial.

---

3. If children were shorter than this line when they first came to Auschwitz, they were immediately murdered by gassing. If they were taller than the line, they were examined for physical fortitude and put to work (Robert J. Lifton, *The Nazi Doctors: Medical Killing and the Psychology of Genocide* [n.p.: Basic Books, 2000], 346).

Samson's face ran ashen. The taller children were being sent to Mengele's right. The younger, shorter children were being sent to his left. Samson slowed his pace a bit, thoughts of his own children running through his mind. He could not help thinking of his daughters, how they were experimented on, tortured, and murdered by this man who was joyfully preparing to kill more children this very moment. Samson fought tears as he approached the line of children. He slowed even more, staring at a little girl who resembled his daughters, the top of the girl's head just shy of the line.

Samson saw an opportunity, and unable to stifle his emotions any longer, he yelled out to Mengele, loud and clear in German, *"Wir werden herausfinden, wer Recht hat! Wir werden ihre Theorie auf die Probestellen, Mengele!"*[4]

The guards on either side of Samson shoved him to keep him moving. They could not be too rough with him given Commandant Höss's orders, but they couldn't let Samson get too caustic either. Befuddled, Mengele turned away from the shy-of-the-line girl and muttered to a nearby guard. With Mengele momentarily distracted from the choosing process, Samson looked directly at the girl and darted his eyes toward the line moving to the right. The girl followed his eye line and got the hint. With Mengele's back turned, she quickly hustled into the other line, the life line of taller, stronger-looking children.

"We will? And which theory is that?" Mengele replied. The doctor looked at Samson curiously.

Samson ignored Mengele and kept on walking. He shot a glance at the little girl whose life he had just saved. He imagined what that girl's future would hold. She might be a nurse, a scientist,

---

4. "We'll find out who's right! We will put your theory to the test, Mengele!"

an engineer . . . a mother. These were the daydreams that Samson had grown accustomed to using in order to give himself hope.

Samson sat near the open door of the barrack at the end of the day, his body weary, his mind reeling at the task that lay before him. Aaron sat next to him. Other inmates gave them space. Aaron reminded Samson so much of his father and his uncles, all of whom were now dead. For some time, the two sat next to each other in silence. Smoke drifted overhead from the crematorium. Ash fell around them, a constant, horrific memorial of those burned every day, an unrelenting reminder of where they were headed.

Finally, Aaron spoke. "Word is spreading about what you are trying to do. We will be praying for you." Aaron laid a hand on Samson's shoulder and gave him a fatherly squeeze, but Samson turned away. His thoughts were heavy, and he had never been the kind of man to talk much when his heart was full. A thought had been brewing in his mind for some time, one that involved Aaron, but he was hesitant to whisper it because of the potential for ruin that it might bring. He decided to test the waters.

"Aaron," Samson said, "it strikes me that you're one of the good ones."

"What does that mean?"

"You're *Sonderkommando*. Yet you haven't forgotten your roots."

Aaron smiled wryly. "It wasn't my first choice to be a *Sonderkommando*. I was always a community leader before the war broke out. When we were in the ghetto, the opportunity was offered to me to work with the Nazis, even though I hated them more with every breath I took. I agreed, hoping it might buy some time, perhaps smooth things over. I'm not sure I would make the same decision today."

"You're liked, though, in the *Sonderkommando*," Samson said. "The others respect you. I can see that."

"I guess," Aaron said. "But their respect doesn't buy me more time. I have great fears for my future . . . Samson, when you step in that ring, you step in for every one of us who will never leave here. You fight for the thousands of us who have died, and for the many more who will undoubtedly die and be buried in the very ditches we have dug . . . including me." Aaron's words were quiet, yet impassioned; he was pouring out his heart to Samson, and Samson could not help but listen to the man.

"You still have possibilities," Samson said.

"Possibilities—me? Yes. My possibilities are what I can do this moment. The next moment is always unknown. Yet in some moments I still have shreds of hope, Samson. You have helped to renew that for me. Your victories have given me seeds of hope that I thought were long dead. You have helped me a great deal. Tell me, is there anything I can do to repay you for the hope you've given to me?"

Samson looked at him with kind eyes before turning away, staring off, pondering the question. "Well . . . you have *allies* in the *Sonderkommando*, don't you, Aaron? I mean, you have others who think the way you do, others you can trust."

Aaron nodded. "I have learned to be wary of any man who is desperate, any man who is not free. But I believe I have some whom I can trust, yes."

Samson took a deep breath, measuring his words carefully to the older man. He wanted to be honest, but he did not want to rob Aaron of hope; in fact, he wanted to do just the opposite. "Well . . .

I have a feeling you won't see me after tomorrow night." Samson's voice was low. "But I want you to do something. No matter what you hear about me after the fight, I want you to gather the few *Sonderkommando* who still have strong, courageous hearts, and together"—Samson took another deep breath—"fight back. Strike the Nazis in a way they will never forget. Strike them in a way the history books will be forced to remember."

Aaron looked at Samson like he had just dived into a pool with no water.

Samson glanced around the room and lowered his voice even further. "Don't go down without a fight, Aaron. There are enough Jewish *Sonderkommando* to get what is necessary. And surely there is a man among you with some military training. A background in demolition or explosives. The guards are often distracted during the fights, so that is when you can steal the necessary ingredients."

"Ingredients?" Aaron's eyes were round, but he was listening very intently. "What ingredients?"

"The ingredients to strike back and slow them down. That is how you can repay me."

"Slow them down?"

"You have access to the crematorium, yes?"

Aaron nodded.

"Then blow it up," Samson said.

Stunned, Aaron could not reply at first, but slowly Samson's words sunk in.

"The Nazis are not unbeatable," Samson continued. "They are not always on their guard. They are human just like us, and they make mistakes, just like us. The distraction of the next boxing match could certainly afford the opportunity to take possession of the necessary materials."

Aaron's brow wrinkled. It was clear to Samson that the man's mental wheels were turning. He nodded.

"I will try Samson . . . but it may take time."

"That is one thing we do not have in abundance."

"Samson, if they really do make the fight happen . . . do you truly believe in your heart that you can beat him? Schmeling was the heavyweight champion of the world just a few years ago."

Samson looked at Aaron and nodded. "Schmeling is not a bad man. I followed his career in the papers for some time before we were brought here. He will be fighting for money or perhaps because they order him to fight for Nazi glory. But I will be fighting for my life and the lives of my family. A desperate man, who believes without doubting, is a dangerous man indeed."

"You will win, then?"

Samson swallowed. "The odds are greatly stacked against me, but there is one way it may be possible for me to beat him . . . and that's to let him beat me."

Aaron shook his head, confused.

"Gather the ingredients," Samson whispered. "Do not delay." He stood, patted Aaron on the shoulder, and walked away.

The mass grave seemed to stretch on for at least half the length of a soccer field.

Samson, Zach, Aaron, and other prisoners dug the last shovelfuls out of the deep ditch as the morning sun rose higher in the sky. An overseer ordered the prisoners out of the hole as multiple Nazi army trucks backed up to the edge of the freshly dug grave and dumped hundreds of dead, unclothed bodies into the ditch. The mass grave filled quickly as the prisoners watched, bodies piling high in minutes.

Samson's face dropped. His eyes had no tears left, even when he saw Kolbe's body fall into the twisted heap of human flesh. Samson stared across the ditch at Kolbe's lifeless face.

Samson stood speechless. Stunned, he finally whispered, "I saw him just last night . . . He was alive . . . and strong."

Aaron shook his head. "I did not want to tell you, Samson. A *Kapo* just told me the news this morning. Since Kolbe had lasted longer in the hot box than anyone else ever had, Mengele feared his survival might inspire other prisoners, so he decided to speed things up a bit. He took him to Block 10 and gave him a shot of carbolic acid."

Samson turned to Aaron, a pained, confused look on his face.

On orders, prisoners poured gasoline over the bodies. Samson bowed his head, thoughts of Kolbe racing through his mind. He thought of all the times Kolbe had cleaned his wounds and bandaged him. Of the times the priest had stitched him back together after a fight. Of the times Kolbe challenged and encouraged him with words of faith, hope, and love. Somehow Kolbe had found the strength to buoy Samson up even when he himself was wasting away, starving and in great pain. Kolbe had given his life for Samson willingly and without any fear of death.

Samson slowly took out his father's yarmulke and his mother's mezuzah from inside his shirt. He had secretly kept his treasures there since the day his parents died. He stepped to the edge of the pit and dropped them into the mass grave where Maximilian Kolbe lay dead.

The guards coordinated their moves to the sides of the ditch, torches lit. Gasoline hit Kolbe's face. The flames burned the dead bodies for hours.

TWENTY-FIVE

SIMON'S SMALL FACE WAS PLACID. HE WAS sleeping in a dirty corner bunk inside Block 10 that night when Samson quietly slipped through the door. Samson had bribed a *Kapo* with food in return for ten minutes inside Block 10. It had been a tough deal to make as it included more food going to others in the *Kapo*'s network, but since many were starving, food was a powerful bargaining tool, and they all knew Samson had a small but steady supply coming from the commandant.

Several other children were sleeping in the crowded room, all once and future victims of Dr. Mengele's experiments. Some were missing arms. Some legs. Some were covered in purple splotches, and still others had gangrene setting in.

Samson carefully stepped to Simon's bunk. It was long past midnight, almost morning, and he stared at his little boy. The apple didn't fall far from the tree, and Simon looked more and more like his father with each passing day. As small as Simon still was, Samson remembered when his son was much smaller, when he could hold Simon's entire head in one hand, his infant body no more than the length of Samson's forearm. He was a solid little baby with big eyes and a shock of dark, wavy hair. Gently, Samson laid a hand on Simon's face and brushed his hair away, waking him softly with a hand over Simon's mouth so he would not scream.

Simon's eyes popped open. Samson shushed him quickly with a finger to his lips. He smiled tenderly at his boy. Simon's eyes lit up, smiling back.

"I can only stay for a minute," Samson whispered. He removed his hand.

"Are we going home?" Simon grinned, brimming with excitement at seeing his father for the first time in weeks.

Samson could not hide his true feelings from his son. His facade of emotional strength began to break, and he found himself struggling to stop himself from crying. He could not tell his son everything, but he wanted to bring Simon the deeper things that Kolbe had reminded him of—faith, hope, and love. "Yes, Simon. Very soon. I just came to tell you a few things first." Samson smiled at his boy again. "I love you very much. I want you to know that. The day you came into the world was one of the happiest days of my life."

Simon stared back at Samson's face. He knew his father well. "What's wrong, Daddy?" the boy asked. "Are you hiding a secret from me?"

Samson strained to contain his emotion. Tears welled in his eyes. "Tonight, Daddy must do something that is very hard. And Daddy is scared."

"But you never get scared, Daddy. You're not afraid of anything."

"Even daddies get scared sometimes. I want you to know that no matter what happens tonight, I love you with all my heart."

Simon's eyes brimmed with tears. He reached out and hugged his father tightly.

Samson held on to his son. "I'm sorry for putting our family here. I was trying to do something good . . . I promise you . . . our family will be together again . . . Maybe not here. Maybe not for a long time. But we will be together again. That is my promise."

Simon hugged Samson even tighter. The boy began to cry. "Please don't go, Daddy. Please."

Samson hugged him as he had hugged him the day his son was born—with all his heart and soul. Then, knowing that he had no time left, he slowly and gently laid the boy back down on his bunk. He held Simon's face in his hands, then pulled the thin sheet up to the boy's chin and tucked him in, just as he had so many times before in happier days. Samson kissed his son's cheek. "Promise me you will never forget what I've said. Our family will be together again. One way or another. Be brave, my son . . . have faith."

Simon looked up into Samson's face. He kissed his father's cheek and hugged him one more time. Samson wiped the tears from his son's eyes and then wiped his own. Simon nodded.

"I promise, Daddy."

The day passed slowly. Evening came, and outside Auschwitz-Birkenau the hardened face of a Schutzstaffel officer drove an officious-looking black car through the main gate. It was the first in a long line of German government-issue cars carrying the highest upper echelon of the Nazi Party.

Adolf Hitler sat alongside Heinrich Himmler; *Oberführer* Scherner;[1] *Obersturmbannführer* Rolf Czurda, a senior official in the party; and former SS-*Hauptsturmführer* from the Stuttgart

---

1. Julian Scherner was a Nazi senior colonel who led the SS and Nazi military police during much of the occupation of Kraków, Poland. He was responsible for deporting the population of the Kraków ghetto to the concentration camps.

Gestapo main office, SS-Major Herbert Kappler. This was to be a night of renowned entertainment. A boxing match of this nature, one that pitted Nazi Party beliefs of Aryan superiority against the opposition, was not to be missed.

Several Gestapo-filled cars and trucks preceded and flanked Hitler's car. Guards at the Auschwitz gate saluted as they stared in awe at the dozen or so automobiles on their way in. The cavalcade continued up the road and stopped directly outside Solahütte. Several SS soldiers hopped out of the cars first, ensuring safety . . . and then out stepped a tall, powerful-looking man, a heavyweight, the once-champion of the world.

Max Schmeling.

At that moment, inside the officers' parlor bathroom, Samson knelt by a low bench used as a footstool by the Nazis. His hands were clasped tightly, his eyes closed as he attempted for the first time in many years to pray. Samson started to speak, then stopped, unable to find the words. He was not accustomed to praying. His mother and father and brother had done most of that for the whole family, but now he found himself in desperate need to pray. Words did not come easily.

"Lord God, it is very difficult to talk to someone who you don't believe in . . . Forgive me if my faith seems weak . . . For this moment I will choose to believe. Help me in my unbelief . . . I will make myself believe . . ."

Two knocks struck the door forcefully, but Samson did not even bother to look up. *"Gib mir eine Minute!"*[2] he yelled in German.

---

2. "Give me one minute!"

He figured it was probably the Hut 57 *Kapo* or some other guard. Samson did not care if he offended them. He quickly recomposed himself and continued praying.

"Lord God . . . *Adonai Elohim* . . . if Kolbe is right, then I ask you to receive me as one of your own. But before I do . . . I ask that you would give me strength . . . strength unlike anything I've known before. Strength to prove them wrong . . . strength for my family . . . for my son . . ." Samson paused for a moment before praying the ancient Hebrew prayer he knew so well . . .

"Barukh atah Adonai, Elohaynu, Melekh ha-olam . . ."[3]

Another much louder knock sounded, interrupting Samson's prayer. The knocks were followed quickly by a familiar face. The kindly guard known as Hanz poked his head around the door. He'd been present when Samson first toured Block 10 and had expressed his horror and outrage at what he encountered there. Hanz chewed his bottom lip nervously. He looked frazzled at the responsibility of overseeing Auschwitz's reigning champion.

"Samson, it is time—Oh, I'm sorry," Hanz said, only then realizing that he was interrupting Samson's prayer.

Samson slowly stood and looked at the young guard. "It's okay. You're here to do a job." Samson held out his right glove to him. "Can you tie my glove?"

Hanz nodded. His hands trembled slightly. Rapidly, he began tying.

"When do you think this war will be over?" Samson asked.

"Tomorrow morning," Hanz said quickly.

He finished tying the glove.

---

3. "Blessed are You, Lord, our God, King of the Universe."

In the middle of the officers' parlor in Solahütte, Mozart lilted out from a lone violin player. The crowd milled around, unsettled, anticipating the night's excitement. Samson recognized the music and poked his head out of the changing area, listening. He could see Simon in the middle of the ring. The boy's eyes were closed and he swayed back and forth as he played, pouring his heart into the music, even through the din.

"We must go," Hanz said simply. The guard stood in front of Samson, shielding his view from the crowd.

Samson nodded.

Hanz began to walk forward through the crowd. Samson walked behind him. Heavy booing and hissing instantly erupted. Soldiers craned their necks to see the "Jewish champion." The parlor was packed wall-to-wall with SS, guards, top-ranking officials, and *Obersturmbannführer* galore—a regular who's who of Nazi top brass. Samson spotted Höss, Hitler, Himmler, and Mengele in front-row seats, then shifted his focus away from the officials and focused his eyes on his son.

Samson's physique had grown painfully lean from giving so much of his food away and working all day in the camp. But he was remarkably muscular and solid looking despite being marred with stitches and gashes. His back and the backs of his legs were a crisscross of raised welts, scars, and discolored bruises. Altogether, he was a walking contusion.

A drunken soldier threw a pint of ale at him, splashing Samson in the face. Howling laughter spread throughout the parlor. He wiped his face, blinking to get the stinging dark ale out, trying to see his son. Jeers filled the room. Samson could sense the hatred and contempt.

"Deutschland, Deutschland über alles, über alles in der Welt . . ."[4] The crowd broke into singing the national anthem. Simon stopped playing and was escorted away by a guard. When Samson's eyes were cleared, he saw the source of the Nazi's joy and pride, the reason for the sudden outbreak of patriotic song. Heading toward the ring was the former heavyweight champion of the world—well over six feet tall, lumbering in at an off-season 230 pounds, yet still muscular and solid. Max Schmeling climbed into the ring and waved to the crowd.

Samson continued to work his way through the parlor. He considered what he knew of Schmeling. The famous heavyweight champion had been forced to join the Luftwaffe, the German air force, as a *Fallschirmjäger*—an elite paratrooper. It was rumored he'd become a puppet for the Nazi Party due to his international boxing fame. Undoubtedly, Hitler had befriended him to such an extent that Schmeling could not refuse an invitation to show up at an exhibition bout. Samson had also heard of Schmeling's controversial kindness toward Jews. Undoubtedly, the German boxer had no idea of the life-and-death circumstances Samson was being forced to fight under. Had Schmeling known, he would never have agreed to the fight, no matter what political pressure had been put on him.

Back at camp, Zach, Aaron, and every prisoner in Hut 57 kneeled in a circle at the corner of the barrack, praying for Samson, hands clasped together.

---

4. The first line of the German national anthem is translated as "Germany, Germany above all, above everything in the world." Since World War II, only the third verse is typically sung, due to the rest of the song's connections with the Nazi Party. See "Germans Stop Humming, Start Singing National Anthem," DW.de, June 24, 2006, http://dw.de/p/8fOw.http://en.wikipedia.org/wiki/German_national_anthem.

"Lord God, we pray you give Samson strength for victory," prayed Zach.

"Amen," said the group in unison.

All over Auschwitz, small groups of prisoners were praying the same prayer, all asking God to give Samson an uncommon, surpassing strength—a God-given strength like the biblical Samson had been blessed with.

Just as Samson stepped up to the ring ropes, Commandant Höss caught his arm. "Kolbe was already gone when I got to him. But our deal stands. I'll even include you, Samson," Höss said, gripping Samson's arm.

"I don't doubt your word, Commandant."

"I promise. If you win, then you will go free too. Now remember, Max does not know what you are fighting for, and he does not know what happens if you lose. So you cannot tell him. Understood? If you say anything to him, then our deal is off."

Samson eyed the commander, nodded his assent, and stepped up and into the ring.

Schmeling stopped his pacing for a moment. He looked down on his much-smaller opponent and shook his head, trying not to chuckle.

The ref-guard stepped into the center of the ring, and the room began to quiet. The two fighters followed suit and stepped to the center of the ring for the mandatory referee rule setting. The ref-guard spoke to Schmeling in German. There were to be no rounds in this special exhibition match. It was a fight until knockout. Schmeling nodded.

The ref ignored Samson and turned to leave. Samson stepped back toward his corner, but Schmeling stuck out his glove to shake hands. The action caught Samson off guard. Sportsmanship in this ring was unheard of until now. Tentatively, Samson reached out to touch gloves with the German champion, but Schmeling grabbed Samson's glove with his gloves and pulled him forward. Samson attempted to pull his glove back, but Schmeling held on, pulling even tighter. The big fighter leaned forward and spoke in a harsh whisper . . .

"I like Jews, you know. My wife and I hid Jews in our house so they would not be caught. But I need the money . . . and I cannot tell Hitler no."

Samson nodded.

Schmeling let go. As he walked back to his corner, Samson watched Schmeling's long strides and heavy steps shake the canvas-lined floor.

Bets piled high on tables. Officers in the back rows stood, some even on top of their chairs. Hats and soldier caps were quickly removed. Jackets were unbuttoned for Saturday night comfort. Dark beer glasses clinked all around. Samson could see Hitler chatting with Commandant Höss. Himmler and Mengele shared a smug smile, undoubtedly anticipating what they were sure was going to be a quick and painful trouncing of the "little Jew."

Ding! Ding! The bell rang out. The fight began.

Schmeling shuffled forward. Samson watched his stance, his eyes measuring the big man's gait. *Jab, jab.* Schmeling struck Samson twice. The German had quick hands for a big man. He followed with some more stiff lefts, but Samson ducked underneath, the blows glancing off the top of his head and gloves.

Schmeling's footwork was measured and planned. Both his

hands were up to guard his chin. He wasn't throwing anything flashy, just consistent left jab–right cross combinations, a conservative, effective style, tough to get around. But Samson was much quicker. He bobbed and weaved, taking his dodging style to a new level. Schmeling loosened up a bit, throwing another combo. Samson weaved side to side out of harm's way, but now he was stuck in a corner, trying to get out. Too late—

Schmeling threw a solid left hook. Samson slipped under it, but Schmeling followed with a right to the body that caught Samson hard. *Thud!* The crowd screamed in delight. Pain wracked Samson's face. The German heavyweight was far stronger than anyone Samson had ever faced in his life. Schmeling's punches felt like sledgehammers.

Schmeling landed a vicious one-two-punch combo. Samson took cover, both gloves over his face and head, and tried to roll out of the corner, but the German was too savvy and experienced of a boxer to fall for the trick, stopping him immediately. Samson quickly switched strategy. He moved like a snake, working his way off the ropes by bobbing and weaving. The effect caused the onslaught of Schmeling's punches to angle off Samson's gloves and arms so none of the punches connected solidly.

The crowd stood to its feet as if in unison, screaming encouragement in German. A chant began: *"Schlag den Juden! Schlag den Juden!"*[5]

Schmeling breathed deep. As a man used to fighting only heavyweights, he had expended a lot of energy already chasing this lighter, faster middleweight. The lightning-quick Samson was hard to land a solid punch on, and there was no bell to end the round for rest.

---

5. "Beat the Jew! Beat the Jew!"

Samson slipped out of the corner and off the ropes, but he still had not thrown one punch. He paced in the center of the ring. "Come and get me," Samson yelled and motioned Schmeling forward.

A look of surprise passed across the German's face. He wasn't used to deliberate challenges, but the former heavyweight champion of the world did not need to be asked twice. Schmeling rushed in, mixing it up—quick jabs, a right cross, a left hook. Punches rained down on Samson, but most he stealthily deflected off his gloves and arms. The consistent ducking, bobbing, and weaving was forcing Schmeling to miss repeatedly.

Samson had used this strategy in the past but never for this long—making an opponent miss this much was an exhausting task. Tiring, Samson deliberately backed up to the ropes and stopped the shuffles, bobs, and weaves for a moment as he caught his breath. Samson leaned on the ropes to save energy, his back propped up, and caught his wind. But without his lateral movement, he was a sitting duck. *Crack! Thud!* Schmeling nailed him again and again. Samson covered his head. Most of the heavy punches landed on his gloves, arms, shoulders, and ribs.

The guard led Simon just outside Solahütte. "I was supposed to take you back to camp," the guard muttered, "but I'm not missing this fight for the world." He glanced at the boy momentarily and saw he wasn't trying to get away. The guard slung his machine gun to one side and stood on his tiptoes to get a better view of the fight.

Simon spotted a window above him with a broad ledge. The ledge was very wide and flat, and it looked like it was made to have a large vase placed on it. Simon turned his back to the guard, hefted his violin case up on the ledge, then leaped up, caught the ledge, and swung himself up. It took some doing to turn himself around and not fall off, but once he was positioned, the boy had a clear view of the ring. He could see his father against the ropes. The bigger fighter was leaning on him, pounding him with his gloved fists. Simon knew he could not call out for fear of being heard, but in a hoarse whisper he said, "Get off the ropes, Daddy, stop getting hit!" He now knew what his father was talking about when he said he was afraid.

Simon prayed with every breath and every ounce of faith he had. "Please God, help my daddy, help him."

The champ's punches came hard and heavy. They fell on Samson like a pounding rain that swept away everything in its path. Still Samson covered up, deliberately letting Schmeling beat on his arms and shoulders. Samson made no attempt to punch back, a seemingly insane strategy, but it was exhausting Schmeling. The German had ceased even to put on a defense. He was not covering up at all anymore and had abandoned the traditional style of one arm back to protect one's head and midsection while the other arm struck. Schmeling simply let loose and beat away on a seemingly hapless Samson. The crowd booed and hissed, wanting more for their money.

"Not much of a fight, is it?" Himmler stated with a content smile.

"Of course it isn't," Mengele said. "I don't know why our champion was ever even brought in to fight such a pitiful Jew."

Höss cleared his throat and growled at the doctor. "Don't be so sure he's finished yet. Either of you two know anything about boxing?"

"Of course," Himmler said. "I've been following Max's career for years."

"That's not what I'm talking about," Höss said. "I'm referring to fighting strategies. Heavyweights aren't known for their endurance, and—let's face it, gentlemen—Max isn't in the best shape of his life right now. He's used to breaks between rounds too. I'd say that Jew is shrewder than we think." Höss peered closely at Samson and pointed. "Look at that crafty fox. His eyes are focused. He's barely broken a sweat. He's measuring his effort, boys. That's all. Just you wait—we're about to see the best fight of our lives." Höss chuckled low in his throat.

Crack! Schmeling finally got past Samson's twisting, cagey defense and hit him with a hard punch square in the face. Samson staggered back from the blast. The crowd went wild. The champ landed another punishing left cross to Samson's jaw, knocking him to one knee. It was the first time since Samson was thirteen years old that he had been knocked down in the ring. He'd been too hungry for too many days; he'd taken too many beatings from Mengele . . . Samson's strength was sapped.

Hitler, Himmler, and Mengele stood straight. Höss, nonplussed, peered closely at his "horse." A bead of cold sweat rolled down the commander's face. Maybe he had spoken too soon.

The ref counted as Samson leaned on one hand and knee. "One . . . two . . . three . . ."

Höss watched Samson very closely. He saw him breathe deep with even, controlled breaths. Samson's breathing was not the breathing pattern of a man half conscious. Höss wiped his brow and grinned. The commander knew Samson could stand if he wanted to. He was simply enjoying a few moments of rest.

"Six . . . seven . . . eight," the ref continued.

On the nine-count, Samson abruptly stood. He looked focused and ready. The ref rapidly backed away, and in came Schmeling.

It felt like Simon's soul had been caught in a vise. For several moments the boy could not even breathe.

When he saw his father rise, the boy could not stifle himself any longer.

"Go!" Simon yelled. "Go! Go! Go! Go!"

It was the only word he could think of that would blend in with all the cheering for Schmeling and not be considered suspicious. In his heart, Simon prayed even more fervently. His faith in his father was welling up, and his faith in God was pouring out.

"Go!" the boy yelled again. "Go! Go!"

Samson leaned on the ropes, resting his legs. Schmeling came in with a hard right cross, but Samson twisted expertly, turning with the German's punch to minimize impact. Schmeling's gloves kept coming, every second or third punch landing hard despite Samson's dodging style. A hailstorm of pummeling uppercuts and hooks rained down on Samson's body. Fueled by the crowd cheering him on, Schmeling threw blow after blow.

Samson, trying to duck the barrage, got caught with a powerful shot—*crack!* An efficacious wallop right in his eye. *Crack!* Another landed on Samson's nose. *Thud!* The chin. The cheekbone. The jaw. Samson's legs gave out from under him and down he went again.

"One . . . two . . . three," the ref counted.

Höss watched closely, trying to gauge Samson's face, trying to discern if Samson was able to go on.

Samson shook his head. He was seriously hurt, hurt like he had never been before. His jaw was famous for being like a square piece of iron, but he had taken one too many blows to the head from the powerful heavyweight. Samson struggled to rise, crawling on all fours to get to the ropes.

Höss squinted, peering at Samson's face.

The brow above Samson's eyebrows was swollen and cut badly. Blood flowed directly into both of Samson's eyes. His nose was broken and bloody. His breathing was labored. Samson was not faking anymore. He was truly down.

Höss shook his head knowingly, a gesture he did when he was certain a fighter was finished . . . it was over.

"Four . . . five . . ."

The crowd roared.

Samson grabbed hold of the corner ropes. He pulled and strained, trying to stand.

"Six . . ."

Schmeling raised his arms in victory.

Höss moved away from the others and stepped to the ring's edge. He peered at Samson as closely as he could. The commander shook his head. *No . . . There is no way . . . The Jew is finished.*

A thought flashed through Samson's mind. It seemed like so long ago . . . Inside their little apartment in the ghetto, Samson play-wrestled with Simon, the two tussled around on the floor. Samson feigned exhaustion, lying on the floor in surrender, and let go of his son. Simon popped up, laughing heartily. "Come on, Daddy, get up! Get up, Daddy, let's keep playing . . . Come on, Daddy, get up, get up! Come on, get up! Get up!" pleaded Simon, wanting to keep play-wrestling. Samson looked at Simon's smiling face . . .

The sight of his father beaten repeatedly, crushed, and knocked down flat was more than Simon could bear. He forgot himself and screamed in desperation at the top of his lungs.

"Get up, Daddy! Get up! Please get up!"

No one could hear Simon's cries. The thunderous yelling from the Nazi soldiers cheering their champion drowned out everything else.

The memory of Simon begging Samson to get up spurred something deep within him. He struggled anew, desperately trying to pull himself up from the canvas floor again.

"Nine . . ."

A gasp of disbelief rippled through the crowd. A split second before the ten-count, Samson stood. Booing ensued. Samson leaned back against the corner post. He stretched out his arms on the ropes, appearing as if on a cross, and looked up to God for strength.

Schmeling lowered his arms. The champ stood dumbfounded, shaking his head in awe. Schmeling had beaten this man like he had never beaten any man ever in his boxing career. He had hit him with the hardest punches he was capable of, punches that knocked the best heavyweights in the world unconscious. The fight had already gone on for what seemed like an eternity. Neither fighter had been allowed any rest since the bell had first rung, and Schmeling was feeling every ounce of the effort now.

Yet there stood Samson, refusing to yield.

Schmeling had never seen anything like it. It was as if someone or something was holding the other fighter up.

Samson slowly stepped forward, motioning the heavyweight in. "Come and get me," Samson said.

Simon jumped up and down, ecstatic at the sight of his father rising off the floor. He had seen his father taunt opponents before, but he had never seen his father so bloody, so hurt. Still, he knew the look in his father's eye, the unyielding look of a man with a will that couldn't be broken. This fight was far from over.

Samson met Schmeling in the center of the ring. The champ let loose with a barrage of punches, but Samson seemed to have been blessed with a second wind. He ducked and bobbed and weaved, still taking a beating but continuing to cover up, the majority of the punches landing on his gloves and arms.

Frustrated at not being able to beat this smaller opponent, Schmeling unleashed a flurry of blows. Samson's defense was finally penetrated. *Crack!* Samson was knocked down again. He crawled on the ground and wiped the blood from his eyes. His right eye was nearly swollen shut. He waited until the nine-count, then climbed to his feet again. *Crack!* Schmeling struck powerfully, and Samson went to the mat again. This time facedown. He rolled over to his side and slowly crawled up the ropes.

All over Auschwitz, groups were gathered in barracks, praying for Samson. Jews and persecuted Christians alike. Zach, Esther, Sarah, Aaron. All over Auschwitz, men, women, and children were all praying for their champion—arms lifted toward God.

Crack! Crack! Crack! Three shots landed on Samson's head and he went down again.

Tears fell down Simon's face. His father was being beaten to death in front of his eyes. Samson was not moving on the ring's canvas floor. Then, slowly, unbelievably, Samson crawled to his feet again. He was wobbling and dizzy, barely able to stand.

Schmeling stared at Samson once again, stunned. Samson again beckoned him forward. The heavyweight shook his head, not wanting to fight anymore, not wanting to continue beating this man. But there Samson was, motioning the champ in, asking for it again. The fatigued heavyweight lumbered forward, exhausted, but unwilling to give up.

Samson squinted through the blood in his eyes, watching Schmeling's feet. They were moving flat and slow. The bounce had gone out of his step.

Samson lowered his hands to his sides, deliberately abandoning all defense.

Schmeling sighed and looked warily at his opponent. The German hadn't stopped throwing punches for what felt like an eternity. "You giving up?" he called.

Samson stepped forward toward Schmeling. "Are you?" He grunted the words.

Schmeling threw his best left, but it was slow and lumbering.

Samson slipped underneath the champion's tired, fatigued left hook and tied up with Schmeling. In the clinch, Samson spotted Hedwig coming through the side doors. He spoke directly into Schmeling's ear in German, *"Bereit zu kämpfen?"*[6]

"Kein Mensch kahn so viele Schläge einstecken und noch aufrecht stehen ... geschweige denn überleben," Hitler said to Himmler.

Himmler nodded in agreement. "You're right, *mein* Führer. Nothing human could take that beating and still live ... much less stand."

Höss found himself nodding silently. Even he was dumbfounded. He had always looked at Samson as an interesting bet, a means to an end, with the end being reichsmarks in his pocket ... but now that had changed. He had long believed Jews were an inferior form of human, a subhuman, and that Samson's strength was akin to an ape's strength, an odd mix of perhaps mutated genes and unusual ligaments, bone density, and muscle fiber type ... but not anymore.

Höss knew that the strength he was beholding was not derived from flesh; there was something else holding him up, something else galvanizing him. When Höss was being raised as a Catholic boy, before he lost his faith, he had been told that the Jews were God's chosen people, the special remnant of a long-ago covenant with Abraham.

Seeing Samson battle in the ring made Höss think of those lessons in faith he had forsaken long ago. Only one chosen by God, he thought, could do what he was seeing before his own eyes.

---

6. "Ready to fight?"

Samson pushed away from Schmeling, breaking the clinch, then motioned the German to come after him again.

Schmeling, exhausted, threw a slow, tired right hook—a big mistake. He knew to never leave a slow punch "hanging" out there with an opponent as fast as Samson was. Samson slipped under the slow punch. *Crack!* He landed a crushing, bone-rattling punch to Schmeling's jaw with a devastating left hook. The punch snapped Schmeling's head sideways.

It was Samson's first punch of the fight, and Schmeling stumbled back. The crowd stopped cheering. A collective gasp enveloped the room.

Samson charged at the former champ with every ounce of strength he had left. He sent a crushing right hook to Schmeling's body—the air from the heavyweight's lungs escaped. Struggling to backpedal, Schmeling had no vigor left. He was "punched out" from the nonstop effort he had made, exhausted by Samson's stamina-sapping strategy.[7]

Samson nailed Schmeling again and connected with a hard left hook, a right cross, a left cross, and a right uppercut. Schmeling tried to answer with a sloppy left, but his punches lacked sting—he was on empty, and Samson knew it.

Samson pounded away, crushing Schmeling with another combination of battering punches. The crowd looked stunned. Their

7. In 1974, in a fight against George Foreman, Muhammad Ali would make famous a boxing style that came to be known as the "Rope-a-dope." But the technique was around long before Ali made it famous. The strategy is to allow an opponent to hit you in "safer" places, like the arms and shoulders rather than the head and solar plexus, thereby expending all the opponent's energy and weakening him over the course of the boxing match.

jaws went slack as they watched their nightmare play out. Seven . . . eight . . . nine punches landed unanswered to Schmeling's head.

Down to the canvas went the heavyweight like a sack of lead.

"One . . . two . . . three," the ref began counting. He counted as slowly as he could, pausing for a full second in between numbers.

But Schmeling was not going to get up.

Höss lowered his head and smiled. He was about to become a very rich man.

"Eight . . . nine."

The ref paused and looked at Höss with a shrug.

Höss nodded officiously.

The ref looked toward Hitler and Himmler, as if expecting further confirmation before counting the last number, but their heads were down. They looked humiliated and disgusted.

The ref swallowed hard. *"Ten!"*

Simon held both hands over his mouth to muffle his own yelps of excitement—his father had done the impossible. Through an incredible feat of faith, strength, stamina, and an iron will, he had felled the former heavyweight champion of the world in front of a room full of the most powerful Nazis in Germany.

TWENTY-SIX

SAMSON RAISED HIS ARMS IN DEFIANT VICTORY. He was bloody, bone weary, half blinded, and badly injured. No one was cheering for him. Around the room, officers and enlisted men exchanged money, argued, and ordered more beer. Samson lowered his arms, wiped the blood from his eyes with the back of his glove, and stumbled toward the corner of the ring.

"Mengele!" Samson called out, blood sputtering from his lips. "Are you ready to admit your theory is wrong? Are you man enough to admit you're the inferior one?"

Hitler and Himmler exchanged puzzled looks. Mengele's face blanched. Turning the other cheek to comments like that was not one of his skills.

"Watch yourself, Jew," Mengele called back. His voice had lost the calm baritone he was so well known for. Mengele turned to Höss. "Can't you control your performing monkey—?"

"Stop!" Höss said abruptly. "That sounds dangerously close to a command, Doctor. May I remind you that I am your superior officer?" Höss's voice was filled with renewed power. The huge win had

299

brought a bright-red hue to his cheeks, and there was no way he was going to be bullied by a man of lower rank in front of the top brass.

Samson stepped to the edge of the ring. Struggling to see through swollen, bloody eyes, he keyed in on Mengele's voice and called directly to him. "You're a weak Aryan, Dr. Mengele. A disgrace to your country. You're a blemish on the Third Reich. To call yourself a Nazi is to degrade the master race!"

All the activity in the parlor—the exchanging of money for bets and debts, the arguing and drinking of beer—slowed to a screeching halt. The room quieted to a whisper. All eyes turned to the ring.

Mengele stood and pulled out his gun. "I warn you!" The doctor shook with anger. His gun trembled in his hand.

"What's the matter?" Samson shouted the deliberate taunt in German. "Are you afraid of a half-beaten Jew? You're so cowardly you need to pull your weapon instead of getting in the ring. Why don't you prove your superiority the old-fashioned way and step in here with me? Come on—I'm just a performing monkey, a little 'Jew-rat.' Come on . . . get in the ring!"

It was a chess move. Samson was working on a plan. He knew that to call Mengele out in this way, in front of the most powerful members of the Nazi Party, would probably lead to only one result. He hoped Mengele would take the bait.

Mengele raised his gun and pointed it straight at Samson's head. "Say good-bye to this earth, swine—"

"Dr. Mengele, do not disgrace yourself!" Höss commanded. He made a lunge toward Mengele, but he was too far away. Mengele's finger moved on the trigger.

Bang!

A bullet whizzed over Samson's head and hit high on the wall on the other end of the room. Mengele turned to see who had grabbed his arm and forced it upward—it was Heinrich Himmler. The doctor jumped at the sight of the second most powerful man in the Nazi Party. Himmler's hand was underneath the doctor's arm. He glared at Mengele.

"Are you going to let this Jew make you and the entire Third Reich a laughingstock?" Himmler addressed Mengele as one would address a schoolboy who had forgotten himself, a youth who had abandoned his table manners.

Mengele shook his head. "Of course not—"

Samson interrupted, yelling to Mengele, loud and clear, "If you want a chance to prove I'm wrong, to prove that you are indeed superior—here I am, standing in the ring, waiting for you. Half beaten already. Half starved. I can hardly see out of my eyes, much less stand up. A fly could push me over if it landed on my glove. So why don't you climb in the ring with me and prove who's strongest? Come and get me . . ."

Samson could see Hitler staring at Mengele. The Führer's arms were folded, his eyebrows raised in question. Samson's plan was working. The doctor was taking the bait—hook, line, and sinker. Mengele, forced by pride and circumstance, was being goaded to go toe-to-toe with a man whom he had deliberately, maliciously, and meticulously attacked and tortured.

"He is insulting your honor, Dr. Mengele," Höss reminded. "He is challenging your right to be considered a member of the brilliant Third Reich. Are you going to back down? Are you going to let him challenge the precepts of the Third Reich?"

Mengele eyed the room. The eyes of every Nazi bored into him.

"Get in the ring!" someone yelled from the back of the parlor.

"Go on," Himmler said. "The man can barely stand. He can barely see. He is no match for you."

Mengele looked around again. The whole room was watching, waiting.

"I'll make it easy for you," Samson called out. "You don't even need to wear gloves."

Mengele looked at Samson's face. His eyes were swollen and blackening. His body was wracked and torn from the whippings and beatings. Yellow and black bruises scattered about his torso like a bad road map. Blood dripped steadily from the prisoner's face.

Mengele smiled and handed his revolver to Himmler. "Hang on to this for a moment, will you?" the doctor asked. "This will be easy."

Simon could not hear all the dialogue from where he sat on the ledge, but he heard the taunts his father called out to the officials. He didn't understand why his father didn't simply leave and go to the infirmary to get bandaged up. He'd won the fight. So why was his father still in the ring?

Mengele took off his hat and loosened his necktie.

Cheering erupted from the room—two fights for the price of one. New bets hit the tables. Höss circulated around, taking bets again against anyone who thought Samson would lose—which was everybody he talked to. Samson was a bloody mess.

Mengele tossed his shirt aside. The doctor was indeed lean and fit, as all active members of the German army were expected to be. He stepped into the ring on the other side of Samson.

"You don't look so good, Jew-boy!" Mengele called. The crowd laughed.

All Samson could see was a blurred outline of Mengele's body. Blood continued to drip into his eyes.

Mengele paced in his corner. "Even if I lose—which I won't, Samson—nobody here would ever admit this fight even happened," Mengele said just loud enough for Samson to hear. "I'll kill you when we're done. You do know that, don't you?" Mengele had some boxing lessons when he first joined the army, and his footwork was loose and nimble. Mengele called out to his cohorts, "The only good Jew is a dead Jew!" The crowd cheered in agreement.

Samson glanced around at the crowd. A fuzzy-looking room full of Nazis was calling for his blood. He was fairly certain he knew what he was doing, but doubts were edging into the corners of his mind. Despite Samson's bravado, all he really wanted to do was lie down. He backed into his corner and closed his eyes, anticipating the bell. He allowed one solid image to come to the forefront of his mind. The image stayed there, clear and unyielding.

Rebecca.

Ding! Ding!

The ref-guard rang the bell. The roar from the crowd was deafening. Samson charged toward Mengele, swinging wildly. He swung furiously, but his punches were badly wide. Nearly blinded, he tried in vain to wipe the blood from his eyes, focusing as best he could on Mengele's outline.

Thump! Mengele punched Samson square in the face. *Thump. Thump. Thump.* Mengele jabbed at will. His hits lacked Samson's raw power, but they kept connecting with their target. Over and over and over.

All the joy that Simon had felt a minute ago drained out of him.

"No . . . no . . . no!" Simon's cries of desperation were heard by no one. He thought his father had won. He thought they would be going home now based on Samson's cryptic words about "seeing him again." But the boy's hope was faltering—why was his father fighting again? And how could he win when he was so badly hurt? His eyes were nearly swollen shut—how could he fight if he could no longer see?

Samson swung again and again, still unable to connect. He was punch-drunk from having taken too many blows to the head.

Mengele came in close, jabbed Samson on the chin twice with his left, then hauled off and punched Samson square in the groin.

Howls rose from the crowd at the sight of the cowardly low blow. Samson collapsed and writhed on the canvas. He breathed hard, trying not to cry out in pain. But instead of calling the low blow an infraction, the ref started counting, "One . . . two . . . three . . ."

Mengele paraded around the ring, arms raised in victory. The crowd changed their howls to thunderous applause. Mengele's tactics were obviously dirty, but at least he was the clear victor.

Samson fought to get his legs under him. He willed himself to rise and breathed deep to control the pain. The ref continued his count.

"Seven . . . eight . . ."

On the count of nine, Samson stood, reeling. Mengele stared at

Samson. But the sudden look of surprise on Mengele's face quickly melted into grim determination.

Samson still had one glove covering his groin. The crowd shouted and booed, astounded that Samson was up yet again. Some spectators were simply unable to hide their drunken admiration and clapped in support. But the cries of "Mengele! Mengele! Mengele!" soon drowned out any cheers for Samson.

Edgy with the anticipation of more profits, Höss nudged Himmler. "Now we've got a fight," Höss said, barely able to contain his joy.

Samson bent double. He wavered and tried to right himself. Mengele came in quickly, not wanting to waste Samson's weakened state. *Crack-crack. Thud.* Mengele slugged him with a quick left-right combination, then another left to the body. But Mengele made the mistake of getting in too close. Samson threw an arm around Mengele and pulled him into the ropes.

Crack. Samson punished Mengele with a crushing left hook. Rearing back, Samson pinned Mengele against the ropes with his left hand and nailed him again with a right cross. Mengele struggled, trying to break Samson's viselike grip. Samson barred his left arm, holding Mengele in place, and pounded away with his right. His punches were connecting savagely, his sheer power and rage flooded out as if the dam in his soul had just been broken and the floodwaters let loose.

The ref struggled to pull Samson's left glove off Mengele's neck, but Samson's iron-fisted grasp on Mengele could not be broken. *Crack!* Samson hammered Mengele square to the face again and again and again . . . Down to the mat Mengele went.

Booing erupted from the crowd. The ref wrapped both arms around Samson's waist and pulled him back toward his corner.

Samson stumbled backward. The ref proceeded with a deliberately slow count for Mengele. "One . . . two . . . three . . ."

The ref paused and glanced over his shoulder at Hitler and Himmler. Both men wore stern looks. The ref slowed even further. "Four . . . five . . ." Mengele shook and crawled to the ropes. "Six . . ." Mengele rested a moment. "Seven . . ."

On the count of ten, Mengele used the ropes to yank himself to his feet. He still looked shaky but with double the amount of count time, he appeared nearly recovered.

Samson struggled to see Mengele clearly. The last push had drained him. The world was getting hazier. His body was exhausted. He'd pushed far beyond fatigue. He tried to take stock of his extremities. His legs felt wooden. His arms felt empty and numb. His gut and back ached. His face throbbed. He wasn't going to make it. On a good day, he would have made clean work of the doctor. But Samson knew when he was finished.

Samson stood in the center of the ring; a vision of the gas chambers ran through his mind. Mengele stood by the ropes, eyeing the prisoner. The doctor raised his fists in front of his face and stepped forward. Samson shut his one half-functioning eye completely. For one perfect moment he stood, blind and peaceful in the middle of the ring, and prayed.

"If I am going to die, Lord God . . . then grant me one thing . . ."

Far on the other side of the room, Simon turned his face heavenward and begged God to give his father strength.

Samson opened his eyes. Mengele was three feet away and charging hard. Samson dodged to his left, took a swing, and missed, far and wide. Mengele fired back, sticking Samson hard with a smart, cautious bare-fisted punch. *Crack!* Samson's vision was fading. He moved to the center of the ring where the light was brightest. Mengele was nothing but a dark shape. Before Samson could get a punch off— *crack!*—Mengele sent a hard right cross straight to Samson's jaw.

Samson hit the canvas. He did not move.

The room cheered. Guards jumped in the air. Officers toasted with beer steins. Soldiers screamed for blood. Mengele raised his arms in victory. Höss shook his head and grimaced. His newfound fortune was secured, but he'd just lost a lot of last-minute bets. Hitler gave Himmler a crafty smile. Himmler held out his hand to Höss.

"Time to pay up," Himmler called out.

Höss pulled out a wad of reichsmarks . . . but then stopped. At the far end of the ring, Samson struggled up the ropes. His lips were moving, as in prayer.

"*Barukh atah Adonai, Elohaynu, Melekh ha-olam, shehecheyanu vi-kimanu vi-higiyanu la-z'man ha-zeh.*"[1]

"Eight . . . nine . . . ," the ref counted.

———

Simon stared at his father struggling up the ropes. He stared hard.

The lights flickered and the room darkened momentarily as if there was a power surge in Solahütte's generator.

A split second later, Simon could not believe his eyes.

———

1. "Blessed are You, Lord, our God, King of the Universe, who has kept us alive, sustained us, and enabled us to reach this moment."

Samson wobbled and stood. He'd beaten the count yet again. Eerie silence fell across the room. Mengele lowered his arms. All the lights in the room had come back on immediately, but Mengele and the rest of the spectators could not believe their eyes. Samson motioned to the doctor with his bloody gloves. "Let's go," he called out.

Mengele's jaw fell. "You should not be standing, swine!" he yelled back.

"Come, Mengele," Samson called. "I fight for the almighty living God . . . I fight for my people. Come and see if you can beat me!"

Every face in the room was transfixed on the ring.

Mengele's anger snapped. He ran straight in and pounded away on Samson with a torrent of blows—a left, a right, another left. "Go down, you dog!" Mengele shouted. He hit Samson with everything he had.

The room spun in Samson's mind, and everything slowed to a standstill as Samson covered up under the punches raining down. For just a split second, Samson's vision cleared, the blood momentarily out of his eyes, and he saw Mengele's face. The man looked possessed, desperation and evil pouring from his countenance, seething with frustration and rage that he could not fell Samson. A deep guttural scream emanated from the depths of Samson's soul.

Crack! Samson plowed into Mengele's ribs with a devastating right hook to the body. The punch was so powerful that Höss heard the sound of Mengele's ribs breaking. Mengele was thrown into the corner of the ring. Samson followed up. *Crack!* Samson lanced Mengele's other side with a bone-crushing left hook. Mengele shrieked in agony.

Crack! Crack! Crack! Samson followed up with crushing hit after hit, unleashing a deluge of anger, fury, and pain. He was a raging beast, a wild lion ripping at his enemy. The power of faith seemed to rush out of him in a burst of unnatural strength, and he tore Mengele to pieces with punches of blind fury.

Mengele lowered his arms to cover his broken ribs, trying to protect his midsection from more punishment, but he left his head wide open—always a costly mistake in the boxing ring. *Crack!* Samson landed a crushing shot to Mengele's face. Mengele tumbled backward and began to fall through the ropes. Samson reached over the ropes and pulled Mengele's upper body back into the ring, throwing him to the canvas floor. He jumped on top of his opponent, and pounded Mengele's face, over and over and over.

"Why . . . ?!" Samson shouted. "Why . . . ?!! Why . . . ?!!!"

The ref rushed over and tried to pull Samson off of Mengele. He couldn't budge Samson and called for reinforcements. A cadre of guards jumped into the ring and struggled together to pull Samson off, but he kept pounding Mengele's face, breaking his nose and jaw, beating the unconscious Mengele repeatedly.

In the midst of savagery, Samson's mind went to another place . . . he remembered the little Kraków apartment in the ghetto. Rebecca was there. Still alive. Smiling. Samson reached out to touch Rebecca. He gently brushed a wisp of hair off of her beautiful face. She reached up and ran a finger down the side of his cheek. The two embraced, dancing slowly. He kissed his wife softly. She kissed him back.

The guards finally yanked Samson off of Mengele.

"Rebecca! Rebecca! Rebecca!" Samson screamed, seeing her clearly, as if she were right in front of him.

The room erupted in a cacophony of chaos. Men cheered and

booed. Some clapped and hollered. Himmler handed Höss a stack of reichsmarks. Höss motioned Hanz over and whispered into the young guard's ear. "Take them both to the infirmary. Make sure no one gets to the Jew before I see him."

Hanz nodded. "The Jew fought like a true champion, didn't he?"

Höss looked at the baby-faced guard, surprised at his honesty, then dropped his head, staring at the floor. "Yes, he did."

Hitler shook his head and walked directly to Höss. The Führer's arms were still folded over his chest. "No more sporting events. Clear?"

Höss stifled a grin and humbly saluted in assent. Hitler whispered to Himmler, who nodded understanding. Himmler eyed the stack of money in Höss's hands before quietly giving Höss his orders. Himmler pointed his index finger in Höss's face and delivered the message.

"Make sure Samson never tells this story . . . to anyone . . . ever. Make sure Samson never even gets the chance to tell of what happened here tonight . . . Make sure no one ever tells this story." Himmler turned and walked to the exit door surrounded by a squad of guards.

Höss watched them leave. He knew what Himmler meant, and he knew he was now faced with a horrible decision. Höss eyed the spot where Hedwig had watched the fight. She was already gone. It didn't matter—the only thing that mattered now was Himmler's orders and the huge stack of money in Höss's hands. He searched for Samson. Hanz was helping him walk to the changing area, one arm around the prisoner's shoulder.

Samson wore an odd look, one that Höss had never seen on the prisoner's face before.

It was peace.

TWENTY-SEVEN

Throughout Auschwitz-Birkenau that night, subtle sounds of cheering and celebration could be heard. Shouts in Hebrew of praise to God echoed off the walls of the concentration camp. Few sober soldiers were left in the camp to quell the joy, so the prisoners enjoyed a few brief shouts of jubilee. Simon had been trucked back to the camp and had told Zach and Aaron everything that had transpired. The good news traveled quickly.

The next morning, the camp was still buzzing with the various reports of the victory. The news continued to spread, and greater and greater retellings of the bouts ensued. Two *Sonderkommandos* overseeing the ditchdiggers could not help a bit of kibitzing.

"Did you hear the news?" said the first *Sonderkommando*. "Samson fought his way to freedom. Beat the former heavyweight champion of the world and escaped in the midst of the fury."

"Perhaps God has not forgotten us after all," said the second.

"That almost sounds like you're hopeful again," said the first.

"Hope is contagious, my friend. It spreads to anyone susceptible."

That night, deep in Block 10, the bandages were slowly unwrapped from Samson's swollen eyes. He looked up to see Mengele's bruised face, the doctor's broken jaw and swollen nose, yet he wore a mild grin. "Congratulations," Mengele said. "Your God must have answered your prayers." Sarcasm dripped from every word.

Samson looked down. His arms and legs were shackled.

Mengele smiled pleasantly, then turned away, wincing in pain. Heavy bandages were wrapped around his broken rib cage. "Well, perhaps he will answer your prayers again and give you a quick death," Mengele slurred through his broken jaw. "But I don't think so." He pulled out his table of surgical tools. "As I am sure you recall, I believe you are the perfect candidate for my most prized medical experiment, the one that determines how much pain a subhuman can take before he dies from slow torture. I believe I can prolong your death for forty days and nights. My old record is twenty-one days, but I have learned much since then."

Samson glanced around the infirmary. No guards. No commander. The room was completely empty except for himself and the doctor.

"Looking for someone?" Mengele asked. "All the boxing competitions in the camp are over, Samson. The Führer ordered it. And now that there won't be any more competitions here, I'm afraid your dear Commandant Höss cannot protect you any longer."

Samson gritted his teeth and strained at his manacles. "When Commandant Höss finds out where I am—"

"Oh, but he won't," Mengele interrupted. "Not for a good long while, anyway. And when he does, rest assured, it will be too late."

"You're a fool—"

"No, Samson." The doctor's voice was calm. "You are by far the most foolish Jew I've ever encountered. Do you really think Commandant Höss cares about you? He knows as well as I do that your people drain our resources. You steal our food. You taint our bloodlines with intermarriage. You contaminate our businesses, schools, cities, and countries with your philosophy and religion. Face it, Samson, you Jews are one of the earth's foremost plagues. You're a hoard of locusts. An outbreak of vermin. You need to be eradicated from our houses and swept into the fire." Mengele fired up a Bunsen burner.

Samson eyed two branding tools, one bearing a metal Star of David where the cattle brand should be. The other came to a dull point, like the end had once been sharp but had been sheared off.

Mengele noticed him eyeing the branding equipment. "I had it made especially for you," the doctor said. He placed the first of the tools in the searing blue fire of the burner. The metal began to glow.

Samson was strangely serene. "No matter what you do to me, for the rest of your life you will know you were wrong. The 'inferior' beat the 'superior.' The humiliation of knowing all your friends and countrymen watched you be beaten horribly—it must be unbearable. You will have to live with that for the rest of your life."

"No one will ever know what happened in that ring. This is one story that will never be told." Mengele turned away, again wincing at the pain in his ribs. "You know, Samson, the experiments on your people have been very helpful to me. You see, a report came out recently of a strange epidemic in Africa—a deadly virus being spread mostly by monkeys. We've been studying the possibility of defeating our enemies by infecting their cattle and poultry with this virus, thus starving our enemies to death. It would be the first true weapon of mass destruction. If General Rommel can control North Africa, and if we can continue experimenting on my little Jewish guinea pigs, then we should be able to isolate this viral strain and synthetically re-create it in a laboratory. So, you see, your people could actually end up helping us win this war. Isn't that marvelous?"

"Mengele, I want to ask you something. And you owe me an honest answer." Samson struggled with his words. He hated the thought of having a civil conversation with this monster, but the question gnawed at his very bones.

"Ask what you wish, but I owe you nothing." Mengele snorted.

"Why did you shoot the mothers with young children? Because they were Jews and you hated them? Or because they were useless to you? Or do you even know?"

Mengele's smug smile returned. He shook his head as if scolding a child. "It's such a simple answer, Samson, I'm surprised you don't already know. I shot them because I knew they were innocent."

Mengele pulled out the fire-hot Star of David branding iron and walked toward his prisoner.

At first, all he could hear was the slow drip of blood into a metal bowl.

Samson's mind fought the darkness. His sense of smell came back to him next. The odor of formaldehyde. The dank dustiness of wet concrete walls. Samson inhaled deeper, struggling for recognition, his mind becoming clearer with each second of consciousness. The sour smell of an open wound. The bitter reek of decayed flesh. He wondered if a corpse was nearby.

How long had he been like this?

A day?

Two days?

A week?

The last time he'd opened his eyes he'd seen his surroundings in Block 10. He'd seen the surgical tools and blood-soaked rags, scalpels and broken needles, the equipment for a slow death. He'd seen an IV feeding something into his arm—saline to prolong the torture. And he'd caught a murky reflection of himself in a stainless-steel urn on the table. He'd seen the side of his skinless jaw. His skinless hands. Skinless feet. Skinless stomach. He'd seen his Star of David tattoo, forever marred by serial numbers, visible on a skin strip lying on a piece of glass.

And he'd seen a new tattoo that last time.

Into his forehead was now branded a Star of David.

Pain shot across Samson's chest with each breath. A sharp, stabbing ache throbbed in his shoulder joints. Both arms were held at the wrists, arms stretched wide.

This time the pain was unlike anything he had ever felt. Immeasurable, unfathomable pain.

This time he could not see anything at all.

Samson could still move his head from side to side. When he did, air whistled across the empty sockets of his eyes. The memory flooded back, an image in his mind's eye that he'd seen before he fell unconscious from the pain. It was a different day of torture, and Mengele was holding the second branding iron in front of Samson's eyes, joking about how difficult it was to heat it enough, about how he was sorry he couldn't speed up the procedure. Samson's eyes had been burned out.

Nailed as if on a cross to an upright surgical operating table,

Samson let his mind wander. He wasn't going anywhere. Silently, he prayed Mengele would finish him off soon. His mind drifted, and he found himself on the street in Kraków nearly a year ago. Would he be here today if he'd made a different choice? Was it worth everything to do the right thing and show compassion to his fellow man? Had it been worth it to risk his life and the lives of all those he loved, just to help one less fortunate?

Footsteps sounded in the hallway.

Samson shuddered, even nailed to the table as he was. The footsteps approached, then stopped. A door opened, then shut. In a hoarse, beaten voice, Samson strained to speak.

"I won't last forty days like this. Why don't you get it over with?"

For a moment there was silence.

"Oh, dear God," came a voice.

Samson struggled to remember where he had heard the voice before. He heard crying. Then a retch, like someone was vomiting. Then silence. Rustling. A cabinet door opened and closed.

"Hedwig?" he asked. "Is that you?"

"I'm sorry, Samson. I'm so sorry. This is my fault."

"It's not your fault, Hedwig. You tried to help me."

"I came here to apologize. To beg your forgiveness."

"You don't need my forgiveness," Samson said. "But . . . can you bring me some water?"

Samson heard the sound of a cabinet opening again. A water faucet turned on. Something cool and wet touched his lips.

"Drink," Hedwig said. "Drink it all."

Samson drank. Then he tried to smile, but his facial muscles were too badly damaged. "Are they free?" he asked. "My family?"

"I wish I knew, but I don't," Hedwig said. "My husband said he would keep his word to you, but . . . we are not seeing much of each other these days. I am so sorry I can't bring you better news, Samson. Everything in the camp is locked down extremely tightly right now."

Samson struggled to breathe deeply on the metal cross. Tears flowed from his tear ducts below empty eye sockets. He swallowed and spoke, "If he frees them . . . then I've won."

"You won, Samson. Everyone in Solahütte that night will not forget what you did, even if they are sworn to secrecy. And many of the prisoners found out as well. The morning after the fight I was still able to walk freely in the camp. I found an elderly inmate who told me your whole cellblock celebrated the victory. He told me it gave them hope, a glimmer of joy. The people here will never forget. The inmate told me he could die happily knowing you had won. And he said something else to me—he said you were a true champion."

Samson heard muffled crying, as if Hedwig's hand was over her mouth. His mind was fading, and he felt like he might pass out from the pain again soon. Samson struggled to keep himself awake a moment longer.

Hedwig continued through her tears. "Because even after they took everything from you—your parents, your daughters, your wife—you still fought . . . I know that you fought knowing you would die, knowing my husband would never let you go even if you won, no matter what he told you . . . The elderly inmate said a true champion is a savior, fighting even when he knows he cannot win. He fights the battle for others knowing it will cost him his life. He said a savior will rise to the challenge, no matter what the challenge may be. A savior brings hope to his people . . . even if it costs him everything. The prisoner told me that your victories gave them all the precious gift of hope."

Samson listened, fighting to stay conscious, his vocal chords sounding like gravel. "I remember my first day here . . . I was so cold and thirsty I could hardly stand. I saw a perfect icicle outside the window within my reach. I opened the window and broke off the icicle, but just then a guard prowling outside took it from me. 'Why?' I asked him. He said, *'Es gibt kein 'warum' hier.'*"[1]

"I have heard that phrase uttered one too many times in Auschwitz," Hedwig said. "There truly is no 'why' in this place."

Samson felt a warm hand reach out and touch his head, right above his cheekbone. One of the few places on his body, perhaps, where there was still skin left.

"Someday this will all be over," Hedwig said.

"Yes . . . it will . . . ," Samson said. "Tomorrow morning."

Hedwig started sobbing again. She ran her fingers over Samson's hairline. "It took me months to understand that in Auschwitz . . . 'tomorrow morning' meant 'never.' But it isn't true, Samson. There will come a day when all of this horror truly will be over."

Samson swallowed dryly. "Since I will never see that day . . . I have one favor to ask of you." His words were labored.

"Anything," Hedwig said.

Samson paused . . . then answered with no waver in his voice. "Kill me. Kolbe once told me I was afraid to die, and he was right, but I am no longer afraid."

Samson felt Hedwig's hand leave his head. "I cannot kill you," she said. "I have never taken a life. Shh, be quiet." Her tone was pleading, desperate.

Samson listened.

Faint footsteps sounded. Someone was coming down the hall.

---

1. "There is no 'why' here."

"Quickly," Samson whispered. "There is a revolver in one of those cabinets. It was open last time I was conscious, and I saw it. God is merciful, is he not? Kolbe told me that God was merciful, and I believe him. Do you?"

The footsteps grew louder.

"Yes, I believe," Hedwig said in a hush. "But I must not be found here. Samson, I must go. I will try to bring you some relief sometime soon."

"Wait . . . ," Samson said, still in a hush. "No man deserves to die like this, do they?"

"No," she said. "But please don't ask me to do this."

"I beg you . . . do as I ask. I can't endure this for forty days. This is the only way I can be free of this torture. If you don't do it now, then Mengele will continue to pick me to pieces for as long as my heart beats. He'll keep carving into me until there is nothing left."

The footsteps were nearly at the door.

"I can't," Hedwig said.

"You can. Right through the heart. One shot."

The footsteps stopped.

Someone tried to open the door. Samson could hear that it was locked. Keys jingled outside, fumbling against the wood.

"Good-bye, Samson," Hedwig said. "God bless you."

"Please," Samson said. He tilted his face toward heaven.

Samson heard more fumbling. Footsteps in the room. A door opened—whether a cabinet door or the door to the room, he did not know. Flashes of memories ran through his mind—his parents, Hannah and Abraham; his angelic daughters, Rachel and Leah; his sister Sarah's infant son, Elijah; and his beautiful wife, Rebecca . . . He saw himself dancing with Rebecca, holding her, kissing her.

Then a flash of Kolbe appeared in his mind's eye. The priest was standing in a grassy field. His arms were open wide. He was bathed in sunshine, and he was speaking words of faith, hope, and love. "Don't blame God for the evil that men do," Kolbe said. "Focus on a greater love, the love of God." Then the faces of those still living ran through his mind: Yeshua, Esther, Zach, Sarah. His son, Simon. The images lingered in Samson's mind. He could see his son's bright face, his beaming grin so full of joy. Samson broke into a wide, peaceful smile.

Bang!

One shot rang out . . . and Samson breathed his last.

TWENTY-EIGHT

A COVERED TRUCK SLOWLY DROVE OUT OF THE
Auschwitz-Birkenau camp.

Commandant Höss was behind the wheel.

The guards did not even bother to check his cargo as he gave
them an officious wave. He crossed to the other side of the main
gate, then looked back over his shoulder.

Inside the army truck, Zach, Esther, Sarah, Simon, and Yeshua
huddled together in blankets, their eyes hopeful and free.

Simon closed his eyes, and in his imagination he could see
the people of Auschwitz slowly disappear, all the people—Jewish,
German, young, and old—every living thing vanished . . . except
the bird in the birch tree.

The bird sung as the wind blew through the empty buildings.

Over three years later, far away and safe, Simon would hear
the muted, idiosyncratic voice of Winston Churchill over the radio
announcing the end of World War II.

"Tomorrow morning" had finally come.

Newlyweds Zach and Esther soon immigrated to New York City. They raised Simon as well as Yeshua, who was unable to locate any relatives after the war, and had five children. They named their first-born Samantha, nicknamed "Sam," after her uncle.

Sarah never remarried. She returned to New York City along with the rest of the family, became a pediatric nurse, and devoted the rest of her life to caring for sick children.

In 1953, eight years after the war ended, Simon took time off from his studies at New York University and traveled to Israel. He took a taxi to the western slope of Mount Herzl and toured Yad Vashem,[1] the newly constructed Holocaust museum in Jerusalem.

In the Hall of Names, a memorial to the six million Jews who perished in the Holocaust, Simon added to the archives the account of his time in the camp, along with the names of the eight family members he lost: Samson, Rebecca, Abraham, Hannah, Leah, Rachel, Elijah, and the baby his mother lost while at Auschwitz.

In 1962, seventeen years after the war ended, Simon traveled to Israel a second time, this time with his wife and three children. On the Avenue of the Righteous,[2] Simon planted a tree of remembrance and honor for Maximilian Kolbe, the monk who had given so much so that others might have great faith.

---

1. The Central Database of Shoah Victims' Names at Yad Vashem undertakes to collect the names and reconstruct the life stories of each individual Jew murdered in the Holocaust. The database was made available online in 2004. Some 2.5 million pages of testimony have been submitted over the past fifty years. Other names have been learned from additional lists, including deportation, camp, and ghetto records. See http://www.yadvashem.org/.

2. "The Avenue of the Righteous Among the Nations," established in 1962, features trees planted in honor of non-Jews who saved Jews during the Holocaust. The trees, signs of hope, symbolize renewal of life. See "The Righteous Among the Nations," Yad Vashem (official website), http://www1 .yadvashem.org/yv/en/righteous/commemoration.asp.

POSTSCRIPT

THE CHARACTERS OF THE ABRAMS FAMILY ARE
each amalgamations of different, real people, and all of the horrors
they faced were real events that happened to real victims. Jewish
prisoners were in fact forced to box for Nazi entertainment, and for
their lives, and this is well documented.[1]

At least seventy major illegal "medical research projects" took place
in Nazi concentration camps during World War II. Thousands of
people were forced to be a part of these inhuman experiments by
more than two hundred Nazi doctors.[2]

1. Those who have spoken about such experiences include Nathan Shapow
   (Nathan Shapow and Bob Harris, *The Boxer's Story: Fighting for My Life in the
   Nazi Camps* [n.p.: Robeson Press, 2012]) and Victor "Young Perez" (profiled
   in Yosi Kats, *A Voice Called: Stories of Jewish Heroism* [Lynbrook, NY: Gefen
   Books, 2010], 75–78).
2. United States Holocaust Memorial Museum, "Medical Experiments," http://
   www.ushmm.org/research/library/bibliography/?content=medical_experiments;
   Holly Cefrey, *Dr. Joseph Mengele: The Angel of Death* (New York: Rosen
   Publishing Group, 2001), 78; Peter Tyson, "The Experiments," Nova Online,
   October 2000, http://www.pbs.org/wgbh/nova/holocaust/experiside.html.

After World War II ended, Commandant Höss evaded capture until March 2, 1946. His wife, Hedwig, was instrumental in his capture. Hedwig was afraid that her son, Klaus, would be arrested and sent to the Soviet Union, where imprisonment or torture was a strong possibility, so she told British troops where her husband was hiding. Commandant Höss was executed by hanging on April 16, 1947, immediately adjacent to the crematorium of the former Auschwitz concentration camp.[3]

Due to subsequent liquidations of the Kraków Ghetto, the Abrams family would have almost certainly died in Amon Goeth's "cleansing" program had they not been taken to Auschwitz and subsequently freed via Samson's victories.[4]

On October 7, 1944, three hundred members of the *Sonderkommando* packed crematorium IV with explosives they had stolen

---

3. Ruth Rothenberg, "New light thrown on capture of Hoess," Association of Jewish Refugees, June 2012, http://www.ajr.org.uk/index.cfm/section.journal/issue.Jun12/article=10512 (Hoess is an alternate spelling of Höss); "Rudolf Höss, Commandant of Auschwitz," Holocaust Education and Archive Research Team, http://www.holocaustresearchproject.org/othercamps/hocss.html.
4. Jews living in the Kraków Ghetto were subject to several mass deportations. Among the final deportations, on March 13, 1943, the "A" portion of the ghetto was liquidated, with most prisoners sent to Plaszow Concentration Camp, where survival rates were very low. During this same "cleansing," many Jews were killed on the ghetto streets without being deported. On March 14, 1943, the last remaining Jews were deported to Auschwitz-Birkenau ("Krakow Ghetto," Aktion Reinhard Camps, September 11, 2006, http://www.deathcamps.org/occupation/krakow%20ghetto.html).

and blew it up, effectively slowing the rate of "production" down at Auschwitz and saving perhaps thousands of lives as a result.[5]

On January 18, 1945, as the Soviet army arrived in Germany, Mengele fled Auschwitz. Captured in June, he spent time in two US prison camps where he was not identified as a war criminal. Eventually, he escaped and made his way to Argentina. He lived in hiding there, in Paraguay and in Brazil, until February 7, 1979, when he drowned while swimming in the ocean in Bertioga, Brazil.[6]

There are many who believe that, along with the Nazis' myriad dangerous medical experiments, Mengele and others were indeed trying to isolate the virus known as SIV in apes in order to use it in biological warfare against the Allied forces. SIV has been proven to have later mutated into the virus HIV/AIDS.

In due time, the Vatican proclaimed Maximilian Kolbe to be beatified, meaning to be among the blessed and due special religious honor. In 1982, the Catholic Church proclaimed him a saint.[7]

---

5. Chris Webb, "Sonderkommando Revolt—Auschwitz-Birkenau," Holocaust Education and Archive Research Team, http://www.holocaustresearchproject .org/revolt/sonderevolt.html.

6. United States Memorial Holocaust Museum, "Josef Mengele," *Holocaust Encyclopedia*, http://www.ushmm.org/wlc/en/article.php?ModuleId=10007060.

7. "The Cell of Father Maksymilian Kolbe," Auschwitz-Birkenau Memorial and Museum, http://en.auschwitz.org/z/index.php?Itemid=35&id=22&option=com _content&task=view (Macksymilian is an alternate spelling); Pope John Paul II, "Homily at the Canonization of St. Maximilian Mary Kolbe," October 10, 1982, http://www.liturgies.net/saints/kolbe/homily.htm.

Dedicated to the millions of men, women, and children who were victims of the Holocaust. May we never forget them and the strength of their faith in the face of death.

ACKNOWLEDGMENTS

THANK YOU TO MY FATHER, ANDREW, WHO instead of telling me bedtime stories, decided to tell me true Holocaust stories so that I would not forget the persecution of our people. As painful as many of those stories were to hear, it gave me a different perspective, and it was, I am sure, a large part of the reason I wrote this book.

Thank you to my mother, Jillian, for always having faith in me and encouraging me to do what I felt "called" to do.

Thank you to my wife, Teresa, my son, Joshua, and my daughter, Micah, for your patience and understanding during all those nights I could not sit down and eat dinner because I was working on this book. You are the three most precious people in the world to me.

Thank you to Pastor John Dunn, the most brilliant "Jewish Gentile Pastor" I have ever met, and many thanks to the whole Dunn family. Your prayers and support mean more than you will ever know.

Thank you to Stephen Yake for your profound confidence in this project and for never giving up.

Thank you to Matt Baugher for your faith in this story and unending support. You are the type of man that any person would be thankful to have on their team.

Thank you to Marcus Brotherton, my editor, for pushing me to do my very best with this book. Your excellent insight was a blessing to me in the process of adapting my screenplay into this novel; you are a great editor and a man of deep faith.

Thank you to my grandfather, Lester Hoffman, for always telling me, "Find what makes you happy and do it." Grandpa, you are a real "mensch."

Thank you to my grandmother, Helen, for showing me what God's love looks like in everything you did for me. I know you are in heaven now, smiling down on us all.

ABOUT THE AUTHOR

SHAWN HOFFMAN is an actor, screenwriter, and producer whose credits include a leading role in Broadway's *The Survivor*, performing at the Academy Awards, and being a producer on the NBC show *The Apprentice*, as well as appearing in leading roles in films and TV shows for Lion's Gate Studios, Disney, Warner Bros., NBC, ABC, CBS, FOX, and MTV. After going to Stanford University on a full scholarship, Shawn has gone on to write ten screenplays that have sold to various film studios and production companies, and his screenplay *Samson* has won the Best Screenplay Award at the Beverly Hills Film Festival and the Los Angeles United Film Festival.